ALSO BY LEWIS HYDE

Common as Air

Trickster Makes This World

This Error Is the Sign of Love

The Gift

A PRIMER FOR FORGETTING

A Primer for Forgetting

Getting Past the Past

Lewis Hyde

FARRAR, STRAUS AND GIROUX *New York*

Farrar, Straus and Giroux
120 Broadway, New York 10271

Printed in the United States of America
First edition, 2019

Portions of this book originally appeared, in slightly different form, in *Radcliffe Magazine* and *Tin House*.

Owing to limitations of space, all acknowledgments for permission to reprint previously published material can be found on pages 369–70, and illustration credits can be found on pages 371–72.

Library of Congress Cataloging-in-Publication Data
Names: Hyde, Lewis, 1945– author.
Title: A primer for forgetting : getting past the past / Lewis Hyde.
Description: First [edition]. | New York : Farrar, Straus and Giroux, 2019 | Includes index.
Identifiers: LCCN 2018050163 | ISBN 9780374237219 (hardcover)
Subjects: LCSH: Memory. | Psychology.
Classification: LCC B378.F7 H93 2019 | DDC 153.1/25—dc23
LC record available at https://lccn.loc.gov/2018050163

Designed by Richard Oriolo

1 3 5 7 9 10 8 6 4 2

The author gratefully acknowledges the MacDowell Colony, the Corporation of Yaddo, the Austen Riggs Center, the Radcliffe Institute for Advanced Study, the Lannan Foundation, and Kenyon College for their support, and Richard L. Thomas for his support of Kenyon's Thomas Chair in Creative Writing.

FOR PATSY

Contents

A PRIMER FOR FORGETTING

WHAT THIS IS

MANY YEARS AGO, reading about the old oral cultures where wisdom and history lived not in books but on the tongue, I found my curiosity aroused by one brief remark. "Oral societies," I read, keep themselves "in equilibrium . . . by sloughing off memories which no longer have present relevance." My interest at the time was in memory itself, in the valuable ways that persons and cultures keep the past in mind, but here was a contrary note, one that clearly stirred my own contrary spirit, for I began to keep scrapbooks of other cases in which letting go of the past proves to be at least as useful as preserving it.

This book, the late fruit of those gleanings, has turned out to be an experiment in both thought and form. The thought experiment seeks to test the proposition that forgetfulness can be more useful than memory or, at the very least, that memory functions best in tandem with forgetting. To praise forgetting is not, of course, the same as speaking against memory; any experiment worth conducting ought sometimes to yield negative or null results, and mine is no exception. Readers will surely find instances, as I did, where they'll want to draw the line and say, "No, here we must remember" (though, ironically, stirring up resistance to forgetting can itself be one of the uses of forgetting).

As for the form, I decided to build on my scrapbooks rather than mine their content for a more conventional narrative. I have written three long books—*The Gift*, *Trickster Makes This World*, and *Common as Air*—each of which spends over three hundred pages defending its central proposition. Having done that kind of work for years, I found myself weary of argument, tired of striving for mastery, of marshaling the evidence, of drilling down to bedrock to anchor every claim, of inventing transitions to mask the native jumpiness of my mind, of defending myself against imaginary swarms of critics. . . . What a relief to make a book whose free associations are happily foregrounded, a book that does not so much argue its point of departure as more simply sketch the territory I have been exploring, a book that I hope will both invite and provoke a reader's own free reflections.

The citations, aphorisms, anecdotes, stories, and reflections that are the stuff of my episodic form I have grouped around four focal points: mythology, personal psychology, politics, and the creative spirit. Most of the entries are brief—just a page or two—but once I got serious about making a book out of them, it became clear that several would need fuller elaboration. In "Notebook I: Myth," for example, there's an extended portrait of what happened in Athens around 400 B.C.E., when a legal form of forgetting—what we now call amnesty—helped secure the peace after a brutal civil war. Toward the end of "Notebook II: Self," I recount the story of a racially motivated double murder committed in Mississippi in 1964, one that left the victims' kin struggling to lay traumatic memory to rest.

Several of the political cases presented in "Notebook III: Nation" also called for longer treatment, from the struggle over how Americans both remember and forget their Civil War to the "truth and reconciliation" work that followed South Africa's many decades of apartheid. "Notebook IV: Creation" mixes episodes from spiritual life and from artistic practice, the longer of these reflecting on the uses of forgetfulness in Saint Augustine, in Zen master Dogen, and in Marcel Proust (in whose work the famous moments of involuntary memory carry their redemptive force only because they have been at first forgotten).

I have also mixed a number of images into the book's otherwise prose collage. Having always been a bit jealous of artists and art historians who get to darken the lecture hall and adorn their ideas with a magic lantern show, I was led to invent my own imaginary Museum of Forgetting and to stock it with works of art, each accompanied by explanatory wall text.

Readers often ask what drew the writer to the work at hand, seeming to expect it to have arisen from some difficult personal history. To be sure, one sorrow from my own life—my mother's old-age dementia—figures in the book. So do some other marked events—the death of a sibling, my own connection to those Mississippi murders. . . . But none of these gave rise to this book. Its true roots lie in the enigma of its topic.

Memory and forgetting: these are the faculties of mind by which we are aware of time, and time is a mystery. In addition, a long tradition holds that the imagination is best conceived as operating with a mixture of memory and forgetting. Creation—things coming into being that never were before—that too is a mystery. Writers like me who work very slowly are well advised to settle on topics such as these, topics whose fascination may never be exhausted. Such authors do not simply tell us what they know; they invite us to join them in fronting the necessary limits of our knowing.

NOTEBOOK I

MYTH

The Liquefaction of Time

The Aphorisms

Every act of memory is an act of forgetting.

The tree of memory set its roots in blood.

To secure an ideal, surround it with a moat of forgetfulness.

To study the self is to forget the self.

In forgetting lies the liquefaction of time.

The Furies bloat the present with the undigested past.

"Memory and oblivion, we call that imagination."

We dream in order to forget.

TO THE READER. "Whoever wants really to get to know a new idea does well to take it up with all possible love, to avert the eye quickly from, even to forget, everything about it that is objectionable or false. We should give the author of a book the greatest possible head start and, as if at a race, virtually yearn with a pounding heart for him to reach his goal. By doing this, we penetrate into the heart of the new idea, into its motive center: and this is what it means to get to know it. Later, reason may set its limits, but at the start that overestimation, that occasional unhinging of the critical pendulum, is the device needed to entice the soul of the matter into the open," says Nietzsche.

MIRACULOUS. Replying to a question about the effort he put into composing with chance operations, John Cage said, "It's an attempt to open our minds to possibilities other than the ones we remember, and the ones we already know we like. Something has to be done to get us free of our memories and choices."

Or he once said, "This is . . . why it is so difficult to listen to music we are familiar with; memory has acted to keep us aware of what will happen next, and so it is almost impossible to remain alive in the presence of a well-known masterpiece. Now and then it happens, and when it does, it partakes of the miraculous."

In a nod to his long interest in Buddhist teachings, Cage once released an audio disc titled *The Ten Thousand Things*, that phrase being the formula by which the old dharma texts refer to the whole of existence, to the fullness of what is, as in the teaching of the thirteenth-century Japanese Zen master Dogen: "To study the Buddha Way is to study the self. To study the self is to forget the self. To forget the self is to become one with the ten thousand things."

Note the sequence: First comes study, then forgetting. There is a path to be taken, a practice of self-forgetfulness.

THE TWIN GODDESS. Every act of memory is also an act of forgetting. In Hesiod's *Theogony*, Mnemosyne, the mother of the Muses, is not simply Memory, for even as she helps humankind to remember the golden age, she helps them to forget the Age of Iron they now must occupy. Bardic song was meant to induce those twin states: "For though a man have sorrow and grief . . . , yet, when a singer, the servant of the Muses, chants the glorious deeds of men of old and the blessed gods who inhabit Olympus, at once he forgets his heaviness and remembers not his sorrows at all."

Both memory and forgetting are here dedicated to the preservation of ideals. What drops into oblivion under the bardic spell is the fatigue, wretchedness, and anxiety of the present moment, its unrefined particularity, and what rises into consciousness is knowledge of the better world that lies hidden beyond this one.

I MANUMIT. I HIDE. Let us imagine forgetting by way of two etymologies. The roots of the English "forget" go back to Old High German, where the *for-* prefix indicates abstaining from or neglecting and the Germanic **getan* means "to hold" or "to grasp." To remember is to latch on to something, to hold it in mind; to forget is to let it slip from consciousness, to drop it. All things grasped by mistake (a wrong impression, a hidden wasp) or by nature slippery (the eels of the mind) or overworked and confined (mind slaves, caged birds) or useless mental furniture (old phone numbers, hobbyhorses) or worn-out attitudes (self-importance, resentment) . . . , in every case to forget is to stop holding on, to open the hand of thought.

Greek terms present a different set of images, not letting go, but erasing, covering up, or hiding (the trail washed away by rain, the love letter thrown in the fire, the buried scat, the wound scabbed over, the gravestone obscured by vines). Forgetfulness in Greek is *lethe*, in turn related to *letho*, λήθω (I escape notice, I am hidden), ultimately from Proto-Indo-European *leh_2- (to hide). The privative or negative form of this word, *a-lethe* or *aletheia*, is the Greek word usually translated as "truth," the truth then being a thing uncovered or taken out of hiding. In terms of mental life, all that is available to the mind is *aletheia*; what is not available is for some reason covered, concealed, hidden.

MID-AUGUST AT SOURDOUGH MOUNTAIN LOOKOUT

Down valley a smoke haze
Three days heat, after five days rain
Pitch glows on the fir-cones
Across rocks and meadows
Swarms of new flies.

I cannot remember things I once read
A few friends, but they are in cities.
Drinking cold snow-water from a tin cup
Looking down for miles
Through high still air.

—Gary Snyder

IN THE DESERT. Paul Bowles says that as soon as you arrive in the Sahara you notice the stillness, the "incredible, absolute silence," especially if "you leave the gate of the fort or the town behind, pass the camels lying outside, go up into the dunes, or out onto the hard, stony plain and stand awhile, alone. Presently, you will either shiver and hurry back inside the walls, or you will go on standing there and let something very peculiar happen to you, something that everyone who lives there has undergone and which the French call *le baptême de la solitude.* It is a unique sensation, and it has nothing to do with loneliness, for loneliness presupposes memory. Here, in this wholly mineral landscape lighted by stars like flares, even memory disappears; nothing is left but your own breathing and the sound of your heart beating."

A STORY OUT OF PLATO'S *REPUBLIC.* A soldier by the name of Er was killed in battle. Days later, as his body lay on the funeral pyre, he came back to life and told of all he had seen in the Land of the Dead.

When his soul had arrived in the otherworld he was told to watch and listen so that he might return as a messenger to the living. He then witnessed the punishing of the wicked and the rewarding of the just. And he saw how all these souls convened to be born again, sometimes after having journeyed in the underworld for a thousand years.

He saw how all were given a chance to choose their lot in life and how they did so according to their wisdom or their foolishness. Their lots having been chosen, and the Fates having spun the threads of each one's irreversible destiny, they proceeded together in dry and stifling heat across the desert of Lethe. In the evening, they camped by the River of Forgetfulness, whose water no vessel can contain. Great thirst drove them to drink this water—those without wisdom drinking especially deeply. As each man drank, he forgot everything.

Then they slept. During the night, an earthquake came, and thunder, and all were swept up to their next life like a showering of stars.

At the River of Forgetfulness, Er himself was forbidden to drink. He slept, and when he opened his eyes, he found himself lying on the funeral pyre, the sun rising.

"A MUSICAL INSTRUMENT REMINDING YOU . . ." The myth of Er fits neatly with Plato's theory of knowledge, in which the unborn soul, following "in the train of a god," comes to know the "absolute realities," the ideal forms such as beauty, goodness, justice, equality. This knowledge is lost at birth, however, the soul having met "with some mischance," become "burdened with a load of forgetfulness," and fallen to earth.

Born into this life, those who seek to recover their lost wisdom need to find a teacher whose task is not to directly teach ideals but rather to remind the student of what the soul already knows. "What we call learning is really just recollection," says Socrates in the *Phaedo*. It's *anamnesis*, or un-forgetting, the discovering of things hidden in the mind.

Just as when I see a guitar in a shop window and suddenly remember a dream that I forgot when I woke up, so too the student is directed to the particulars of this world that they might trigger recollection of the previously known noble ideals. "At last, in a flash, understanding of each blazes up, and the mind . . . is flooded with light."

TO SECURE AN IDEAL, surround it with a moat of forgetfulness.

AMERICAN EPISTEMOLOGY. An early chapter of Herman Melville's *Confidence-Man* describes an encounter between a man wearing mourning clothes (the con man himself) and a country merchant. When the man in mourning introduces himself as an old acquaintance, the merchant protests: he has no recollection of their ever meeting.

"I see you have a faithless memory," says the con man. "But trust in the faithfulness of mine."

"Well, to tell the truth, in some things my memory ain't of the very best," replies the puzzled merchant.

"I see, I see; quite erased from the tablet," says the con man. "About six years back, did it happen to you to receive any injury on the head? Surprising effects have arisen from such a cause. Not alone unconsciousness . . . , but likewise—strange to add—oblivion, entire and incurable."

He himself, the con man says, was once kicked by a horse and couldn't remember a thing about it, relying on friends to tell him what happened. "You see, sir, the mind is ductile, very much so: but images, ductilely received into it, need a certain time to harden and bake in their impressions. . . . We are but clay, sir, potter's clay."

Drawn in, the merchant confesses that, yes, he once suffered a brain fever and lost his mind for quite some time.

"There now, you see, I was not wholly mistaken. That brain fever accounts for it all," replies the man in mourning. How sad that the merchant has forgotten their friendship! And, by the way, would he mind loaning "a brother" a shilling?

The whole of *The Confidence-Man* is a Platonic dialogue for a fallen age. Every episode hangs on the question, should we or shouldn't we have confidence in the story being told? How are we to know the truth? In the case at hand, the con man's key move is the erasure of memory; that allows him to detach his claim of old acquaintanceship from the world of empirical knowledge whereupon its veracity becomes a matter of faith. Having accepted the con man's suggestion—yes, there was brain-fever forgetfulness—the merchant is left with little to go on but the story at hand. And the con man is an artful storyteller. In another country and another time, he could have been a great novelist, but he is on the Mississippi River in the mid-nineteenth century and he's given himself over to toying with the locals.

Having severed the merchant's ties to his own recollections, the con man moves in close. "I want a friend in whom I may confide," he says, and begins to unfold the sad story of his recent grief. Before too long the country merchant finds himself moved beyond the solicited shilling: "As the story went on, he drew from his wallet a bank note, but after a while, at some still more unhappy revelation, changed it for another, probably of a somewhat larger amount."

In Melville's America, it's not light flooding the mind that's the mark of true belief; it's money changing hands.

TO SECURE A LIE, surround it with a moat of forgetfulness.

"THE PRECIPITATE" of a sixteen-year exploration, thoughts written down "as *remarks*, short paragraphs, of which there is sometimes a fairly long chain about the same subject" while at other times "a sudden change, jumping from one topic to another," says Wittgenstein of his *Philosophical Investigations*.

"Writer is weary unto death of making up stories," writes David Markson on the opening page of *This Is Not a Novel*, adding, more than a hundred pages later, "Nonlinear. Discontinuous. Collage-like. An assemblage."

CIRCLES. Dinner at the round mahogany table that Mother and Father bought in London fifty years ago. Father has read a book about the erosion of ocean beaches on the East Coast. Mother says, "That book never mentions the hurricane of '38." She was nineteen that year and in college at Mount Holyoke. "I don't know how I knew it," she says, "but I knew there was an eye to the storm, and so I made my way to Safford Hall." Two minutes later she says, "That book never mentions the hurricane of '38. I don't know how I knew it, but I knew there was an eye to the storm, and so I made my way to Safford Hall." Later she says, "That book never mentions the hurricane of '38. I don't know how I knew it, but I knew there was an eye to the storm, and so I made my way to Safford Hall."

"You're going in circles," Father says. They say the CAT scan showed some atrophy of her frontal lobes, but the old material is still there. She is very much her old self. Her verbal tics and defenses remain. "Well, now, Mrs. Pettibone," she says to herself, staring into the refrigerator before dinner. "We'll cope." "We'll get along." She is the shell of her old self, calcified language and no organism alive enough to lay down new layers.

Would it be possible to live in such a way as to never acquire habits of mind? When my short-term memory goes, I don't want to be penned up in the wickerwork of my rote responses. If I start being my old self, no heroic measures, please.

SPEECHLESS. In Chinese myth, Old Lady Mêng sits at the exit from the underworld serving the Broth of Oblivion so that all reincarnated souls come to life having forgotten the spirit world, their former incarnations, and even their speech (although legend has it that occasionally a miracle child is born talking, having avoided Lady Mêng's broth).

REMEMBER WHO YOU ARE. Says Jorge Luis Borges, "I should say I am greedy for death, that I want to stop waking up every morning, finding: Well, here I am, I have to go back to Borges.

"There's a word in Spanish. . . . Instead of saying 'to wake up,' you say *recordarse*, that is, to record yourself, to remember yourself. . . . Every morning I get that feeling because I am more or less nonexistent. Then when I wake up, I always feel I'm being let down. Because, well, here I am. Here's the same old stupid game going on. I have to be somebody. I have to be exactly that somebody."

AGAINST INSOMNIA. In an essay in the journal *Nature*, Graeme Mitchison and Francis Crick (one of the men who discovered the shape of DNA) once argued, "We dream in order to forget." Each of our days is so filled with particularity, we are so swamped with sensory detail, that the mind needs some sort of filtering mechanism to sort out the trivial and retain the essential. Dreaming, Crick argues, serves this function. In fact, without some such process we would all be like the monstrous title character of Borges's short story "Funes, the Memorious," who is unable to forget even the smallest details of his day, so that a tree at 3:06 p.m. with the light just so on its leaves stays with him as wholly distinct from the same tree two minutes later shaded by a cloud. Funes "was . . . almost incapable of general, platonic ideas," Borges's narrator remarks, for "to think is to forget a difference, to generalize, to abstract." It is required of us to forget many particular trees before we can know Tree itself. The ancients broadened the stroke, saying that it is required of us to forget entire worlds—the Age of Iron, these eons of hearsay—before we can recall to mind eternal things.

STATE-TRANSITION AMNESIA. The old mythmakers often puzzled over how a person might either preserve memory or induce forgetfulness when moving from one state of being to another, focusing usually on the transition between life and death (entering the underworld / emerging from the womb) but also on crossing the boundaries between different eras (the golden age / the Age of Iron), places (home/away), moods (rage/equanimity), and levels of consciousness (waking/sleep).

The ancients also showed an interest in the amnesic effects of various drugs and thus of the line between sobriety and intoxication. (In Homer, we hear of nepenthe easing men's "pains and irritations, making them forget their troubles," and of the home-forgetting power of the lotus plant; or in China, think of the Broth of Oblivion Old Lady Mêng serves to the child about to be born.)

Nowadays, we might frame the boundary effects of such transitions in terms of "state-dependent memory," the idea being that memories drop away as we move from one state of being to another but can then be recovered when we move back. In the folklore of memory, the story is typically told of the drunk who hides his car keys while on a bender and can't remember where he put them until he gets drunk again. Empirical research has never produced such a clear-cut case, but studies done with various drugs—alcohol, amphetamines, barbiturates, marijuana, nicotine, and more—nonetheless show that state-dependent memory is not just folklore.

In one experiment, college students smoked marijuana—half of the joints nicely laced with psychotropic THC and the other half inert—and then studied a dozen sets of words grouped into categories. Under "flowers," for example, appeared two common names ("pansy" and "rose") and two less common ("jonquil" and "zinnia"). Days later, the students were tested on how many words they could remember. When the previously stoned students got stoned again, their ability to recall improved by 10 or 15 percent.

So, yes, state-dependent memory exists, although, as the small percentages of such studies indicate, the drug effects are weak and limited.

And no matter the strength of the drug effects, state dependency has a fairly simple explanation: recollection is often tied to context, and drug intoxication is itself a context. Just as a return to the site of an event—either in mind or in fact—will bring back memories, so too will a return to being stoned.

And it is by focusing on changes of context that we'll find the positive value not so much of memory reclaimed as of the initial forgetting that accompanies the move from one state to another. Memories that endure no matter how our contexts change can be a hindrance, not a boon, if the history they carry forward obscures the new setting rather than illuminating it. In such cases, what one study called "the amnesic effect of state change" allows a welcome attention to the new and unexpected. It would be all to the good if the drunk could school himself in sobriety and never remember where he hid the car keys.

GRANDMA HYDE VERSUS FOUCAULT. "The analysis of descent permits the dissociation of the self," rather than its unification, writes Michel Foucault. The truth about who you are lies not at the root of the tree but rather out at the tips of the branches, the thousand tips.

In 1937, my grandmother published *The Descendents of Andrew Hyde*, himself the "sixth in descent from William Hyde of Norwich, Connecticut," this William Hyde being born in England, probably in 1610, and coming to the colonies in 1633.

Twelve generations separate me from William Hyde. I have two parents, four grandparents, eight great-grandparents. . . . My forebears from 1610 may number 2,048. Grandmother's book remembers William Hyde but forgets 2,047 other ancestors, including William's wife.

To practice subversive genealogy means to forget the idealism of a singular forefather and remember these thousands. With that remembrance you must multiply the sense of who you are, multiply it until it disappears. Even Foucault studies the self to forget the self.

Gold Orphic tablet and case found in Petelia, southern Italy

FROM THE MUSEUM OF FORGETTING: THE TWO WATERS. The Petelia tablet is a thin sheet of gold inscribed with lines of somewhat muddled Greek—verses taken from a longer Orphic poem of great antiquity. Discovered in a tomb in southern Italy and dating from the fourth century B.C., this gold sheet was rolled up and placed in a cylinder hung on a chain around the neck of the dead. It contains instructions on how to travel safely through the underworld. These say to the initiate,

> In the halls of Hades you will find on the right, by a ghostly cypress tree, a spring where the dead souls descending wash away their lives. Do not even draw close to this spring for it offers the Waters of Forgetfulness.
>
> Farther on you will find the pool of Memory. Over this stand guardians. They will ask with keen mind what is your quest in the gloom of deadly Hades. Tell them the

whole truth straight out. Say: “I am the child of Earth and starry Heaven, but of Heaven is my true lineage. I am parched with thirst and perishing: give me quickly chill water flowing from the pool of Memory.”

Assuredly the kings of the underworld take pity on you, and will give you water from the spring; then you, when you have drunk, traverse the holy path which other initiates and bacchants tread in glory. After that you will rule among the other heroes.

THE TEST. The doctor asked Mother to remember three words, two concrete and one abstract: "rose, virtue, shoe." Ten minutes later, he asked if she remembered them. "Virtue" had slipped away. Father told the story at dinner, repeating the words himself. Mother looked trapped, distressed. She went to bed early in those days, and Father was perplexed. "What did we use to do in the evenings?" he asked.

THE TWO WATERS—AN ORACLE. In his second-century *Description of Greece*, the historian Pausanias tells us that a certain Trophonios—perhaps a hero, perhaps a god, but in any event a power (the name means "Nourisher of the Mind")—had an oracle at Labadie. Any man wanting to inquire about the future would descend into Trophonios's cave having first purified himself for several days, bathing only in the river Herkyna and making sacrifices, especially the sacrifice of a ram whose entrails would reveal whether the inquiry would be graciously received.

On the night of his descent, the petitioner would be taken to the river by two young boys who would wash and anoint him with oil. Priests would then lead him to two fountains standing near each other. From these he would drink the Water of Lethe so as to forget his past and the Water of Mnemosyne so as to recall all he saw during his descent. Dressed in linen, he would then climb a ladder down into the chasm, lie on his back, thrust his legs feetfirst into a hole, the rest of his body being swiftly drawn in like that of a man pulled under by the current of a fast-flowing river.

Later, having learned of the future, he would be swept upward again, his feet darting first out of the same opening. The priests would set him on the Chair of Memory, where, paralyzed with fear and unaware of himself and his surroundings, he would speak what he had seen and heard. Then he would be given over to his relatives, who would care for him until he recovered the ability to laugh.

The two waters of Trophonios's oracle differ from those of the Petelia tablet and other Orphic poems giving instruction to the dead. In the Orphic case, a choice has to be made:

forgetfulness must be avoided, memory alone offering a path out of this world. In the case of this oracle, on the other hand, the two waters appear in a sequence and are complementary, not contradictory. They bespeak the conjoining or the ambiguity of Forgetting/Not-Forgetting, Covering/Discovering, *Lethe/Aletheia*, each power inseparable from and shadowed by the other. Supplicants do not choose between the two but instead become vessels in which the waters are held in a single solution.

What is the sign or the mark of those who have drunk that blend of Memory and Forgetting? Here it is laughter.

BADMINTON. "One who has perfected himself in the twin arts of remembering and forgetting is in a position to play at battledore and shuttlecock with the whole of existence," says Søren Kierkegaard.

APOPTOSIS. As the human embryo develops, its organs are shaped by a process known as "programmed cell death." Two flipper-like appendages turn into hands as the cells between the fingers die off, separating the digits. Sometimes the cells just fall away, and at other times they are devoured by other cells, there being at least two forms of natural cell death—autophagy, or self-eating, and apoptosis, from the Greek for the "dropping off" of petals from flowers or leaves from trees. Both of these must be distinguished from the cell death that results from traumatic wounds, disease, or old age. Trauma simply damages the body, whereas programmed cell death carves useful organs and tissues out of otherwise undifferentiated flesh. It is a shaping force, an aesthetic force.

Normal forgetting is the programmed cell death of mental life. It winnows the day. It shapes experience into a useful story.

MÍMIR'S SKULL. All-Father Odin, leaving one of his eyes as a pledge, acquired his ancestral knowledge and runic wisdom by drinking the waters that bubble up in Mímir's spring at one of the roots of the World Tree, the great ash Yggdrasil. The giant Mímir (the name means "memory") guards that spring, and he too "is full of ancient lore" for having drunk its waters. Some of the Norse stories have it that Mímir was decapitated in a battle with the Vanir but that Odin kept the head alive with herbs and magic spells and, as with the severed head of Orpheus singing still in a cave at Lesbos, this head went on sharing its secrets whenever Odin was in need. Says the seeress in the *Völuspá*, "Odin murmured with Mímir's head" as Ragnarok—the doom of the gods—drew near.

Some have suggested that what is found in Mímir's spring is not only water but also the giant's severed head or, rather, his skull, there being Celtic and Germanic traditions in which skulls placed in wells give curative and prophetic power, especially if the skull itself is used as the drinking vessel (as one once was by the poet Byron, who, discovering on his estate the bones of "some jolly friar," had the skull mounted as a cup for wine—"the drink of Gods"—so as to "rhyme and revel with the dead" in imitation "of the Goths of old").

WATERS BUBBLE UP. Bruce Lincoln, a historian of religions at Chicago, once gathered a range of Indo-European myths and tried to reconstruct from them a single proto-Indo-European myth about what happens to the souls of the dead as they travel through the underworld. His essay "Waters of Memory, Waters of Forgetfulness" lays out this proto-myth; in it, the dead must first drink from a spring or cross a river or lake whose waters wash away all their memories. Their memories are not lost, however: dissolved in the water, they are carried to a spring where they bubble up to be drunk by certain individuals—bards, prophets, seers—who become infused with wisdom, knowing, as it were, the collective experience of all who came before.

In the Greek case, the river Lethe carries the waters of forgetfulness; in the Orphic tradition, they are found in a spring marked by a white cypress "to the left of the house of Hades." In the Upanishads, the early Vedic texts from India, the dead come to the river Vijara—"Apart for Old Age"—and cross it "by mind," shaking off their past deeds both good and bad. In the Norse stories, the waters of forgetfulness plausibly belong to the river Gjöll, which flows "next to the gates of Hel," the realm of all the dead but for the battle-slain.

For an example of where this water might emerge, Lincoln turns to Mímir's spring, for it was there, by drinking the waters of memory, that All-Father Odin acquired his wisdom.

TWO CATEGORIES. A lively imagination requires a balance of memory and forgetting. “You should go in for a blending of the two elements, memory and oblivion,” says Jorge Luis Borges, “and we call that imagination.” Because Mnemosyne is the mother of the Muses, all arts require her double power, her ability to record or erase as the need may be. There are then two ways for memory to destroy imagination: by retaining too many abstractions (thus failing to perceive fresh detail) and by retaining too many details (thus failing to perceive abstractions, as with Borges’s Funes). The point is worth repeating because two beneficial categories of forgetting recur throughout these notebooks: in one, a mind has become too attached to its concepts or thought-habits and needs to drop them so as to attend again to detail; in the other, a surfeit of detail clogs the flow of thought and must be winnowed so as to reveal the larger shapes of concept and abstraction.

NO FAMILY, NO MOTHER. Roland Barthes, looking at photographs, made a rule for himself so as to avoid the first of the two ways that memory might deaden imagination: he tried never to reduce himself to the "disincarnated, disaffected" kinship categories popular in the social sciences. "This principle obligated me to 'forget' two institutions: the Family, the Mother."

Barthes made himself drop such categories so as to preserve the particularity of his mother, who had recently died and whom he was trying to call to mind by looking at photographs. Most of the images he found failed to bring her back. "I never recognized her except in fragments"—a part of her face, the way she held her hands—"which is to say that I missed her *being*."

Yet finally he found an image that was "indeed essential," that achieved, "utopically, *the impossible science of the unique being*." "The photograph was very old. The corners were blunted from having been pasted into an album, the sepia print had faded, and the picture just managed to show two children standing together at the end of a little wooden bridge in a glassed-in conservatory. . . . My mother was five at the time."

In the book in which he tells this story, *Camera Lucida*, Barthes illustrates his argument with many images, but he never reproduces this essential photograph. "It exists only for me." Others might see in it the late nineteenth century—its clothing, its architecture—they might even see "the Family, the Mother," but none would see the unique being, the one that mattered to Roland Barthes.

Sometimes a considered forgetting is the first step toward bringing the memory of the dead to life.

The real constitution of each thing is accustomed to hide itself.
—HERACLITUS, FRAG. 123

FORGOTTEN IS ALSO TRUE. How odd that the Greek word now translated as "truth" is a *negative—a-lethe*, the *not*-forgotten, the *un*-concealed—the implication being that the ground condition of the world (or of the mind) is obscurity and mystery and that persons who speak the truth have done the work of (or been given a gift for) un-hiding, calling to mind what is otherwise veiled, covered, dark, silent.

Marcel Detienne's *Masters of Truth in Archaic Greece* lists three persons thought capable of such work in the archaic age: the poet, the prophet, and the just king. These were the vessels through whom a power called *Aletheia* spoke. The knowledge she offered was "a form of divinatory omniscience"; she gave the poet "the power to 'decipher the invisible,'" to recall not the past exactly but the atemporal suchness of things, their otherwise obscure being.

And although this divine power may overcome or negate obscurity and mystery, by Detienne's reading she is not split or separated from those ground conditions: "*Aletheia* and *Lethe* are not exclusive or contradictory . . . ; they constitute two extremes of a single religious power."

In archaic Greece, these twin forces belonged to a set of related dualities, *Aletheia* aligned with memory, justice, sung speech, light, and praise, and *Lethe* aligned with oblivion, hiddenness, silence, darkness, and blame. *Aletheia* "was not the opposite of lies or falsehoods"; she was the opposite of all these other things, or rather she is one portion of an ambiguous force that can enlighten or darken, can lead to speech or silence, praise or blame. The Muses are agents not just of memory but of memory-forgetting (as in Hesiod, where their song brings both memory and "the forgetting of ills," or in the *Iliad*, where they punish a boastful Thracian singer by making him "forget his artful playing").

Let us then reclaim forgetting as a component of truth, there being "no *Aletheia* without a measure of *Lethe*." When a diviner or poet penetrates the invisible world, Memory and Oblivion both are present. And what is the name of this double thing found at the seam of silence and speech, praise and blame, light and darkness? Call it imagination, call it poetry.

THE BIRTH OF A MEMORY ART. Cicero's book on oratory recounts the origin story of the Memory Palace tradition, the one in which an orator commits to memory the elements of his speech by mentally placing an image for each of his points in a sequence of locations, as if in the rooms of a palace. Cicero has a certain Antonius express his gratitude "to the famous Simonides of Ceos, who is said to have first invented the science of mnemonics," and then has Antonius tell the story:

> Simonides was dining at the house of a wealthy nobleman named Scopas . . . , and chanted a lyric poem which he had composed in honour of his host, in which he followed the custom of the poets by including for decorative purposes a long passage referring to Castor and Pollux; whereupon Scopas with excessive meanness told him he would pay him half the fee agreed on for the poem. . . . The story runs that a little later a message was brought to Simonides to go outside, as two young men were standing at the door who earnestly requested him to come out; so he rose from his seat and went out, and could not see anybody.

It seems that the young men were in fact Castor and Pollux, grateful for being noted in Simonides's poem and protecting him from a punishment about to be inflicted on the stingy patron:

> In the interval of his absence the roof of the hall where Scopas was giving the banquet fell in, crushing Scopas himself and his relations underneath the ruins and killing

them; and when their friends wanted to bury them but were altogether unable to know them apart as they had been completely crushed, the story goes that Simonides was enabled by his recollection of the place in which each of them had been reclining at table to identify them for separate interment; and that this circumstance suggested to him the discovery of the truth that the best aid to clearness of memory consists in orderly arrangement. He inferred that persons desiring to train this faculty must select localities and form mental images of the facts they wish to remember and store those images in the localities.

TESTES. A second Latin book on rhetoric, the *Ad Herennium*, gives instructions for forming Cicero's "mental images." Above all we're told to make them dramatic. Don't just imagine your friend's face; imagine the face smeared with blood. "Ordinary things easily slip from the memory while the striking and novel stay longer."

Sometimes "one entire matter" can be recorded by composing a single such striking image, the example given being that of a lawyer called to defend a man charged with poisoning another in order to gain an inheritance, a crime committed despite the presence of many witnesses. To remember this case, the lawyer is advised to form an image of the murdered man lying in bed with the defendant at his bedside holding a cup in his right hand, tablets in his left, and, hanging from the fourth finger of that hand, a ram's testicles.

How to decode that image? Apparently, the cup is there to recall the poison, the tablets to indicate the inheritance, and those ram's testicles, well, maybe *testiculos* is meant to suggest *testes*, witnesses, or perhaps—because ram scrota were used to make purses—the image suggests money used to bribe the witnesses.

Whatever the case, out of such curious and crazy seeds eventually grew the arts of memory that were to dominate European rhetoric and religious speculation for centuries to come.

DRAWN DOWN INTO TIME. While these stories out of Latin rhetoric are of interest in their own right, I offer them in the context of Marcel Detienne's sketch of the archaic *Lethe-Aletheia* mythology, for it is Detienne's argument that in the history of memory and forgetting it was especially the sixth-century Simonides of Ceos who took those twinned powers away from their archaic masters—the bard, the diviner, and the just king—and gave them over to the sophists and rhetoricians, practitioners of persuasion and illusion. In Cicero's account, notice that Simonides is a hired hand, writing for a fee, and that as such, he is the literary equivalent of a court painter, his employer being a wealthy aristocrat. "By the classical period," writes Detienne, "the system of thought that privileged sung speech as a religious power had become no more than an anachronism. . . . The poet's job now was to exalt the nobility and praise the rich landowners." With Simonides, "memory became a secularized technique" and forgetting consequently a failure of technique, a mental deficit rather than a shaping power working in tandem with its twin.

Whereas in the archaic age these powers belonged to certain special persons, in the classical age they are available to any student of "the science of mnemonics." Whereas previously the poet spoke without artifice ("speaking *Aletheia* came as naturally as breathing"), now there are schools of rhetoric. Whereas previously the voice had been singular and efficacious, atemporal and commanding, now it is but one among many and bent not on assertion but on persuasion. Where previously the goal was a release from human time, now time became "the best of things," Simonides said, because "it is in time that one learns and memorizes." Where in the archaic age the sequential waters of memory and forgetfulness organized the petitioner's quest for prophetic knowledge, in the classical age a set of memory tricks helps an absentminded lawyer remember that his client is accused of murder.

BOREDOM. Writing about the cosmology of the Trobriand islanders, the anthropologist Susan Montague tells us that the Trobriand universe is a vast disembodied space filled with both minds and energy. Cosmic minds are all-seeing, all-knowing, and all-powerful, able to manipulate the energy of the universe toward whatever end they desire.

But in spite of, or rather because of, these remarkable endowments, cosmic minds have a problem: cosmic boredom. They have the power to do anything they wish, but because they have no needs, that power has no purpose. They may be all-knowing, but to be all-knowing means there's nothing to think about. So they sit around bored to death or, rather, bored to life, because as it happens, they have invented a way to relieve cosmic boredom: it is to play the amusing game of life.

To play, you must be born into a human body, and to be born as such, you must forget the fullness of what you knew and work only with what can be known through the body. A human being is someone who has abandoned the boring surfeit of knowledge so as to come alive.

LIQUIDATION. Working to heal herself of the trauma of rape, Sohaila Abdulali took it upon herself to counsel young women, teaching them about rape's dangers and effects. At first she found it upsetting to include her own story in these classes, but after many tellings the intensity of feeling faded. She even surprised herself during one class. Someone asked her what was the worst thing about her experience: "Suddenly I looked at them all and said, the thing I hate the most about it is that it's *boring*." Time had passed, the work had been done, and she wasn't interested anymore. The French psychologist Pierre Janet once suggested that we think of memory not as a thing fixed in the mind but as an action, "the action of telling a story," and when it is successful, that action leads to "the stage of liquidation." Forgetting appears when the story has been so fully told as to wear itself out. Then time begins to flow again; then the future can unfold.

TWO BURIALS. Given that the etymological root of the Greek *lethe* suggests that forgetting is the covering up or hiding of something, we could extend the image and say that to forget is to bury. And to differentiate some kinds of forgetting—especially in regard to trauma, both individual and collective—let us say that there are two kinds of burials: in one, something is hidden because we can't stand to look at it; in the other, it is buried because we are done with it. It has been revealed and examined, and now it may be covered up or dropped for good. This latter is proper burial, burial after attention has been paid and funeral rites observed.

SORTING THE DEAD. Those who never receive proper burial are denied the relief of state-transition amnesia, their memories sticking to them even in death. In Virgil's *Aeneid*, Aeneas travels to the underworld in search of his father. Coming to the rivers where Charon ferries the dead to the otherworld, he sees that the ferryman is refusing passage to some of the thronging souls. "What divides the dead?" he asks the Sibyl, his guide; she replies that those denied passage are the "helpless and graveless." Charon will not carry them across the waters "until their bones have found a resting place. A hundred years they roam and flit about these shores; then only are they admitted and revisit the longed-for pools."

IN FIJI, according to Basil Thomson, the souls of the dead, after various adventures, come to a spring and drink to forget sorrow. Why, exactly? Because the relatives of the dead in the daylight world are tired of mourning and "savage etiquette" prescribes that as long as the dead soul remembers, his relations must remember too. They find this tedious, so the shades drink the Water of Solace and the living are released.

IN ANNE MICHAELS'S NOVEL *Fugitive Pieces*, the parents and sister of the young Holocaust survivor Jakob Beer have been killed, but he remembers them in dreams. When he wakes, he feels a particular anguish: "the possibility that it was as painful for them to be remembered as it was for me to remember them; that I was haunting my parents and Bella with my calling, startling them awake in their black beds."

"LET GO." In a long 2017 Facebook post, the Diné, or Navajo, activist, artist, and ceremonial leader Pat McCabe—also known as Woman Stands Shining—explained her resistance to the call to "never forget."

McCabe had once worked with a shamanic healer to address her serial depressions. During one session, she had a vision of living in Canyon de Chelly on Navajo tribal lands and witnessing a massacre of her people at the hands of "beings who had the appearance of humans, who were all identically dressed in blue." Over the years, her vision kept returning until she finally sought out a place where the events might have in fact occurred—a place aptly named Massacre Cave. There she unexpectedly found herself praying.

"I began to address my ancestors. . . . I said to them, that we would love them always, and forever, but that somehow we must forget, or let go of, all of the violence that had come before now, or we ourselves would complete the job of genocide that the U.S. government began. I begged them, my ancestors, to let us go free. I told them they must find their way all the way home to the Spirit World.

"And then I prayed with all my heart, and all my tears, and asked for Creator to open the gate for them to travel, and to leave us in peace, and for them to find peace beyond the gate, and for each of us to travel in the correct way once again, each in our own world, me in this Earth Walk world and they, true ancestors in the Spirit World. I saw part of this take place, I saw them traveling in long lines out of this place and into the world beyond."

"TEACH ME I AM FORGOTTEN by the dead / And that the dead is by herself forgot," wrote Emerson at the age of twenty-seven, his young wife, Ellen, having died.

In his biography of Emerson, Robert D. Richardson points out that this prayer came at a turning point in Emerson's life. He soon left his Concord home and traveled to Europe. He wanted to live again, and to do so, the boundary that separates the living from the dead must be sealed. In a case like this, "never forget" would be a deadly curse.

BLOOD AT THE ROOT. There's something odd worth noting in Cicero's account of the invention of artificial memory. Remember: the poet Simonides was insulted at a banquet; called away, he briefly left the banquet hall; while he was out, the roof collapsed, crushing the host and all his relations, mangling their bodies so completely that none of the corpses could be identified except by the returning poet. Simonides could recall where each guest was sitting and thus discovered, wrote Cicero, that anyone wishing to train the memory "must select localities and form mental images of the facts they wish to remember."

What's strange about this story going forward—for it is the beginning of a centuries-long interest in the place system of memory—is how much is made of the method and how little of those unrecognizable, oozing slabs of human flesh and bone. The "completely crushed" bodies add a memory-enhancing hook of horror to the otherwise benign localities and images.

In the rhetorical tradition, the tree of memory set its roots in blood.

AN ALTAR TO OBLIVION. If the arts of memory are rooted in blood, could there be an art of forgetting that puts an end to bloodshed?

In the Erechtheum on the Acropolis in Athens, there once stood, says Plutarch, an altar to *Lethe*, to Forgetfulness, meant to remind Athenians to forget a mythic dispute between Poseidon and Athena. Each god had sought to win the city's favor with a gift, Poseidon offering a spring of salty water and Athena, the winner, an olive tree. Defeated, Poseidon did not begrudge the loss, however, but took it, says Plutarch, with "an easy-going absence of resentment." The dispute between Poseidon and Athena supposedly took place on the second day of the last month of summer (Boëdromion), and Athenians have ever since omitted that day from their calendar. The erased date and the altar to Forgetfulness are reminders that the foundational divine discord should be left to the past, not brought forward.

ENDLESS. Perhaps all nations have their foundational discord. In the United States, it was the debate over slavery, not solved by the compromises written into the Constitution and not solved by the War Between the States. Terry Alford, author of a 2015 biography of Abraham Lincoln's assassin, John Wilkes Booth, reports that even as he was working on his book—a century and a half after the event—a custom had arisen in which people put Lincoln pennies faceup on the Booth family crypt in Baltimore, as if to seal the assassin in his grave. But others had reversed the ritual, leaving pennies with Lincoln's face down in the alley behind Ford's Theatre, the site of the assassination. "That Civil War," Mr. Alford said, "is still going on."

MIXING MYTH AND HISTORY. The Athenians omit the second day of Boëdromion from their calendar so as to remember to forget the founding discord between Poseidon and Athena. In noting this, Plutarch observed that Poseidon exceeded Thrasybulus in civic spirit, for the god agreed to bear no grudge in his hour of defeat, whereas Thrasybulus's similar graciousness appeared only after a famous victory in a battle against tyranny.

THE TYRANNY. At the end of the Peloponnesian War, the citizens of Athens, thoroughly beaten and starving, surrendered to Sparta, whereupon the Spartans appointed thirty Athenians of oligarchic leanings to write a new constitution. But, as Xenophon tells us, the Athenians "continually delayed framing and publishing this constitution" and instead initiated a civil war against the city's democrats and resident aliens.

Beginning in September of 404 B.C., the Thirty Tyrants, as they are now called, arrested and put to death all who had previously offended them or who now aroused their enmity. They encouraged collaborating citizens to inform on their neighbors, thereby sending them to death. They disarmed their enemies and seized their lands and property; they killed resident aliens, then sold their goods to pay a mercenary militia; they occupied the village of Eleusis and, to make it a refuge for themselves alone, executed all male inhabitants. When one of their own questioned the excesses of this reign of terror, they passed him the bowl of hemlock. By the end, thousands had been driven into exile and fifteen hundred killed, more than during any decade of the war just passed.

As might be expected, resistance to the Thirty Tyrants soon arose, and in May of 403, in a final battle at the Piraeus, Thrasybulus and his fellow democrats defeated the oligarchy.

As that battle drew to a close, Cleocritus of the democratic resistance called for reconciliation with his fellow Athenians. "Citizens . . . , why do you want to kill us . . . ? We have joined with you in the holiest rituals, in the most beautiful sacrifices and festivals. We have been fellow dancers with you, fellow students, and fellow soldiers. . . . For the sake of our kinship, our marriage ties, and our fellowship . . . , put a stop to this crime against our city."

THE DEATH OF POLEMARCHUS. Lysias, one of the great Attic orators and a resident alien in Athens at the time of the tyranny, tells the story of how Eratosthenes, one of the Thirty, came upon Lysias's brother Polemarchus in the street, arrested him without charge, and carried him off to prison. The Thirty sent down their customary order, that Polemarchus was to drink the hemlock. They allowed him no hearing, gave him no chance at self-defense, would not tell him why he was to die. After his family carried his body from prison, the Thirty forbade them to hold his funeral rites in their own homes, and so they laid Polemarchus out in a hired shed. Though they were rich in cloaks, the Thirty made them wrap Polemarchus in a borrowed shroud and rest his head on a borrowed pillow. The Thirty confiscated his property—slaves, gold and silver, ornaments and bronze, furniture and clothing. When Melobius, another of the Thirty, came into the house, he immediately tore from the ears of Polemarchus's wife her earrings made of gold.

Multiply such thieving and such murder by fifteen hundred dead and again by thousands exiled, and you will have an estimate of the grief and rage endemic to Athens on the day the tyrants fell, of how hard it might have been to heed Cleocritus's call for reconciliation.

THE UNFORGETTABLE. Some emotions grip us, then fall away. A great happiness can bring sleepless nights when first it blooms, but the possession eventually fades. Two years out, no one says, "I cannot shake my joy!"

Grief and rage, however—these can go on and on. Decades go by and still a loss or wound from childhood colors our days. Two decades have passed since Odysseus left for war, and still the old swineherd Eumaeus grieves "unforgettingly" for his absent master.

Rage may be the more troubling of the unforgettables, and especially rage knit together with grief because these don't just persist; they call for action, and in action taken, they reseed themselves generation after generation. All the years of the Trojan War have passed, and still Clytemnestra cannot forget how Agamemnon sacrificed their daughter to put a wind in his sails, and so she takes her revenge, a revenge that plants the seed in turn for their children, Orestes and Electra, to seek vengeance against her.

In Sophocles's play that bears her name, Electra speaks of her father's murder as a sorrow (or evil) that cannot be forgotten and describes her own passion (or anger) in similar terms, though in this case the Greek for "not forgetting" (*our láthei*) might better be translated from its root meaning—"it does not escape notice," "it is not hidden." The image is of anger as a thing that the mind cannot bury, cannot help being aware of. Electra's passion won't let her alone. It's intrusive. It bugs her. We do not control the unforgettable; it controls us.

The spirits of such unforgetting are called the Furies, the Erinyes. They cling to the memory of hurt and harm, injury and insult. Their names are Grievance, Ceaseless, and Bloodlust. Their names are Grudge, Relentless, and Payback. They bloat the present with the undigested past. "Most dreaded of the forces of insomnia," they harry the mind, demanding for its release a ransom paid in blood.

THE TERMS OF PEACE. At the end of the Athenian civil war, after the democrats had defeated the oligarchs, negotiations led to what Aristotle in *The Athenian Constitution* calls "peace and reconciliation." By the terms of the agreement, the Thirty and several small groups of their supporters were exiled to nearby Eleusis (and could be subject to criminal prosecution if they returned). All others, no matter their involvement in the tyranny, were granted amnesty. They were allowed to stay in Athens provided that each took an oath, swearing "not to remember the recent misfortunes."

The oath is the crux of the Athenian amnesty and, before we unpack its complexity, it should be said that, by all accounts, it worked; it put an end to the fighting and to any ongoing cycle of revenge killings. "On this occasion," writes Aristotle, "the Athenians reacted to their previous misfortunes . . . better and more public-spiritedly than anyone else at any other time."

FORGET ABOUT IT. A family has saved for a trip to Carthage, only to find that all the money must go to pay a tax bill. Says the wife to the husband, "We can forget about Carthage."

A teenager has misbehaved and his parents say, "You can forget about using the car tonight."

When we say, "Don't forget the milk," we indicate an act that should follow from the thought. It wouldn't do to say, "I was thinking about milk the whole time; I just didn't buy it."

In one of his endless meditations on language, Ludwig Wittgenstein writes, "Suppose someone points to a vase and says 'Look at that marvelous blue—forget about the shape.' Or: 'Look at the marvelous shape—forget about the color.' No doubt you'll do something *different* in each case."

One category of forgetfulness has to do with putting a thought aside, as it were, and with *the nonaction* that follows. "To forget about the shape" of the vase means to refrain from putting it in play, mentally, and thus not to make it part of whatever "you'll do." "Forget about Carthage" doesn't mean you can't think about it, just that thinking about it can't lead to a trip.

In all such cases, forgetting is a lack of action, not a lack of thought. You can think about driving the car all you want, but you won't be driving it tonight. Forgetting in these cases severs the otherwise reflexive link between thought and action. Many things may come to mind, but when they do, nothing happens. The seeds of karma are not sown.

THE OATH. The key phrase in the Athenian amnesty oath is variously translated as "it is forbidden to recall the recent misfortunes" or to "recall the past misdeeds" or to "harbor grievances against any citizen." The Greek phrase itself is *mê mnêsikakein* (μὴ μνησικακεῖν), *mê* being "not," and *mnêsikakein* being a compound built from *mnes-*, indicating memory, and *kakein* from *kaka*, indicating any bad or evil thing. As Nicole Loraux argues, the "bringing back to memory" that the oath forbids is not simple recollection but rather a summoning of memory against an opponent: "*Mnêsikakein* implies that one wields a memory like a weapon, that one attacks or punishes someone, in short, that one seeks revenge."

The language echoes the old tradition of blood vengeance. In the *Oresteia*, for example, the Furies describe themselves as those who "hold the memory of evil (*mnemonics kakôn*)," the point being that the amnesty oath is *an inversion of that epithet* and, as such, should be seen as a speech act directed against everything the Furies represent, the primordial forces of unforgettable grief and rage.

That being the case, the negation the oath declares is a bit of an oxymoron for, given what we know about the Furies, we might now translate it as a promise "to forget the unforgettable"—a contradiction in terms unless, that is, we add the distinction just made between symbolic action (thought, speech, writing) and actual action (for example, acts of revenge). Athenians swore to forget about "recent misfortunes" in terms of action, but that didn't mean they couldn't speak or write about them.

In fact, as the legal scholar Adriaan Lanni has pointed out, the amnesty was quite leaky when it came to the actual airing of grievances, especially in court cases about matters wholly unrelated to the civil war. Athenian courts had neither judges as such nor lawyers, cases being heard by randomly selected juries of several hundred adult male citizens. In addressing the jury, litigants were allowed to bring up all sorts of evidence that we would now think of as irrelevant or prejudicial: how the accused treated his parents, for example, or—to the point here—how he had behaved during the tyranny. Amnesty did not mean amnesia or silence; gossip and shaming proceeded heartily outside the prohibition on litigation directly related to civil war crimes. The amnesty worked in part because there was a way for grief and anger to be spoken even as everyone swore to forget about actual action. Speech was the charm deployed against the incarnate violence of the unforgettable.

"ACTS OF OBLIVION" was the name given in later centuries to grants of amnesty such as, for example, the 1560 Treaty of Edinburgh, signed after Reformation hostilities in Scotland ("All things done here against the laws shall be discharged, and a law of oblivion shall be established") or the 1648 Treaty of Westphalia signed at the close of the Thirty Years' War ("There shall be . . . a perpetual Oblivion . . . of all that has been committed since the beginning of these Troubles." All "shall be bury'd in eternal Oblivion").

Sometimes those who would not forget "the recent misfortunes" were threatened with punishment. Upon the restoration of Charles II to the throne, the 1660 Act of Oblivion levied fines upon anyone who, for the next few years, "presume[d] maliciously," in speech or in writing, "to revive the Memory of the late Differences." Things were even tougher in the British colonies. After Protestants rebelled against Maryland's Catholic proprietor, the 1650 Act of Oblivion singled out all whose "reviling speeches" might disturb "the Amity desired" and threatened them with "any one or more of these": imprisonment, fines, banishment, pillory, and whipping.

THE PHILTRUM. In Jewish legend, the Angel of the Night, Laïlah, places the fertilized soul of a child in the womb and, kindling a light so the soul can see the world from end to end, teaches it about the just and the wicked, those who follow the Torah and God's commandments and those who do not. When it comes time to be born, the angel lightly strokes the child's upper lip, leaving a small indentation. Immediately, the newborn forgets all it has seen and learned and comes into the world crying.

BABBLE. The prattle of babies displays an amazing range. The linguist Roman Jakobson writes that the babbling infant voices phonemes "which are never found within a single language or even a group of languages—consonants of any place of articulation, palatalized and rounded consonants, sibilants, affricates, clicks, complex vowels, diphthongs, etc." During their age of "tongue delirium," infants are capable of uttering "all conceivable sounds."

Then comes the fall into language, the "passing over . . . to the first acquisition of words." In order for there to be intelligible speech, there must be "stable phonemes . . . capable of becoming impressed on the memory." All the rest of the polyphonic natal tongue must not be so impressed, must be dropped. The forgetting that is birth does not end the day the baby is born, but continues until the inborn font of phonemes has been sluiced into the narrow flow of local speech.

FOLDING LAUNDRY ON THE PLAINS OF LETHE. The retirement community had an arrangement with a day care facility where Father could leave Mother so that he could have some time to himself.

One of the facility's tricks for engaging the demented was to set them to work folding laundry. Mother stood at a table with a large basket of dry wash before her, folding the sheets, folding the towels.

"WATERS NO VESSEL CAN CONTAIN." Much of the mythological material offered so far presents memory and forgetting together, sometimes as twinned or equal powers, though more often with memory placed above forgetting as the thing to be valued and sought. Moreover, by "memory," the old stories don't mean what we mean today. Mythological memory refers not to mundane recollection (what happened yesterday or last year) but to the mind's awareness of eternal truths. In Hesiod, memory brings the golden age to mind; in Plato, memory recalls the ideal forms; even with the mixed waters of Trophonios's oracle, it is the Waters of Memory that help the petitioner to keep in mind the oracle's prophetic insight. Often, then, forgetting is a falling away from the ideal, a falling into birth and into time.

And yet, if we are seeking out those situations in which forgetting is more useful than remembering, it's worth flagging places where the old stories themselves suggest that troubles follow if memory triumphs at the expense of forgetting. Nothing good happens when unforgettable Furies make revenge the ideal you can't get out of your head. Or when memories of injury stoke an endless civil war. Or when the dead never drink the Water of Solace and the living know no end to grief. Or when, as with Borges's sleepless Funes, no detail of daily life is too trivial to let go of. By implication, if forgetting is a fall into birth and time, then a pure, triumphant memory will mean an end to emerging life and a fixing of time, everything stuck just where it is (stuck, we might say, in those eternal, unchanging forms).

As much as memory is to be valued and sought, there is clearly some limit. Only some right relationship between the two powers can assure constant rebirth and the liquefaction of time. True, when time flows, we are in the world of sickness, old age, and death, but we are also in the world of fertility, new life, and fresh action, and it is these that call for an allowed forgetting. In Plato's myth of Er, the man returned from the dead says that souls soon to be born must drink from the river Lethe, "whose waters no vessel can contain." What exactly are those waters? Perhaps they are life itself, for life is a thing no vessel can contain. Every body it inhabits will in time be broken. These are one and the same, the waters of life and the waters of forgetfulness. To be born is to be stripped of all atemporal knowledge and left henceforth to know this world through that time-bound mortal vessel, the human body.

THE UNDERWORLD NOW. In a modern, secular world, how are we to understand those old stories about the landscape through which the souls of the dead must travel? Suppose we do not believe that the soul survives the body, that it makes a journey, that it will be born again? Are all the old tales empty, then, disposable? Or can we bring them forward, translated into a current tongue?

One way might be to say that the forgetting that belongs to state-transition amnesia, as I've called it, is suffered not by the newly dead but by the newly bereaved who struggle to hold the dead in mind, only to find their memories eroded as they cross into that new state of being known as mourning. Slowly the tide of tears thins the substance of the past.

Another way might be to say that the old stories are not about life after death but about life after sleep. Every night we travel through the underworld, and in the morning we will have to see what has been discarded and what preserved from the day just passed, which dreams are remembered and which forgotten, and what training there is for those who wish to take the path of artful sorting, forgetting, and remembering in a useful way.

Or perhaps a night-and-day cycle is too long. Let us say that the self is reborn with every breath we take, that it is constantly dropping away and coming into being as conditions alter. Every human thirst draws us toward the waters of forgetfulness and the waters of memory, and the old stories tell us that there is schooling as to how to quench our thirst such that the voice might speak with bardic authority. Between every in-breath and every out-breath, there is the underworld with its various waters. The ghostly cypress that the Orphic poets sang about is not in the future. It is right in front of you.

NOTEBOOK II

Self

"A Perfectly Useless Concentration"

The Aphorisms

Changes of identity call for large doses of forgetfulness.

"The Atlantic is a Lethean stream."

Nothing can be forgotten that was not first in mind.

"One *tock*! and I have forgotten all I knew."

"Make the grass grassy and the stone stony."

"Mnemosyne is a very careless girl."

You may visit a grave but you do not have to.

Live steeped in history but not in the past.

Liquefy the fixed idea.

"We drink light."

THE EMPTY STUDIO. Said John Cage to the painter Philip Guston, "When you start working, everybody is in your studio—the past, your friends, enemies, the art world, and above all, you own ideas—all are there. But as you continue painting, they start leaving, one by one, and you are left completely alone. Then, if you're lucky, even you leave."

THE DARWIN LETTER. "Reading Darwin, one admires the beautiful solid case being built up out of his heroic observations, almost unconscious or automatic—and then comes a sudden relaxation, a forgetful phase, and one feels the strangeness of his undertaking, sees the lonely young man, his eyes fixed on facts and minute details, sinking or sliding giddily off into the unknown.

"What one seems to want in art, in experiencing it, is the same thing that is necessary for its creation, a self-forgetful, perfectly useless concentration," says Elizabeth Bishop.

THE PLAIN BUN. I am about seven years old, and I have read a book containing the moral that it is better, when offered a choice of things, not to take the very best but to take something modest. I am in a bakeshop with Mrs. Brown, who offers to buy me any bun I want. There are hot cross buns with white frosting and buns studded with candied fruits, but I choose a very plain bun, much to Mrs. Brown's surprise (and, as I eat it, to my own disappointment).

I am about ten years old. I am standing in the kitchen after school, and my mother—by the sink, in sunlight—suddenly asks me if I think she should get her hair cut. I have no opinion whatsoever on this matter, but I can tell that she wants to get her hair cut, and so I tell her that, yes, she should.

But why do I remember these events? Because in them I am performing someone else's script. When I perform myself, that's forgettable, and rightly so, the actions of the unself-conscious self leaving no necessary mark on memory.

RESISTANCE. In a dream, I have forgotten to write my term paper. I am in a seminar led by the famous professor C——, and I suddenly realize that it is the end of the semester and I have done absolutely nothing about the paper. I wake in the usual panic.

Reflecting on the dream of forgetting, I decide to honor the forgetful me. There must be a good reason he has not written that paper. He seems trapped under false obligation—able neither to do the task nor to deny it.

I myself am now teaching a college class. The semester is beginning as I have this dream, and now I feel sympathy for my students. Years from now, will I appear in their dreams, expecting the unfinished work? I revise my syllabus, removing three of the assignments.

A SHORT HISTORY OF HABIT. For centuries, the cultivation of habit was considered a virtue. "Habit is . . . the enormous fly-wheel of society," wrote William James, approving of its stabilizing force. "It is well for the world that in most of us, by the age of thirty, the character has set like plaster, and will never soften again."

Not so, said Walter Pater, arguing instead for constant unique alertness, free action as opposed to automatism. And not so, said Henri Bergson, arguing that habit doesn't produce ethical conduct, only its appearance, a steadiness not enabling but enslaving.

Whatever the reason (perhaps resistance to all that set plaster called to serve industrial production), this virtue flips over at the end of the nineteenth century, whereupon *the forgetting of habits of mind* becomes the thing to be desired and an inability to forget the sign of mental illness, as in Proust, circa 1910, wherein "certain victims of neurasthenia . . . present year after year the unchanging spectacle of the bizarre habits they believe, each time, they are about to shake off and which they retain forever . . . , caught in the machinery of their maladies."

Francis Picabia, *M'amenez-y* (1919–20);
oil on paperboard, 50" × 35"

FROM THE MUSEUM OF FORGETTING. The command at the center of this painting, "*M'amenez-y*," translates as "Take me there," but if spoken aloud, it also suggests "*mon amnésie*," "my amnesia," and so lays claim to the *don d'oubli total* attributed to Picabia by his friend Marcel Duchamp: "Francis had . . . a *gift of total forgetting* which enabled him to launch into new paintings without being influenced by the memory of preceding ones." The work's geometrical design is taken from a 1919 science magazine rendering of a new type of boat rudder. In employing such found-object patterns and punning inscriptions, Picabia signals his desire to be released from his own and his culture's received ideas as to beauty, sense, and subject. A Dada manifesto that appeared in 1920 carried the signature of "Francis Picabia who knows nothing, nothing, nothing." *M'amenez-y* is itself a manifesto: it declares the artistic goal of having nothing in mind when the work begins.

TRIBAL SCARS. Odysseus is in disguise when he returns to his home in Ithaca, his true identity realized only by his old nurse, who, washing the stranger's feet, comes across a scar on his leg, the mark of a wound inflicted by a hunted boar many years earlier. The old nurse takes Odysseus's leg in her hands to wash it, sees the scar, knows what it is, and drops the leg in surprise, Homer wonderfully inserting between the recognition and the leg drop the full story of how the scar was acquired, how the young Odysseus once went hunting with his grandfather.

When my brother went off to prep school, he was assigned a roommate from Uganda, a boy whose cheeks bore three long parallel scars, tribal scars, the marks of his people. "Trauma" in its simplest sense means "wound," and wounds have a wide range from the mere nick on a finger that heals without a trace to more serious scarifying cuts to what we now think of as true trauma, wounds to body and mind so severe as to forbid any easy healing.

I recall the story of Odysseus's homecoming not just to note the essentially harmless boar hunt wound but to say that the resulting scar is tribal or familial: Odysseus is of the people who hunt the boar. No family or culture leaves its young unmarked; by a thousand cuts, we shape the bodies and minds of our progeny. All human communities have a sense of what an ideal man or woman looks like, and all children—even those with the happiest of childhoods—emerge locally marked or, to say it more positively, inscribed with a serviceable identity to be carried out of childhood into the given world, happily so if the child is lucky and loved, and necessarily so, as well, for—as much as we might value the spiritual practice of thinning out the self, of noticing its contingency and transience, of muting its fears and greed—there can be no forgetting the self until there is a self. As one Buddhist psychotherapist has said, "You have to be somebody before you can be nobody." It helps to actually be a painter or a scientist before "sliding giddily off into the unknown."

TRIBAL SCARS: THE READER. Serious traumatic memories make for easily understood, paradigmatic examples of the usefulness of forgetting. But to focus on the worst kinds of wounding hides the more subtle work—the self-forgetting—required to detach from the more or less benign scarification acquired as we grow. To illustrate with a case close at hand, my own father and mother never stinted in their child-shaping duties or, to tell the tale with a bit of distance, Lem and Betty left sufficient tribal markings on young Lewis that he might well remember who he was when he left home.

They were both big readers, Lem and Betty, as was my older brother, Lee, who would lie on his bed with a book (*The Scarlet Pimpernel*, *The Father Brown Stories*), while Lewis begged him to come out and play. Lewis was not a reader; he was a collector—butterflies, coins, rocks—and he liked to be outdoors building a lean-to in the woods, or playing baseball, or walking with his butterfly net or his rifle (for he was of the people who hunt the swallowtail and the woodchuck).

Urging him to read, Betty once told him that someday he would be in the army and that he would be crushingly bored unless he had the habit of reading. The admonition conjured a mental image in which he saw himself, a young soldier lying on his cot in the bunkhouse, reading. Sunlight streams in the windows. Deep silence. Where are the other men? They are scattered around the camp, lying limp beneath the cannons, collapsed on the mess hall tables, slack-jawed in the gym, zombified with boredom. Not Lewis. He is reading a book. He is not like other people.

Betty once paid him to read—fifty cents per book. She told him not to tell his father. The next time they went to the library he checked out *The Story of Ferdinand* and read it in one clip. Betty paid up, but allowed as to how she had had something more substantial in mind. Then he read *Farmer Boy* (a real fatty; he got a fifty-cent bonus). He read that one aggressively, flamboyantly, deliberately. The school bus came at 8:00, and he would get up at 6:30 to log a few pages before leaving the house. In later years, he could still see the image: dawn light (always that light!) fills the front hall of the house, he is on his way to the kitchen, but he has paused to read his book. Memory now splits the image, for he is both holding the book and looking down at himself from the landing of the stairs, the Reader performing for his elevated audience.

These are my own memories of young Lewis, but I have other testimony as well, for, week after week, decade after decade, Lem and Betty used to write to their own parents a "Family Letter" that gave accounts of all their doings. These I now have in my possession, and from them I learn, for example, that the year Lewis turned ten, Lem read Saul Bellow's *Adventures of Augie March* ("a heavy book," he wrote to his parents, but "showing great talent"). He read a biography of Lord Melbourne, the first volume of *The Shorter Cambridge Medieval History* ("fascinating; 643 pages"), *Anna Karenina*, *The Old Wives' Tale*, *The Way of All Flesh*, *The Aztecs of Mexico*, *The English Middle Classes*, *Medieval People*, *Flower Gardening*, and a book "about the Roman Empire around Constantinople at the end of the eleventh century."

Meanwhile, during the winter holiday, they "worked on [Lewis's] reading endlessly, or so it seemed to me," wrote Betty, "as he is a scatter-brain, not stupid I keep saying to myself, but certainly not very well organized." In early summer, "Lewis was down sick for a week," she reported, "but managed to read a 200 page book and seemed to enjoy it, and this gives us some delight because it seemed all too probable he would grow up illiterate." But by August he is said to be in the tree house "reading comics" (while "all the time" his older brother "reads more books").

SWEEPING THE TOMB. The *Mumonkan*, or *Gateless Barrier*, is a collection of Zen koans, or "cases," gathered in the thirteenth century. Case 5 tells the story of Hsiang-yen, a smart young monk who, like many intellectuals, had a hard time with the practice. One day his teacher said to him, "A cerebral understanding of Zen is not much use. I suggest you work on this koan: *Who were you before your parents were born?*"

Hsiang-yen couldn't figure it out. He went back to his room and looked through all the notes he had taken during his years of training, but he found nothing. He tried to get his teacher to tell him the answer, but the teacher said, "I really have nothing to say. I could tell you, but later you would revile me. Whatever understanding I have is my own and will never be yours."

Hsiang-yen gave up. He burned his notes and decided he'd just be a rice-gruel monk and face the question moment by moment rather than trying to think it through. Hearing that the tomb of Nan-yang was being neglected, he said to himself, "I'll go there, tend the garden around the tomb and lead a simple life. I can't do any better." He did that for years. He gave up trying to approach the Way through study. He didn't give up completely: he didn't kill himself or lead a life of debauchery. He just lived as simply as he could, keeping the koan in mind.

One day, while he was sweeping fallen leaves, his broom sent a stone flying. It hit a stalk of bamboo: *tock!* What a sound! The universe opened up. He understood. It was as if for all those years there had been ice melting invisibly from below and then, of a sudden, the ice was gone.

Hsiang-yen composed a poem that opens with the line "One *tock*! and I have forgotten all I knew."

TRIBAL SCARS: THE SPELLER. There is a touching moment in a French movie about little children going to school when we see a young boy writing the number 7 on a blackboard: he draws the horizontal top line and then pauses because he can't remember if the downward slash comes from the right or the left side of the line. He gets it wrong, but of course what we're seeing is how utterly arbitrary is the correct form, how conventional and local for an as-yet-unmarked mind.

Just so with spelling, especially in English. Lem and Betty preserved a note that Lewis wrote when he was turning ten: BE SURE TO ATTEND LEWIS'S BIRTHDAY SELIBRACHON / ADDMISHON 15¢.

Not that getting Lewis to read and teaching him to spell wounded him in any way that didn't soon scar over, but that's the point. Gentle as their touch might have been, these folks were shaping the boy. He still remembers the tune by which they got "bicycle" lodged in his mind, and the tip Lem offered for remembering the difference between "principal" and "principle" (the princi*pal* of the school should be your *pal*). Nor did Lem defend the English language or lack in sympathy for its victim. One report reads that "poor Lewis got only 90 in spelling today because he knew that as between 'bridge' and 'canal,' one of them ends with an 'e' and the other doesn't. But he got the 'e' on the wrong one. He tries without success to apply logic to spelling."

Lucky child to have that sympathetic father, but still, both man and boy are of the people who celebrate the principle that "bridge" ends in an *e* and whose children, if they are to thrive in this tribe, must leave home with that and all the other weird (wierd? weerd?) words on the weekly test incised on the mind like tattoos on the shaved head of a slave.

"EASE AND CHEER." Emanuel Lasker was one of the greatest chess players of all time, holding the world championship for a full twenty-eight years beginning in 1894. His classic *Manual of Chess*, published in 1927, ends with some "final reflections on education in chess" that include this remark: "Chess must not be memorized. . . . Memory is too valuable to be stocked with trifles. Of my fifty-seven years I have applied at least thirty to forgetting most of what I had learned or read, and since I succeeded in this I have acquired a certain ease and cheer which I should never again like to be without."

TRIBAL SCARS: THE HANDYMAN. In later years, one of Lewis's friends, a successful Ivy League literary critic, passingly described him as being "handy," a remark that irked him, for it felt as if it named a mere eccentricity, as if he knew Hittite grammar, say, or could recite the Pledge of Allegiance backward, whereas in the Hyde family being handy was a mark of the truly human (or at least of the truly human male). Visiting one of his daughters-in-law, Lem once asked if she had a hammer in the house. She did not know. In his later telling of the tale, it was clear that for Lem it was as if the woman did not know if her house had a bathroom.

Lem himself was exceedingly handy, a fixer and a tinkerer. It wasn't only that there were half a dozen patents under his name (No. 3001450: the improved rearview mirror; No. 3246507: the puff tonometer; and so on); it was that every house they lived in was an extension of the lab, full of cunning devices like the pulley that allowed the rooftop TV antenna to be rotated from a ground-floor closet or the wiring that put a phone in the tree house or the switches that let you control the garage light from any of three locations. The acquisition of a quarter-inch drill was literally something to write home about. In the mid-1950s, their first-ever TV set had to be accompanied by a complete set of replacement vacuum tubes so that Lem could be the in-house repairman. For decades, a Bendix washing machine traveled with the family from house to house with Lem constantly fixing it. July 1955: "I took apart most of the Bendix to fix the valve which got in trouble with rust. I know all there is to know, now, about mixing valves in Bendixes." When the thing finally died, it became an organ donor, the solenoid salvaged from the carcass making an automatic garage-door opener for the village fire department; as the sirens wailed, the firehouse door would fly up to greet the arriving volunteers.

When people asked Lewis how he became "handy," he used to say that he really didn't know beyond being curious and paying attention. But the Family Letters tell a different story. Lem buys Lewis a kit from which to make an electric motor. Lem pays Lewis three cents per shingle to help roof the garage. Lem's quarter-inch drill is not for him alone: Lewis and his brother Lee are to run the wiring through the studs of the newly built guest room. Lewis builds model airplanes. He builds a birdhouse for Betty. He is given polarizing lenses, and Betty writes home, "Lewis spent a long time pasting various thicknesses of cellophane together so that he would have a varicolored butterfly when he put it between two polarizers. He will probably make a good scientist since he cares essentially nothing for the material things of this world and becomes absolutely engrossed in such projects. I never knew anyone so consistently oblivious to his surroundings." Lem once bought Lewis a lens-grinding lap, "a tremendous piece of machinery which the two of us can scarcely lift," Betty wrote. The gift arrived one Christmas Day, "and Lewis has spent almost all his time since then polishing agates that he found in Minnesota last summer. His hands turn blue from the abrasive, and he is perfectly blissful."

TRIBAL SCARS: THE SMARTY. Like an invisible electric fence by which a dog can be kept to its proper yard, in Lewis's childhood a surround of offhand remarks about intelligence ("not stupid I keep saying to myself") marked the line between the Dummies and the Smarties of this world. The Family Letters bear some traces: a carpenter's helper described as "a little lacking mentally"; a cousin's daughter graduating from college with "honors in chemistry though not cum laude"; Lewis in the fourth grade testing at the sixth-grade level; brother Lee in the seventh testing at the tenth.

The substance of these observations is not the point but rather that they were worthy of speech in the first place, that it mattered to mark the categories, to sort the population, hand out the uniforms, and begin the endless back-and-forth of wits and half-wits, show and shame, the copulatory friction of identity-by-difference that repeats itself again and again into the future, there being no final resting place once the weary game has begun, for the tenth grade is followed by the eleventh, eleventh by twelfth, twelfth by college, graduate school, a job, another job, the horizon of Smartville receding with every achieved approach. The only relief would be to quit the game entirely; ah, but that would mean self-expulsion from the very tribe that brought you into being, exile from the one homeland whose citizens can always be counted on to remember who you are.

In the last week of freshman year at the state university, Lewis slept through the final exam in chemistry, and although the kindly professor allowed him to take the test late, he ended up with a D in the course. This was a case not of a sleeper dreaming that he has forgotten an exam but of dreams themselves allowing the sleeper to forget an exam in fact. Betty said she had hoped that after a successful first year he could transfer to an Ivy League school, but now it was hopeless. He'd crossed the line. As the sun rose, some subtle, resistant force had deposited the slumbering youth on the shores of Dumbville.

Years later, when he was accepted as a fellow at the Radcliffe Institute for Advanced Study, his hosts bragged to the incoming fellows that percentage-wise it was harder to get into the Institute than it was to get into the freshman class at Harvard. Back across the line! What an honor! And yet an honor, it turned out, that brought an unexpected grief, for when Lewis got the news, his first impulse was to pick up the phone and call home, to close the loop with the authors and original audience of this element of Who He Was. But it was too late. Lem and Betty were both ten years dead.

FEED ON THE PRESENT. Larry Rosenberg, a dharma teacher from the Insight Meditation Center in Cambridge, Massachusetts, tells of the time he was in New York City with a free afternoon and his wife suggested that they visit the Tenement Museum, on Manhattan's Lower East Side. Untouched for over fifty years, the museum's apartments present preserved examples of the housing offered to immigrant families in the early twentieth century. Rosenberg himself had been born and raised in a similar building in the same neighborhood and found himself unexpectedly transported into the past.

"Suddenly certain things started to come back to me about my past, and I couldn't talk for quite a while." Asking himself, "Did I come out of this? Did I grow up here? How can that be?" he was mostly struck by the great distance between the life he had come to live and that long-ago childhood. "Seeing the size of what was called the bathroom, which was more like a telephone booth—no bathtub, no shower, et cetera. And my memories of living with my parents, my mother's three sisters and brother, and both my grandparents in a space like this."

Rosenberg told this story in the context of a talk about a distinction he draws from Buddhist teaching between "real time" and "psychological time." With real time, we do not dwell on (or dwell in) the past or the future but simply note them (saying, "I grew up in New York" or "When I retire I'm going to Florida," and so on). With psychological time, on the other hand, past and future take over the present; we live in them, identifying with their pleasures and pains. As the Buddhists say, we "make self" out of them (as I might make self out of my pride in publishing a book or my shame over having flunked a chemistry exam).

In Rosenberg's case, what struck him in this regard was not the Tenement Museum itself but the way his account of the visit changed over time. At first it had been a bare experience. It "sort of opened me up, and I saw something about my origins and a sense of myself. . . . Right on the spot I was quiet. I didn't want to talk for a while. I was very moved by it. Some of it was painful, a lot of it was pleasant, but . . . it conveyed to me the distance I had traveled, socially, psychologically."

Later, however, when he got home and recounted the story to various friends, "the telling started to change a bit, from it just being a straight report of a fact and what I went through. I saw that it was promoting the self. What it was saying was, 'Aren't I wonderful! I started here, and then I was a professor, and I dropped out, and now I'm a dharma teacher, and I know how to dress—I'm a real American guy!'" The story had picked up self-importance along the way; "there was some mileage coming from it."

Rosenberg is clear that this kind of self-making may be unavoidable and often harmless, but as a matter of Buddhist practice it should at least be noticed, be brought to mind. "I saw what the mind was doing; the mind was taking materials from the past—at first they were just 'factual' but then it immediately started to use them for the present, the present sense of myself. . . . The self is constantly using the materials of the past and the future to nourish itself, to build itself up. . . . I didn't do it consciously. . . . It just happened. The ego is going to work, and that's what it knows how to do."

Rosenberg likes to use a food metaphor to describe how the ego functions: it feeds on the past and the future. There is a

Buddhist scripture from the Pali canon, the Samyutta Nikaya, that says of practitioners who are "peaceful in mind,"

> They do not lament over the past,
> they yearn not for what is to come,
> they maintain themselves in the present,
> thus their complexion is serene.

In Rosenberg's own reading of these verses, the third line becomes "they *nourish* themselves in the present." Such is the food of a serene self-forgetfulness. Self-making, on the other hand, feeds on time past and time to come. "The continuation of psychological time and the survival of the ego are really the same thing," says Rosenberg.

CHANGES OF IDENTITY. "Forget your past, your customs, and your ideals," reads a Yiddish guidebook printed in Odessa and given to Jews on their way to New York in the 1890s. The waters of the river Lethe feed directly into the oceans surrounding the American continent. Americans have always claimed the right to reinvent themselves, and all changes of identity call for strong doses of forgetfulness. Emerson's "Self-Reliance" stands as one of our earliest odes to forgetfulness in the service of a shifting self: "Why drag about this corpse of your memory, lest you contradict something you have stated in this or that public place? Suppose you should contradict yourself; what then? It seems to be a rule of wisdom never to rely on your memory alone . . . but to bring the past for judgment into the thousand-eyed present, and live ever in a new day."

The transcendentalists wrote their own guidebooks to the New World, eager as they were to forget European culture and establish their own. "The Atlantic is a Lethean stream, in our passage over which we have had an opportunity to forget the Old World and its institutions," wrote Henry Thoreau in a typical passage. "If we do not succeed this time, there is perhaps one more chance for the race . . . , and that is in the Lethe of the Pacific, which is three times as wide."

IN TIBET. In 2000, *The New York Review of Books* carried a report by Ian Buruma about his trip to Tibet. The Chinese have been diligently trying to wipe out the Tibetan language and culture, making it impossible for young Tibetans to study their own history, especially their religious heritage. Their efforts are a species of the "organized forgetting" that Milan Kundera described in regard to Soviet propaganda in Eastern Europe.

And yet Buruma meets a Tibetan Muslim in a restaurant for whom religion has a different meaning: in the past, as in Myanmar more recently, the Buddhists, intent on maintaining their own purity, had persecuted the Muslims such that they and Tibet's other religious minorities view Buddhism with a sense of unease.

This Muslim turned out to be the only Tibetan with whom Buruma spoke who didn't care about the diminishment of the Tibetan language "or the new dominance in urban areas of Chinese low life and pop culture." This man spoke "like a true modernist. It was inevitable, he said, that traditions were hollowed out by modern life. . . . The crude new cosmopolitanism of Lhasa was . . . part of his liberation."

The story echoes that "forget your traditions" advice given to America's immigrant Jews. It seems to promise a secular, pluralist state that welcomes the forgetting of difference and its consequent fluid identity. In this case, it's a false promise, of course, a swapping out of one set of differences for another, of a purely Buddhist agenda for a purely Communist one.

"KENOSIS" means an emptying out, as in Saint Paul's charge to the Philippians: "Let each of you look not to your own interests, but to the interests of others. Let the same mind be in you that was in Christ Jesus, who, though he was in the form of God, did not regard equality with God as something to be exploited, but *emptied himself*, taking the form of a servant, being born in human likeness."

To "look . . . to the interests of others" means to forget about the self that knows itself in opposition to those others, which is to say that the passage is commonly read as a teaching: self-emptying is the cure of pride. In that line, one point of the pages about tribal scarring was to say that "Lewis" is of the people who take pride in their literacy, their mastery of tools, and their intelligence. And that with such pride comes identity—*identity through difference*. "I" am "I" because I am *not* one of those who've never heard of a solenoid, who have no interest in Constantinople at the end of the eleventh century, who never made it to the Ivy League.

If such difference amounts to self-elevation, then kenosis calls for descent into some humbler form. On the other hand, but just as important, if difference amounts to self-debasement ("I" should be ashamed!), then kenosis calls for a move in the opposite direction, an emptying out of servitude and assumption of some less marked way of being. Either way—proud or ashamed, high or low, master or servant, literate or illiterate, smart or dumb—this emptying finally means letting go of all such oppositions. The crossroad where dualities meet and cancel each other out—that is the site of the self-forgetfulness whose consequence is the death of identity by difference. Concludes

Saint Paul, "Being found in human form, [Jesus] humbled himself and became obedient to the point of death—even death on a cross."

NOT TO BE REPEATED. I sometimes have a book on my nightstand and read a bit every night, but the next day, when someone asks what I'm reading, nothing comes to mind. Some books set us thinking on our own terms, not under their command; they leave us with our own reflections, not with the author's. In an interview published in *Bomb* magazine, a journalist admitted to Adam Phillips, the British psychoanalyst and writer, that though he loved Phillips's many books and essays, he could "never actually remember anything" that he read in them. Phillips was delighted. "That's the reading experience I've always loved. Certainly, when people say to me, as they often have done, 'I can't remember anything afterward,' I think, Great, that's the point! The work is not there to be repeated or identified with, but something works on you." Such was my experience in reading Phillips's book *Equals*, especially its chapter called "Superiorities." It was an important inspiration for my last book, *Common as Air*, but I could never remember why.

"SIMULTANEOUS COMPOSITION AND DECOMPOSITION." In a collection of essays, *Echolalias: On the Forgetting of Language*, Daniel Heller-Roazen reproduces a story about Abū Nuwās, the great eighth-century Arabic poet. When first setting out, the young Abū Nuwās approached a local master, Khalaf al-Ahmar, and asked permission to compose. A much later biographer tells the tale:

> Khalaf said: "I refuse to let you make a poem until you memorize a thousand passages of ancient poetry, including chants, odes, and occasional verses." So Abū Nuwās disappeared; and after a long while, he came back and said, "I've done it."
>
> "Recite them," said Khalaf.
>
> So, Abū Nuwās began, and got through the bulk of the verses over a period of several days. Then he asked again for permission to compose poetry. Said Khalaf, "I refuse, unless you forget all one thousand parts as completely as if you had never learned them."
>
> "That's too difficult," said Abū Nuwās. "I've memorized them quite thoroughly!"
>
> "I refuse to let you compose until you forget them," said Khalaf.
>
> So Abū Nuwās disappeared into a monastery and remained in solitude for a period of time until he forgot all the lines he'd learned. He went back to Khalaf and said, "I've forgotten them so thoroughly it's as if I never memorized anything at all."
>
> Khalaf then said, "Now go compose!"

In his commentary, Heller-Roazen ends up wondering if the telling of this tale isn't the biographer's way of understanding Abū Nuwās's achievement, as if true poetry emerges only from a region "in which memory and oblivion, writing and effacement," cannot function unless they work together.

REFOCUS. In mid-July 2013, the Boston Red Sox led the American League and were set to start the second half of the season with a return to Fenway, their home ballpark. When a reporter for the Associated Press asked the team's manager, John Farrell, what he found most impressive about the team, Farrell replied, "Our ability to forget—forget what yesterday had in store for us, good, bad or indifferent—and to refocus on our goal for today."

ANATTĀ. "A sturdy lad from New Hampshire or Vermont who in turn tries all the professions, who teams it, farms it, peddles, keeps a school, preaches, edits a newspaper, goes to Congress, buys a township, and so forth, in successive years, and always like a cat falls on his feet, is worth a hundred of these city dolls. He walks abreast with his days and feels no shame in not 'studying a profession,' for he does not postpone his life, but lives already," says Emerson, in whose writing self-forgetting is also constant self-renewal. That given, a question arises as to whether there is any stable thing behind the masquerade of professions. Emerson often sets out to name that thing, but when he does, his writing always becomes more and more elusive. (For example, in trying to describe "the aboriginal Self," he ends up speaking of a "deep force, the last fact behind which analysis cannot go.") The transcendentalist experiment in serial self-forgetting begins to suggest that there is no permanently enduring self.

PREPARING for my own dementia.

LESS STRESS. One day the Dutch novelist Daan Heerma van Voss woke up with almost no memory—a sense of his name and little more. The loss of memory struck him as a loss of causality, the sense of how one word leads to the next, for example. "It was a profound not-knowing, and it was terrifying."

Transient global amnesia is the name neurologists give to what struck Heerma van Voss. They have no idea of its cause. Luckily, it usually lasts less than a day, as it did in this case. And as terrifying as it was for Heerma van Voss, it did have a curious upside. "There were moments," he writes, "in which countless causes for daily stress and fear simply did not exist, moments when I felt enlightened." Former patients, he's been told, recall their immersion in oblivion as being light and carefree. "And they go on living their lives with a vague but everlasting sense of homesickness."

DON'T LOOK BACK. These sturdy lads trying all the professions, these immigrants abandoning their ideals, these students emptying out the teachings—not everyone can lead a life of such limber flexibility. In his *Dissertatio medica de nostalgia* of 1688, Johannes Hofer elevated homesickness to a medical condition worthy of a physician's attention. He replaced *Heimweh*, the everyday German word for homesickness, with a scientific-sounding neologism stitched together from the Greek *nostos* (home, return) and *algos* (pain). In those who suffer from nostalgia, Hofer wrote, "the nervous sap always takes the very same direction," flowing only toward "the desire to return to one's native land."

Young Swiss soldiers serving far from home were particularly prone to suffering, even dying, from nostalgia. They missed their mothers' care, the bread and cheese they used to have at midday, the rich milk that tasted of their own fields. Certain rustic melodies triggered fits of nostalgia, especially the tunes played as the herds were driven to pasture in the summer Alps.

Hofer having identified this dread disease, the great national armies of Europe struggled to control it. Many generals, hoping to prevent suicides, gave nostalgic soldiers immediate permission to return home. Others took a harder line. In 1733, one Russian general decreed that nostalgic soldiers would simply be buried alive. After several had been so dispatched, the affliction disappeared from his ranks.

My comrades . . . mingled with the Lotus Eaters . . . , and whoever of them ate the honey-sweet fruit of the lotus no longer wished to return home, but there they wished to remain . . . , feeding on the lotus and forgetting their homecoming.

—*ODYSSEY* 9.82–97

THE LOTUS EATERS TELL THEIR VERSION. "All we knew at first was that these three sailors appeared out of nowhere, haggard and battle weary. They wanted to know who we were and 'did we eat bread?' Of course we eat bread! Bread and rice, apples and plums, pork and beef . . . , the whole gamut. When these strangers stumbled into town we did what all civilized peoples do: we didn't ask their names, or where they came from, or who their forebears were—we fed them. We let them bathe and change into clean clothes and join us at the table. We did notice, of course, that of all the delicacies offered at that first banquet, they were unusually attracted to that flowery food the lotus (served that evening in a soufflé and as a garnish for the ices).

"The men had just come from a horrid battle, so it was no wonder they found the lotus attractive. They had been fighting the Trojans for ten years; that war over, setting sail for home, they landed first in Ismarus, home of the Ciciones. Immediately their crazy captain started another war! They sacked the city, killed the men, raped the women, and spent the evening getting drunk—only to find the next morning that the Ciciones had regrouped and ruthlessly attacked, killing at least six men from each of their dozen ships. The Achaeans fled in horror, fear, and grief.

"Their apologists always insist that the lotus made them forget about their journey home, and of course it does that, but we prefer to say that the lotus helped them come into the present moment. They stopped having flashbacks to the war, they stopped daydreaming about a town they hadn't seen for years, and they noticed what was going on right then, right there.

"One thing they surely noticed was how different our land is from the homeland they told us about. Ithaca! It seems it was an aristocratic patriarchy, the kind of place where men make all the decisions, where a king with impunity can slaughter a maid servant who crosses his path. Servant? Better to say slave. Read Homer closely; he's not ashamed to say it. Eurycleia, always described as 'the old nurse of Odysseus' but in fact: a slave! Eumaeus, 'faithful swineherd of Odysseus': a slave! The sailors we welcomed never said as much, but we suspect that at least one of them was a slave as well. Not that Lotus Land is perfect, but we are at least an egalitarian democracy, and slavery has been outlawed since time immemorial.

"The sailors confessed themselves much charmed by our primary school of philosophy, one of whose tenets dispenses with the entire 'homeland' postulate, the one so clearly stated in later centuries by Novalis: 'Philosophy is properly homesickness; the wish to be everywhere at home.' It's an understandable longing, to be sure—that there might be a place of origin, a secure first principle from which all else follows, so that once the 'home' is discovered, the world is never again a foreign land. But it's a daydream, and a dangerous one at that, for what it really does is to estrange us from the world as it is. No, Lotus Philosophy *does not seek to define a unique threshold of emergence, the homeland* toward which the pilgrim travels. It seeks, rather, to be at home everywhere. No wonder our island appeals so deeply to immigrants and wanderers, those who arrive already disposed to forget their past, their customs, and their ideals and to take up residence in the thousand-eyed present.

"It isn't hard to understand why those sailors were weeping when their captain dragged them to the ship and tied them beneath the rowing benches. It wasn't just that they were to be deprived of the lotus, though that was part of it. It was their intuition of what lay ahead. Their captain had the full-on weeping sadism of unthinking nostalgia, the cruelty a man must have if he's bent on shaping the present to the past. Lotus insight had shown his men the folly of assuming that what waited for them would be untouched by time. More likely the sweetheart will have married another man, creditors will have seized the old homestead, the faithful hunting dog will have long ago died. Drought may have come, or famine, or plague; the palace may have been overrun by some hostile enemy. Agamemnon got home, and look at what happened to him.

"We have often thought of bringing a libel suit against the endless slanders that the centuries have settled on us Lotus Eaters, but in fact we are not a litigious people and besides, all this happened long ago and we have our 'Lotus Laws,' our statutes of limitation."

NOSTALGIA AMUSED. Vladimir Nabokov's memoir *Speak, Memory* is steeped in "a hypertrophied sense of lost childhood," but its nostalgia is of a particular strain. For one thing, it recognizes the imperfections of memory. Mnemosyne is "a very careless girl," says Nabokov, admitting that "when, nowadays, I attempt to follow in memory the winding paths . . . , I notice with alarm that there are many gaps, due to oblivion or ignorance, akin to the terra-incognita blanks map makers of old used to call 'sleeping beauties.'"

Accepting of such gaps, Nabokovian nostalgia celebrates the collaboration of memory and imagination. Our most vivid recollections, the author elsewhere says, demonstrate "Mnemosyne's mysterious foresight in having stored up this or that element which creative imagination may use when combining it with later recollections and inventions." Nabokov never indulges in fantasies of homecoming; nor does he suppose it better to avoid the pain of loss: "I wonder . . . whether there is really much to be said for more anesthetic destinies, for, let us say, a smooth, safe, small-town continuity of time, with its primitive absence of perspective, when, at fifty, one is still dwelling in the clapboard house of one's childhood."

In *The Future of Nostalgia*, Svetlana Boym places Nabokov's work in a category of "reflective," as distinct from "restorative," nostalgia. Restorative nostalgia thinks it possible to go home again. It sets out to re-create the past precisely and impose it on the future. It power-washes the moss from the brickwork and scrubs the marbles white. The stuff of religious revivals and ethnic nationalism, it has a simple story to tell about getting back to origins and roots (or about the conspiracies that stand in the way). Insisting on the impossible task of re-creating the past, it descends easily into humorless cruelty. Under the sign of Make Our Country Great Again (or *Heimat, Heimat, über alles*), restorative nostalgia will jail, deport, or kill all those who do not fit its imagined story of past grandeur.

Reflective nostalgia, on the other hand, may dream of an end to exile, but knowing that the home is in ruins and return impossible, it keeps delaying its departure. Yes, it longs to go back, but the stress falls on the longing, not on the home. It has learned to find pleasure in the marks that time leaves on all things—the patina on the bronzes, the candle soot on the frescoes. It has little story to tell going forward, past loss having made it clear that the future is various and unknown. Its tone is wistful, humorous, even playful, as in this moment from *Speak, Memory* when Nabokov tries to recall one of his boyhood tutors: "How readily Mr. Cummings would sit down on a stool, part behind with both hands his—what? was he wearing a frock coat? I see only the gesture—and proceed to open the black tin paint box."

THE LIQUEFACTION OF THE FIXED IDEA. Twenty-year-old Irène nursed her mother devotedly as she lay dying of tuberculosis. And yet when the mother died, Irène seemed oblivious. She told none of the relatives; she made no plans for a funeral. When the family stepped in and arranged a burial, Irène behaved as if it weren't happening. Pressured into attending, she laughed during the ceremony, explaining that her mother was on a trip and would soon return, that this was not her funeral. As if her mother had not died, Irène went on as before; she continued to clean and prepare the sickroom, to lay out the medications, to cook the meals, and in all respects proceed as if her mother would soon return.

Early in the twentieth century, writing about Irène's case as an example of "dissociative amnesia," the French psychologist Pierre Janet proposed that we should think of memory not as a record of the past but as something more dynamic: "*Memory* . . . is an action; essentially, it *is the action of telling a story.*" In Irène's case, the story stalled; her mother's death was so shocking that the young woman was "incapable of associating" it with an ongoing life history. "Strictly speaking, then," writes Janet, someone in Irène's situation "cannot be said to have a 'memory'" at all. "It is only for convenience that we speak of it as a 'traumatic memory.'" That being the case, it might be better to speak of "dissociative agnosia" (non-knowing) rather than "amnesia." Nothing can be forgotten that was not first in mind.

In dissociation, narrative collapses. In the short term, that can be a useful, healthy defense against the kind of shock that threatens a person's very identity. Long term, to move beyond dissociation requires building the capacity to tolerate the shocking thing, but until such capacity appears, an internal pact of oblivion can be most salutary.

In the case of Irène, the mother's death left the girl inhabiting a species of hallucination, performing actions that everyone else could see belonged to another time and place. How to dispel the hallucination? How to unfix the idée fixe? Turn agnosia into knowing by taking up again "the action of telling a story"; then the event may be remembered, and what can be remembered may also be properly forgotten.

"After much labor I was able to make [Irène] reconstruct the verbal memory of her mother's death. From the moment I succeeded in doing this, she could talk about the mother's death without succumbing to crises or being afflicted with hallucinations. . . . Irène . . . threw off her depression . . . and became capable of bringing about the necessary liquidation."

UNLESS IT CONTEMPLATE.

To be forgot by thee
Surpasses Memory
Of other minds
The Heart cannot forget
Unless it contemplate
What it declines
I was regarded then
Raised from oblivion
A single time
To be remembered what—
Worthy to be forgot
Is my renown

—Emily Dickinson

"REMEMBERING IN A WAY . . ." In a 1914 essay titled "Remembering, Repeating, and Working-Through," in language that matches that of Pierre Janet, Sigmund Freud writes that in psychoanalytic work, it "often happens that something is 'remembered' which never could have been 'forgotten,' because it was never at any time noticed, never was conscious." A thing cannot slip from the mind that never was held in mind.

And yet even unnoticed events leave traces. The patient for whom "nothing comes to mind" will commonly suffer a "compulsion to repeat," Freud writes, and repetition "is his way of remembering." As Adam Phillips writes, "People come for psychoanalytic treatment because they are remembering in a way that does not free them to forget." They are remembering by way of their symptoms, the compulsion to repeat being a kind of stuttering toward speech, toward the symbolization that can be held in mind and therefore worked upon until forgotten.

Freud says, "We have to treat [the patient's] illness as an actual force, active at the moment and not as an event in his past life." Which is to say, the work is about not remembering the past but bringing attention to the now, or rather, creating awareness during the only time available, the present moment.

Finally, Freud writes that "one must allow the patient time to get to know [the] resistance of which he is ignorant, to 'work through' it, to overcome it." And what does it mean to "work through"? Through to what?

The essay never says, and in a way, that is the point: truly free from the past, the future will arise in ways that are new and unpredictable.

THE HORSE'S MOUTH. In a diary entry from 1897, Leo Tolstoy records noticing something he had not noticed. He was cleaning up his study and came to the divan: Had he dusted it or not? He couldn't remember. Then comes the commentary—how much we hardly notice, how much of life we forget as soon as it happens, and how, in a sense, the unattended life is not a life at all, how there are surely people whose entire quotient of years passes absentmindedly so that "such lives are as if they had never been."

If we have forgotten whether we dusted the divan, something other than dusting must have occupied the mind as the body went through the motions, and how might we forget *that* thing so as to attend to what's right in front of us? How might we quiet the habitual mind buzz that so often stands between us and the actual world?

One trick would be to make the divan strange enough to snap us to attention. Move it to the other side of the room. Put a dead mouse on one pillow. Have it give a mild electric shock. Cover it with petals of the pink hawthorn. Or, to dispense with this dusted or not-dusted divan and state the general case, in order to recover direct attention, to have perception be conscious instead of unconscious, simply make the familiar unfamiliar. Such, in any event, was a key suggestion offered in regard to art by the Russian formalist critic Victor Shklovsky in a 1917 essay that used Tolstoy's diary entry as a point of departure.

"Art exists that we may recover the sensation of life, to make us feel things, to make the stone *stony*," Shklovsky wrote. "The purpose of art is to impart to us the sensation of an object as it is *perceived* and not merely as it is *recognized*." Taking the usual and making it unusual is one of the tricks by which an art can accomplish this end, "defamiliarization" freeing us from "the automatism of perception."

In Tolstoy-the-artist rather than Tolstoy-the-duster, Shklovsky found many examples of this technique in operation. In a story called "Strider," Tolstoy has a long critique of private property but rather than having it spoken by some left-wing activist, he gives us the voice of a horse trying to puzzle out what humans mean when they say "my own" or "mine":

> Many . . . who called me their own never rode on me—although others did. . . . The coachman, the veterinarians, and the outsiders in general treated me kindly, yet those who called me their own did not. . . . A man says "this house is mine" and never lives in it. . . . There are people who call a tract of land their own, but they never set eyes on it and never take a stroll on it.

The horse is forced to conclude that he is witnessing a language game and that the main difference between humans and his fellow horses is that "the actions of men . . . are guided by *words*—ours, by deeds."

For Shklovsky, the message of such a passage is of less interest than the formal move that makes it engaging. Note what he's after in art: *the sensation of life*, *perception* rather than *recognition*. Unconscious automatic awareness engages only with the recognizable already known, that is to say, with things that match existing memory traces, those whose roots lie in the past, not the present, and the present is the only place where life is actually available.

For Shklovsky, fresh perception is sufficient. Perhaps attention to the real will lead to something else—to transcendent truth, political insight, hope, or despair—but Shklovsky's formalist aesthetic serves no such ends. Paying attention is what matters, the good life being that in which one is simply alert. When most of our learning is learning to ignore (as when you've learned the way to the grocery store), when objects appear "as though enveloped in a sack," when sentences go unfinished because everyone knows . . . , when lives are as if they had never been lived, then we need a path back to simple awareness, a technique to help us shed, however briefly, the mind's buffering blubber of routine so that the stone may again be stony, the grass grassy, the divan divany, the life lively.

NO . . . , NO . . . The British psychoanalyst Wilfred Bion believed it "important that the analyst should avoid mental activity, memory and desire. . . . If the psycho-analyst has not deliberately divested himself of memory and desire, the patient can 'feel' this and is dominated by the 'feeling' that he is possessed by and contained in the analyst's state of mind."

Bion's is a discipline of the present moment: "Psychoanalytic 'observation' is concerned neither with what has happened nor with what is going to happen but with what *is* happening." In that regard, the quieting of desire is key, "'memory' [being] the past tense of 'desire,' 'anticipation' being its future tense."

A particular theory of knowledge underlies Bion's method, especially his belief that both memory and desire arise from sense impressions and that the senses cannot be trusted to tell the truth. Nor can they help us apprehend psychological states (depression, anxiety, fear, and so on); only intuition can do that, and to make room for intuitive knowing, every analytic session "must have no history and no future." The therapist who knows something from the past may as well forget it to make room for the unknown.

As for this "unknown," Bion regularly speaks of it in terms of "evolution." "Out of the darkness and formlessness something evolves," something that the analyst must interpret. He is unlikely even to be aware of it, however, unless he follows two rules.

First, "do not remember past sessions." Especially don't remember supposedly significant events or crises, for when such things occupy the mind, "the evolution of the session" won't be seen at the only time it can be seen, in the present moment.

Second, avoid all desire, especially "desires for results, 'cure,' or even understanding."

PENSÉE. That spring, someone bought Mother some pansy sets to put in the garden. From the living room window, I could see the half-empty box—a few pansies planted, the rest abandoned. The simple stitching together of time needed to move from start to finish had abandoned her. Flowers in small plastic pots, on the ground but not in the ground. Their colorful pansy faces seen from indoors, from above looking down.

You can tell a true war story by the way it never seems to end.
—TIM O'BRIEN

SOMETIMES I THINK IT'S HOPELESS, this quest for beneficent forgetting. When I was six, my sister Edith—eighteen months old—died of viral encephalitis. On Sunday she fell sick; on Friday she was dead. To this day I feel that those I'm close to may simply slip away. I come home expecting to find my wife, but she is not there. Anxious fantasies flood the mind. The news says a woman has been killed by a snowplow north of town. Not my wife, surely—too far north—but still, these things happen. Fully aware of how crazy it is, I check each room of the house. What if she had a stroke and fell to the floor in the laundry room? I try a simple meditation, watching the breath and noting the panic for what it is. I study the self, but all I find is this restless, intrusive Unforgettable.

"People come to therapy because they are remembering in a way that does not allow them to forget." Ah, but when does the therapy or meditation practice work and when does it not?

David J. Morris, a former marine infantry officer, was working as a reporter in Baghdad in 2007 when an improvised explosive device nearly killed him. Some years later, sitting in a movie theater with his girlfriend, he had a sudden blackout; when he came to, he found himself "pacing the lobby of the theater, looking at people's hands to make sure they weren't carrying weapons." What had happened? There had been an explosion in the movie, his girlfriend said, and he fled.

Eventually, Morris went to the VA for help and began a program of "exposure therapy" in which the story of trauma is told over and over in hopes of wearing it out, stripping it of its toxic charge. But it didn't work. He couldn't sleep, couldn't read, couldn't write. He would suit up and go running through his neighborhood, but his calves would seize up, his body "at war with itself. One day, my cellphone failed to dial out and I stabbed it repeatedly with a stainless steel knife until I bent the blade 90 degrees."

ACHILLES AND THE UNFORGETTABLE. In one old story, as the Greeks sail toward Troy, they come to the island of Tenedos, where a certain Tenes tries to keep them from the harbor by hurling rocks from a cliff. Achilles swims to shore and kills him. The problem is that Tenes is a son of Apollo, and Achilles's mother had made it clear that if Achilles ever killed such a man, he himself would die by Apollo's hand. In fact, a slave named Mnemon—let's call him "Mindfulness"—traveled with Achilles with no other task but to help him remember this warning. Now, when he realizes what he's done, Achilles kills Mnemon. By the time the Greeks arrive at Troy, Achilles has no servant of the mind to help him forget his wrath.

Man does not die in a ditch like a dog—but at home in history.
—Boris Pasternak

Living in history without living in the past
Is what the task is.
—Charles Wright

OTHER BODIES (A MURDER STORY). When I began this book, I thought to include a short section examining my own fragmentary recollections of a season of political engagement from my college days. As it turned out, there was no way to tell the story briefly, for my personal point of entry into that history soon led me to another man's much more complicated and traumatizing experience. Thomas Moore, an African American man a few years older than I, had a brother who was murdered by the Ku Klux Klan in the early 1960s. Moore's struggles with the legacy of that violence eventually led him to participate in the conviction and incarceration of one of the killers, to engage with and offer forgiveness to another one of them, and finally to give his murdered brother what I think of as a proper burial. Pertaining as it does to civil rights history, the story of the Moore brothers could easily appear in the more political notebook that follows this one. I place it here under "Self," however, to highlight the individual struggle that political narratives sometimes obscure, the difficult journey one man must take if he is to lay a traumatic memory to rest.

As for my own connection to this history, I spent the summer of 1964 as a civil rights worker in the state of Mississippi, one of a thousand or so volunteers who traveled south that summer to register black voters and to help organize the Mississippi

Freedom Democratic Party in hopes of unseating the all-white delegation that the state's Democrats would inevitably be sending to the party's August nominating convention in Atlantic City.

When I started writing these pages, I found to my surprise that I couldn't remember how I had traveled to get to Mississippi. I knew I started from my parents' home in Rochester, New York, and that I went first to Memphis. My parents had stalled my departure, insisting I come home from college before going south, so I missed the initial "Freedom Summer" orientation in Oxford, Ohio, and instead attended a second one, in Tennessee.

I must have taken a bus. I had a vague memory of a layover in Columbus, Ohio, during which I went to a burlesque show, where I was disappointed to find nothing very sexy on display. I was eighteen. The orientation in Memphis must have been on a college campus; I remember a basement classroom where a man named Staughton Lynd taught us something. Perhaps I got to Laurel, Mississippi—where I was to work all that summer—on another bus, or perhaps we took a bus to Jackson, then drove to Laurel. It's all lost.

Luckily, Mother and Father kept newspaper clippings and the letters I wrote that summer, so I have documents to supplement living memory's shabby record. Inspired by Martin Luther King Jr.'s "Letter from Birmingham Jail," I had, while still in Rochester, responded to an editorial in the local paper with an idealistic letter to the editor announcing that "injustice anywhere is a threat to justice everywhere." My father, having read the letter, advised me that one trick to good writing was to cut the flamboyant parts (racism was "like a boil," I'd written, and "the pus must continue to drain," and so on), but it was too late—I had posted my manifesto.

And I *did* take a bus, one of my letters calling the trip a twenty-nine-hour "torture." The Memphis orientation was at LeMoyne College; a "strange fellow," Richard Beymer, "the guy who played Tony in *West Side Story*," was in the group; Staughton Lynd taught us that the "Removal Statute of 1868," under which "a case can be removed from the state courts to fed courts," might be invoked when we got arrested, but that it was "more of a stall than a workable means." When I got to Laurel, we tried to rent a car, and the local Avis outlet offered us a hearse; I read a book by "Bert. Russell," whom I described to my parents as a "very cool cat." The three-page mimeographed "SECURITY HANDBOOK" we were given warned, "When getting out of a car at night, make sure the car's inside light is out," to which I added in pen: "unscrew it."

Of all my scattered and fragmented memories from that summer, one in particular stands out: when Lyndon Johnson sent four hundred sailors into the state to walk the swamps and drag the rivers searching for the bodies of three volunteers—Mickey Schwerner, James Chaney, and Andrew Goodman—murdered by the Klan on June 21, these sailors found other bodies, dead men no one had been looking for, no one had reported missing. "So this is Mississippi," I thought, a place where a walk through any swamp might uncover the invisible dead, unnamed, unsought.

When I began work on this book, I decided to see if there was any truth to this memory. I began searching *The New York Times* online and on microfilm. The reading was slow: other events drew my attention (Barry Goldwater was running for president, a country called Vietnam appeared occasionally), and the papers were voluminous (Sunday editions ran to hundreds of pages). I worked for several days and found much about the missing volunteers but nothing about other bodies. Perhaps this was a false memory or a rumor that we circulated that summer, a projection of our fears.

And yet, cranking through the old microfilm, looking for coincidentally discovered murder victims, I finally came upon a UPI report dated July 12 that told how "a fisherman found the lower half of a body, its legs tied together, floating in the Mississippi River." It seemed that Mickey Schwerner had been found. "It was the body of a white man," the UPI declared; "the belt buckle carried the initial 'M,'" and there was a gold watch in the blue jeans pocket. "Civil rights workers . . . said Mr. Schwerner had a gold watch."

So I had misremembered. A body found in the river, not a swamp. Near the Delta, not in Neshoba County. A white, not a black, man.

But no, the news from the following day corrected the story. The body of Charles E. Moore, a black youth from Meadville, Mississippi, had been found, so badly decayed that his race was not apparent. And a second body had been found nearby, that of Henry Dee, also young and black, also from Meadville. The boys had been missing since early May. "Rope and wire found around their bodies indicated they had been bound and thrown into the river."

After this, however, *The New York Times* dropped the story. There is hardly another word about Dee and Moore until the following winter, when three short articles appeared. November 7: "2 Whites Seized in Negro Slayings"; November 8: "2 Whites Released on Bond in Killings"; January 12: "Whites Freed in Slayings."

James Ford Seale and Charles Marcus Edwards, both members of the Ku Klux Klan, had been arrested and charged with willful murder. Their families posted bond; the men were released; at a January hearing, the charges were dismissed, the Franklin County DA saying that "additional time" was needed to solve the case.

SAMBO AMUSEMENT. In Mississippi in those days, the White Knights of the Ku Klux Klan believed that they were Christian soldiers opposing the forces of Satan on this earth and that the civil rights workers invading their state were the newly fashioned betrayers of Jesus the Galilean. The Imperial Wizard of the Mississippi Ku Klux Klan, Sam Bowers of Laurel, part owner of a jukebox and vending machine company called Sambo Amusement, had devised a secret code to tell his crusaders when to burn a cross or to whip a man or to firebomb a church or to eliminate a heretic, eliminate him without malice, in complete silence, and in the manner of a Christian act. In Mississippi in those days, the White Knights of the Ku Klux Klan believed that young Negro men had signed agreements promising to rape, weekly, one white woman, that there was an impending Negro insurrection, that the Black Muslims in Chicago had smuggled five thousand automatic weapons, "and maybe a machine gun," into the state and had hidden them in churches and graveyards. In Greenville, Mississippi, the Klan convinced Washington County deputies that by the act of "felony grave tampering" these guns had been hidden in the cemetery of a black church. "Working in the dark, foggy graveyard, heavily armed police pried the lid from a wooden vault," finding no guns but disturbing the rest of one James Turner, only recently buried.

"What divides the dead?" Aeneas asks the Sibyl, his guide; she replies that those denied passage are the "helpless and graveless." Charon will not carry them across the waters "until their bones have found a resting place. A hundred years they roam and flit about these shores; then only are they admitted and revisit the longed-for pools."

ON SATURDAY, MAY 2, 1964, Charles Moore and Henry Dee, both nineteen years old, were hitchhiking across from the Tastee-Freez on the outskirts of Meadville, Mississippi. Moore was a student at nearby Alcorn College, at the time suspended for joining a protest about the lack of social life on the campus. Dee worked at a local sawmill. Neither had any involvement in the civil rights movement.

James Ford Seale of the Bunkley Klavern of the Ku Klux Klan picked the boys up and took them into the nearby Homochitto National Forest, where he and four other Klansmen tied them to a tree and beat them savagely with sapling branches. Dee had recently returned from a trip to Chicago; he wore a black bandanna: surely he knew where the guns being smuggled into the state were hidden. One of the Klansmen, Charles Marcus Edwards, asked if the boys were "right with the Lord," the implication being that they were about to die. In desperation, one of them invented a story: yes, there were guns; they were hidden in Pastor Clyde Briggs's church, over in Roxie.

The Klansmen split up, one group going to the courthouse in Meadville to get Sheriff Wayne Hutto to go with them to Briggs's church (where they found no guns). The others took the beaten boys to a nearby farm. They were bleeding so profusely that the Klansmen spread a tarp in the trunk of a Ford sedan before stuffing the boys into it and driving them ninety miles north to Parker's Island, a backwater bend of the Mississippi River.

When they opened the trunk, they were surprised to find the boys alive. One of the men asked if they knew what was going to happen. They nodded. James Ford Seale taped their mouths shut and their hands together. He bound their legs with rope and wire. He and another man chained Henry Dee to a Jeep engine block, loaded him into a boat, rowed him out onto the river, and rolled him into the water, alive. Charles Moore watched from the shore. The men returned, chained Moore to another weight, rowed him out onto the river, and rolled him into the water, alive. Later they were to say that they dumped Dee and Moore alive rather than shoot them because they did not want to get blood all over the boat.

It is an ancient theme, the consequences of denying the dead a proper burial. In Sophocles's play *Antigone*, the prophet Tiresias speaks to the stubborn king Creon, he who will not bury the body of Polyneices, now lying outside the gates of Thebes, picked at by carrion birds and dogs:

> As I took my place on my ancient seat for observing birds . . . I heard a strange sound among them, since they were screeching with dire, incoherent frenzy; and I knew that they were tearing each other with bloody claws, for there was a whirring of wings that made it clear. At once I was alarmed, and attempted burnt sacrifice at the altar where I kindled fire; but the fire god raised no flame from my offerings. Over the ashes a dank slime oozed from the thigh bones, smoked and sputtered; the gall was sprayed high into the air, and the thighs, streaming with liquid, lay bare of the fat that had concealed them.
>
> Such was the ruin of the prophetic rites.

The Klansman who owned the boat used in the murders of Dee and Moore had a brother who knew nothing about their

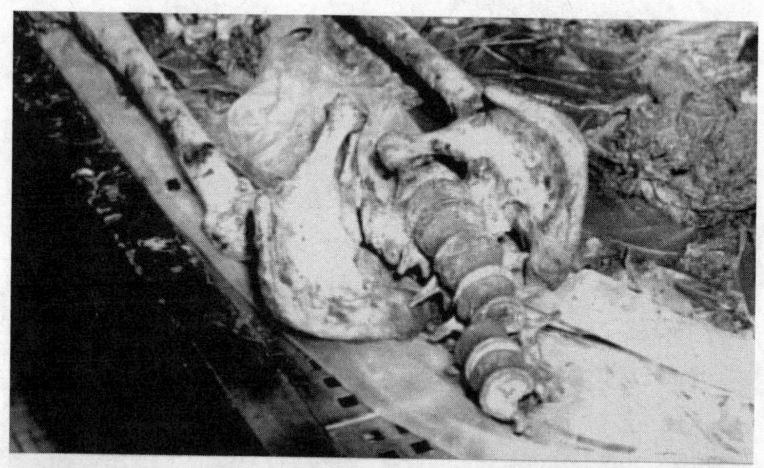

drowning. But this Klansman felt he should tell his brother what had happened because at the point where the brother frequently crossed the river, he had the habit of dipping up water to drink and he should be warned that he was "drinking water off a dead Negro."

In the Dee-Moore murder case, historical memory—the contemporary written record—is almost as shabby as my personal memory. To take but one key example, the newspapers at the time reported that the Franklin County sheriff, Wayne Hutto, made some phone calls and located the boys in Louisiana. "I can't figure it out," Hutto is quoted as saying. "If these boys had been in any trouble around here I think I would have known about it."

But Mississippi in 1964 was a police state, meaning simply that the police were complicit with the Klan terrorists, Hutto in this case having helped the Klan search for weapons in the church in Roxie.

We know all these details because the Dee-Moore murder case was in fact solved by the FBI within months of the discovery of the bodies. The FBI had a paid informant in the Klan, a man to whom the killers told the whole story of what happened on May 2, 1964.

That is why in late October of that year the FBI was able to send navy divers into the muddy waters around Parker's Island and find the skeletal remains of the victims, along with the Jeep engine block. Charles Moore's skull was found—identified because he had lost some teeth playing football. Henry Dee's skull has never been found.

THE SECOND DEATH. They say that one way to lay a traumatic memory to rest is to create a particular kind of symbol: a grave marker. Once a grave has been marked, you can visit it, but you do not have to. Once a trauma has been properly buried, you can call it to mind, but you do not have to. It's available but not intrusive, not haunting.

"The first symbol in which we recognize humanity . . . is the burial," writes Jacques Lacan. "It is man who invented the sepulcher. . . . One cannot finish off someone who is a man as if he were a dog. . . . [His] register of being . . . has to be preserved by funeral rites."

This is from Lacan's seminar on *Antigone*, a play in which we find no proper burial. *Antigone* ends with three suicides, and suicide can be thought of as an attempt to signify through action what ought to be named through inscription. Lacan calls naming through inscription "the second death." "The symbol . . . [is] the killing of the thing," he writes, drawing on Hegel, whose idea was that conceptual understanding is a kind of erasure of the particular.

Take a living dog that runs and barks and eats and shits. As soon as that dog passes into the word "dog," its particular embodiment disappears: the word "dog" doesn't run and bark and so forth.

Let us put this in terms of trauma. A very particular, horrifying thing happens to someone—as happened to the families of Dee and Moore. How to recover from (or at least work with) such horror? The advice is to erase (or liquefy) the particular by putting it into symbols. If the story cannot be fully told, then the trauma persists. Time stops. Twenty years later, the dead still appear in dreams.

The grave marker is the symbol that makes it clear that whatever has happened need not live forever. The symbol lives on, but the real, once properly inscribed, is temporal and can be buried.

Forgetting is the erasing angel that murders particularity so that concepts can be born, so that time can flow again.

COLD CASE. In January 1965, for various reasons (the local DA stalling for "additional time," the FBI refusing to reveal its informant), the murder charges against James Ford Seale and Charles Marcus Edwards were dismissed for "lack of evidence," and law enforcement at every level—county, state, and federal—abandoned the case. Several journalists showed some interest in it during the 1990s, but nothing began to move until the summer of 2005, when the Canadian filmmaker David Ridgen got in touch with Charles Moore's older brother, Thomas.

Thomas Moore is the central character in the rest of this tale.

He was in the army when his brother was killed, and though he came home for the funeral, his mother told him that there was nothing he could do, that he had to forget about it and go on with his life. The army sent him to Vietnam, and he later served in the first Gulf War. He retired to Colorado Springs in the 1990s. During all his years in the military, Moore had nightmares about his brother's death. He would hear Charles calling out for help, asking, "Why?" The killing left him feeling trapped, he has said, "chained by pain, guilt, hate, and shame."

Ridgen persuaded Moore to go back to Mississippi and work on the case. Within weeks they had remarkable success: they found James Ford Seale (who had been reported dead), and they found what were supposedly lost FBI files. Soon they confronted Seale's conspirator, Charles Marcus Edwards, directly, approaching him one morning as he and his wife came to open the church where he was a deacon.

In Ridgen's film, *Mississippi Cold Case*, we see Moore hand

Edwards a manila envelope of FBI files, and we hear him ask Edwards why the files contain his name. Edwards protests, "I'm not on the FBI report." (He had in fact never seen the files.) "I did not kill your brother," he says. "The FBI dropped all this case and you know that. They dropped the case because there wasn't any evidence. I've never been on that Mississippi River in my life," he says, shooing Moore and Ridgen away. "You all get off this church ground and quit stirring up trouble here on the church."

Not long after this encounter, Moore and Ridgen persuaded a U.S. attorney in Jackson to give Edwards immunity in exchange for his testimony and to indict Seale for conspiracy in the murders. In 2007, Seale was convicted and sent to jail, where he died four years later.

"MY BROTHER'S GOT PEACE." In the spring of 2014, I went back to Mississippi, and on May 2—fifty years to the day after the kidnapping, beating, and murders of Charles Moore and Henry Dee—Moore, Ridgen, and I visited the site in the Homochitto National Forest where the boys had been tied to a tree and whipped until one of them invented the story about guns hidden in a nearby church. Two sticks leaning against a tall yellow pine marked the spot of the beating. I dropped a digital recorder into my shirt pocket, and Moore and I, standing on the dirt road amid the filtered sunlight and the bugs, began to talk.

What was of most interest to me was not Seale's conviction—that was simple justice—but something surprising that happened at the trial: Edwards asked the families to forgive him for his part in the crime. In her book *The Human Condition*, Hannah Arendt addresses "the predicament of irreversibility," our "being unable to undo what [we have] done" such that the deeds of the past hang over every new generation. "Forgiving," she writes, offers a "possible redemption from the predicament of irreversibility."

I knew in general what had happened at the Seale trial, but I was glad to hear Moore tell it in his own words:

> The first day of court . . . it was about four o'clock . . . and he [Edwards] said, "Can I address the court?" and the judge says, "Well, let me dismiss the jury"—and I was sitting right on the front seat—he was still in the witness box and Thelma [Collins, Henry Dee's sister] was sitting next to me . . . and he looking right at me, he asked me, he said, "Mr. Moore and Mrs. Collins," he said, "I wants

to apologize for what I was involved in forty-one years ago, in the killing of your brother." And he said, "I ask your forgiveness." Those were the words. And that was it.

Everybody's mouth was just, *whup!* an' I said, "Holy shit."

So then, I had several family members there . . . and I went to each one and I said, "What do you think?" They said, "That's up to you. You got to deal with it." I said, well, I was readin' the Bible—'cause I was brought up in Sunday school—and I read where it said, "How many times do I forgive my brother? Shall I forgive my brother seven times? No, seventy times seven." And then I said, "I'm goin' to forgive him and give him a handshake." So we did, next morning.

Moore's decision to forgive Edwards would have been hard to predict. The U.S. Army had trained Moore as a rifleman, then as a machine gunner, then as a sniper. "You were a dangerous man," I said as we drove down the back roads, and he agreed. In fact, when it became clear that his brother had been killed simply for being black, Moore began to plot revenge against whites in Franklin County. He stockpiled automatic weapons. He imagined climbing the water tower and poisoning the town water supply. Only when his mother found out what he was up to, and told him not to do it, did he forbear.

Standing with Moore on that dirt road in the forest, I kept circling this change of heart, wondering how he had moved from being a trained, revenge-seeking rifleman to being a man willing to forgive. He kept putting off a direct answer, or so it seemed until I realized he was building it up slowly, for it had many parts.

The first had to do with finding out what had actually happened. In 2005, when Ridgen approached him about filming, Moore asked, "What's in this for me?" and Ridgen replied, "Maybe a little truth." Until that time, Moore had not actually known how his brother had been killed or by whom.

In short, in describing his change of heart, Moore began by speaking of truth and justice (or, as he said to me, "some justice"; of the many men involved in the murders, only one went to jail). It was especially the Seale indictment, and the fact that Moore himself was instrumental in securing it, he said, that had "redeemed [him] from being angry."

"Forgiving," writes Arendt, "is the only reaction which does not merely re-act but acts anew and unexpectedly." That day in the courthouse, Moore and Edwards had quoted back and forth to each other the Christian Gospel about forgiveness, a common language known to both men but belonging to neither, what a psychologist friend of mine calls "the third," that is, a thing that allows two people to step beyond themselves into something other than opposition.

Nor was that the end of it. After Seale's conviction, Moore "continued to read about forgiveness":

MOORE: Research, research, research. Get an understanding. And I read this thing where it said it was a three-part process. Two of them you have a whole lot to do with—you got to want to do it . . . it talks about what you holding in—Who is it really hurting? And then I said, then the third part must be the Holy Spirit, to come in and take the place of all that violent mind. And of course I was in the church then; I was moving, I was moving. Marcus [Edwards] opened the door, gave me the key. Now, a lot of people have asked me, "Do you think Marcus was serious?" I don't know. And I really don't care. I really don't care whether he was trying to make himself look good. I don't care. I don't know. He dangled some keys in front of me, and I took 'em. And I let myself out of my own suffering, my poor prison. And I was able to let it go . . . and let my brother lie, just settle down. I think my brother's got peace.

HYDE: But do you still dream about your brother?

MOORE: No. No, no, no, no. No, I look at the work that I'm doing in church, in the community. I look at it as my brother and my mom, they lookin' down on me and sayin', "He doin' some good stuff." So, as horrible and as brutal as it was, I have come—through the spiritual life—to accept the fact that this was something that I was destined to do, and go *through* in my life in order to be who I am today.

In the Erechtheum on the Acropolis in Athens, there once stood, says Plutarch, an altar to Lethe, to Forgetfulness, meant to remind Athenians to forget a mythic dispute at the founding of their city.

"COME ON IN THE CHURCH." James Ford Seale was convicted in 2007. Three years later Thomas Moore returned to Mississippi, this time to seek out the Klansman Charles Marcus Edwards to see if it was possible to move beyond truth and justice to something closer to true reconciliation. David Ridgen filmed their encounter. After some preliminary greetings, the two men sit on Edwards's porch swing, and Moore initiates the conversation:

MOORE: I don't know how you feel about it but when you stood up in church, I mean stood up in the court and asked for forgiveness, that gave me *an avenue.*

EDWARDS: Yeah, right.

MOORE: Man, I hated you, dude. I'm gonna tell you right off, I said, "I'm gonna get him," you know, and I didn't even know you.

EDWARDS: You know, when I did that, being in the church, and I'd prayed about that a lot of times, for forgiveness, you know. And it lifted a burden off of me, yes sir, it lifted a burden off of me. That was a black mark in my life, I can't tell you. I'm sorry for it to this day. I was sincere when I asked you and Miss Dee to forgive me too, you know. I didn't deny being a member of the Klan. I didn't deny that.

RIDGEN [*voice-over*]: Soon the conversation turns to the beating itself.

EDWARDS: I reckon you could say Curtis [Dunn] and myself, we did the little strapping that went on. James Seale says I—he held a gun on these guys. . . .

MOORE: I try to think that the shock and that they was on the, uh, how bad they were beaten up I don't know, but just the fact that, I know . . .

EDWARDS: They got a pretty good whuppin' but I—they was nowhere near dead nor nothing like that, I mean, they were good and alive when they left [*unintelligible*] and took them back down to Mr. Seale's place down there before those other people came out there.

MOORE: Did you ever think about: "What if that had happened to *my* son?"

EDWARDS: Well, sure I did. And I wondered, you know, I wondered, I had four boys, and I wondered, and I said, "What if some of them people might retaliate and take one of my sons," you know, and I wondered about that.

RIDGEN [*voice-over*]: After two hours, and the conversation becoming ever more personal, the coffee comes out.

We see Edwards bringing coffee mugs from his kitchen; then he and Moore are standing by Moore's car.

MOORE: What does this talking that you and I are doing do for you today?

EDWARDS: Well, let you know that we can be friends.

MOORE [*nods*]: Yeah.

The scene switches back to the men sitting on the porch swing. Moore recalls the time he approached Edwards at his church, trying to get him to talk; Edwards had refused and shooed him off the property.

MOORE: We didn't come to see you until 2006 because I'm gonna tell you why. I'm gonna tell you why: because I didn't have the *nerve* to come talk to you. So I, me and David rode by here a couple of times, and I said, "No, I'm not goin' in there." That was in 2005.

EDWARDS: I tell you what, and I look back at the day that you all came to church up there and [*unintelligible*] I thought about it a thousand times since then: "Why didn't I just ask them people to come on in the church with me?"

MOORE: What time is your church service on Sunday? The service.

EDWARDS: The service is at eleven o'clock. [*Pause.*] If you want to come, you come.

MOORE: I think—you and I, sittin' up in church, is going to be a testimony for our people.

EDWARDS [*nods*]: Okay.

The men go into the garden to pick peaches and tomatoes. They shake hands by the car.

MOORE: We'll be seeing you, fellah.

EDWARDS [*nodding*]: Uh-huh.

MOORE: I remember the words you said, "You all get off of here now, go home." All right, sir, we'll see you Sunday.

Moore and Ridgen drive away, Moore shaking his head in disbelief.

MOORE: I'm damn near speechless, myself. Five years ago, we talkin' this kind of shit, you crazy as hell. [*Smiling.*] And instead I'm telling the man that "I planned to kill you. I plotted." And the biggest thing is that he invited us to his church. I didn't expect that. I didn't expect him to say, "You all come on to the church." That's going to be a *story*. God damn it, black and white *do not* attend church together.

"A GREAT MILLSTONE." Years before this encounter, at the time of the Seale trial, when Moore forgave Edwards, the two men quoted to each other Jesus's answer when asked how many times a man should be forgiven. Seven times? No, says Jesus, not seven but seventy times seven.

By the time I interviewed Moore, I had read Matthew 18:2–6, where this counsel is found: Jesus has a child brought before him and tells the disciples that they should humble themselves "and become like children." Then he says, "Whoever causes one of these little ones . . . to sin, it would be better for him if a great millstone were hung around his neck and he were thrown into the sea."

How would Moore read that line? I wondered. Isn't Jesus saying that some sinners should be put to death rather than be forgiven? Didn't the Klansmen cause one another to sin? It was Edwards who had pointed out Henry Dee to Seale; didn't he in fact set the kidnapping in motion and "cause" the murders?

In her meditation on forgiveness, Arendt allows that there is such a thing as radical evil and unforgivable crimes. Jesus connects forgiveness and repentance, but what exactly is repentance? Arendt points out that the biblical Greek for "repentance" means "change of mind." It isn't enough to say, "I'd like to apologize." What is called for is a conversion, and true conversions are rare; one or two in a lifetime would be unusual. What exactly, I wondered, had Charles Marcus Edwards done to show that he had become a different person? In the filmed conversation, he is remarkably passive; Moore does all the work.

And as for reconciliation, isn't what we're seeing an American individualist form—*one* person guilty, *one* person apologizing, *one* person forgiving? What about a legal system that allowed a century of American apartheid, that allowed county, state, and federal law enforcement to ignore two murders for forty years?

I had been thinking about all of this before I met Thomas Moore and had papers in my pocket with notes to help me fill out my questions. But as we stood talking in the forest where the boys were tortured, my questions seemed out of place, almost rude, thought experiments for some other day.

Instead of pestering Moore about that great millstone, I thanked him for the work he had done. It wasn't my brother who had been killed. I was not the man whose nightmares had been quieted.

IT DISAPPEARS. "To study the Buddha Way is to study the self," writes Dogen Zenji, thirteenth-century Japanese Zen master. And "to study the self is to forget the self. To forget the self is to be verified by all things." "To study" could be translated as "to become intimate with." Translating the second line has its own complications. Some say that forgetting the self is "to become one with the ten thousand things"; some say it's "to be enlightened."

In the Chinese version of Dogen's original text, the character for "forget" is made of two elements: the lower half indicates "heart/mind," while the upper half means "to become invisible, perish, lose." The oldest rendering of this upper part, found on oracle bones dating back three or four thousand years, is a bit of a pictogram: it inserts a vertical line beside the sign for "person" so as to indicate a person hidden behind something and thus invisible.

When something is forgotten, the heart/mind no longer sees it. You could therefore translate Dogen's "self-forgetting" this way: "When we study the self . . . it disappears."

THE WORK. The story of Thomas Moore's journey from vengeance to forgiveness has two kinds of memory and thus two kinds of forgetting. Some things can be called to mind at will, and some intrude upon the mind no matter what we will. It is one thing to get angry when thinking back on an injury; it is quite another to be invaded by nightmares whenever sleep lowers the threshold of consciousness.

The Furies are embodiments of unforgettable grief and rage. *Their names are Grievance, Ceaseless, and Bloodlust. Their names are Grudge, Relentless, and Payback. They bloat the present with the undigested past.* They harry the sleepless mind, demanding blood for its release.

There are certain parasitic fungi that invade the brains of tropical ants, making them climb to the top of trees and die there so the fungus can grow from their bodies and widely spread its spores. In the same way, the Unforgettables control their hosts and seed themselves anew. The curse of the house of Atreus descends generation to generation. The story has no easy closure, each of its bearers being compelled to add another chapter and act it out in the incarnate world.

In the case at hand, the U.S. Army put weapons in Moore's hands and taught him how to kill; add to that his brother's restless, nightmare ghost, and before long you have a man plotting to murder white men in Meadville, Mississippi.

Of the many forces that combined to alter and close that plot, three stand out. First there was the truth: in 2005, after forty-one years, Moore got access to the FBI files and knew for the first time what had actually happened to his brother. Then there was justice ("some justice"): the government indicted James Ford Seale, a Mississippi jury convicted him, a federal judge sent him to prison. Only after all of that did forgiveness enter the picture, and forgiveness, as we saw, turned out to be an object of study for Moore: "Research, research, research. Get an understanding."

To enter the work of forgiveness it may not be necessary for the truth to come out and justice to be done, but it helps. It helps because it then becomes easier for the traumatized man to see the degree to which the wound has become part of his identity, his sense of self. If he is to change, he will first of all have to study that self, become intimate with it. ("Who is it really hurting?") That doesn't mean a literal forgetting of the crime, but it does mean letting go of the person the crime brought into being. "Why drag about this corpse of your memory?" asks Emerson in one of his great odes to American self-renewal. Said Moore, "As hard and as brutal as it was . . . this was something that I was destined . . . to go *through* in my life in order to be who I am today." Who he is today is a man who has laid the ghost to rest ("my brother's got peace"), freed himself from servitude to the Unforgettable, and become the agent of his own recollections.

From the point of view of the parasitic fungus, seizing the ant's brain is a wonderful thing. The fungus community endures and spreads. From the point of view of the ant, it's a disaster. In the human community, the spirit of the Unforgettable is useful when it comes to asserting self against other. The desire for revenge can be an expression of basic self-respect, and as the legal scholar Martha Minow writes, "Vengeance is also the wellspring of a notion of equivalence that animates justice." But revenge without justice too easily descends into unending violence, blacks and whites killing one another year after year as each race claims and defends an identity rooted in *not* being the other.

For those whose goal is an end to conflict, then, better to become intimate with the self that clings to difference. And better to forget about it.

INTO BROAD DAYLIGHT. With Marcel Proust in mind, an interviewer asks the sculptor Louise Bourgeois, "What is your madeleine?" She replies that it isn't a taste or a smell. "It is most of all light. Time is a tributary of the light of the day, of the sunset, of the night, of the dawn. *Le plein jour, ça c'est ma madeleine.*"

James Turrell, *One Accord* (2000),
Live Oak Friends Meeting House, Houston, Texas

FROM THE MUSEUM OF FORGETTING: "NO IMAGE, NO OBJECT, NO FOCUS." A James Turrell "skyspace" is an enclosure meant to be entered to observe the unobstructed sky through a large rectangular opening in the ceiling. Turrell says that people often ask him, "Why do I have to go inside to see the sky? I can see it anywhere I want to!" His reply: "But that's not telling the story of *how* we see the sky," of how very much our "prejudicial perception" forms what we see. "We award the sky its color."

Prejudicial or not, all sight depends on light, and it has been Turrell's long-term project to create situations in which we might drop perceptual habits and see light simply as light. Turrell was born into a Quaker family and remembers the time when, as a child, he was first allowed to attend Sunday meeting: "My grandmother was trying to tell me what you did. Her explanation to me was: 'you go inside to greet the light.'" Of the Live Oak building in Houston, he has said, "That was the kind of Meeting House I always wanted to see. I like the literal quality or feeling or sensation, in that I want to feel light physically. We drink light as vitamin D; it's actually a food."

The light in all Turrell's skyspaces is as unmediated as possible in contrast to the long Christian tradition in which light enters the sanctuary through stained glass, often illuminating a story depicted there. Turrell prefers light itself as the message, a Quaker light, "a straightforward, strict presentation of the sublime." "If you use light to tell a story then you're not using the power of light, you're using the power of the story." Turrell's light is not subordinated to narrative or image. His "locations" dispense with all the demands of the old blood-smeared memory palaces. "If you have no image, no object, no focus—what do you have left? For me, it takes you to this primal relation to light. We drink light."

NOTEBOOK III

NATION

"Everyone Has Forgotten Many Things"

The Aphorisms

Study the nation to forget the nation.

Chosen traumas die hard.

The Unforgotten, destroyer of nations.

"Out of oblivions spring narratives."

Amnesty is a cold forgetting.

The struggle against power is the struggle against the memory of difference.

OGIER THE DANE. Grief swept the kingdom of Denmark, for the queen had died giving birth to her son. The ladies-in-waiting took the babe and, naming him Ogier, laid him on a royal bed of down. And lo! Six shining fairies appeared by his bedside and endowed him fully with gifts of bravery and beauty. Morgan le Fay, queen of the fairies, came last, promising a life of earthly glory to be followed by eternal ease as her consort in Avalon, the land of the fairy.

Years later, when Ogier the Dane had come of age, he pledged himself a knight in service to the emperor Charlemagne. So it was that when Rome was overtaken by the pagan hordes of Islam, Ogier joined the crusade to regain that holy city. Battle upon battle followed, Ogier galloping into the fray fierce as a lion, hewing his way through the paynims, reaping among the enemy until he ramparted himself with a wall of the slain.

So unfolds the legend of Ogier the Dane. Hindu princes convert to the cross under his spell; women, their white dresses sewn with pearls, love him; Saracen giants fall to Courtain, his invincible sword; grateful nations crown him king of Britain, then of Babylon, then of Jerusalem.

Finally, sailing home from the Holy Land, Ogier's ship ran aground on a lodestone reef. The warrior, old and weary, had come to Avalon, where, in her shining white kirtle, Morgan le Fay, queen of the fairies, awaited.

"Welcome, dear knight, to Avalon. A weary time have I longed and waited for thy coming. Now thou art mine; my lord, my love. So let the restless ages roll, and the world totter and decay! We will dream on forever in this changeless vale."

Then she put an enchanted ring upon his hand; so the years

slipped from his shoulders and he stood before her in the prime of youth and vigor. And she placed upon his brow a priceless golden crown of myrtle leaves and laurel, a crown no mortal treasure would suffice to buy—the Crown of Forgetfulness. Then Ogier remembered no more the things that were past. His old loves, toils, and battles faded from his mind, and in place of a dead memory a living love was given him, and he joined the fairy queen in a land that knows neither time nor death.

Two hundred years slipped by as if they were a single day.

Trouble came again to France and Christendom. Chivalry was dead; the pagan hordes of Islam had conquered the Franks on every side. The people cried for help, and Morgan le Fay, queen of the fairies, heard them and took pity. She lifted from the head of Ogier the Dane the Crown of Forgetfulness, and as if waking from a dream, he cried out, "My sword, my horse, my spear! Oh, let me go, sweet Queen!"

Then, once again, the mighty warrior appeared among the disheartened Franks, and once again the battlefield was tracked with lines of slain, until France was free, the Church secure, the spirit of chivalry reborn. Then Ogier the Dane assumed the throne that had long ago belonged to Charlemagne and prepared to marry—only of a sudden to be spirited away again by Morgan le Fay, queen of the fairies.

But Ogier the Dane is not dead. His brow wreathed by the myrtle and laurel of oblivion, he sleeps in Avalon, and in the days that come, whenever their foes draw near, Morgan le Fay, queen of the fairies, will take pity and lift his crown and send her paladin to fight again for France and Christendom.

SHAM GRANDEURS. Though it is true that the Danish resistance in World War II (Christians fighting Christians in that case) took its name, Holger Danske, from the legendary hero, there is really little to admire in this disgusting nineteenth-century fairy tale. Neither of its worlds appeals, not the temporal land of memory and warfare nor the timeless land of oblivion and peace. The latter is too dreamy, with no study of either self or nation; it offers at best an artless forgetfulness, regression without reflection.

As for "France and Christendom," I am reminded of Mark Twain's complaint that the American Civil War could "in great measure" be blamed on romance novels, especially those of Sir Walter Scott, stuffed "with dreams and phantoms; with decayed and swinish forms of religion . . . ; with the silliness and emptinesses, sham grandeurs, sham gauds, and sham chivalries of a brainless and worthless long-vanished society." Just so the tale of Ogier the Dane and its jejune daydream.

And yet two things do interest me here. That Crown of Forgetfulness, of course, but also the way it is set against conflict, and not just any conflict but the centuries-old division between Christianity and Islam. "Ogier the Dane" is pure Orientalism, that politics of difference animating the violence of Christian imperialism.

The twinned pattern of the legend—forgetfulness and conflict in recurring sequence—is also of interest, its vision of history in which differences mean nothing for centuries, then suddenly come back into play, then as suddenly disappear. By turns the heroes are shoring up their identity with enemy corpses and letting it dissolve in fairy idleness.

Where is the politics or the spiritual teaching that might end such a cycle? Is there any statecraft such that nations might forget their wounds? And what, for that matter, is a nation?

"THE ESSENCE OF A NATION." In the late nineteenth century, the philologist Ernest Renan published an essay, "What Is a Nation?," in which he argued that "the essence of a nation is that all its individuals have many things in common, and also that everyone has forgotten many things." The point need not be limited to nations; all group identity, all abstract knowing, has such origins. Families know themselves by mixing recollection and elision; so do oral societies (which, says Walter Ong, keep themselves "in equilibrium . . . by sloughing off memories which no longer have present relevance"). Still, for centuries now nations have been perhaps the largest theaters for the practice of collective forgetting. "No French citizen knows whether he is a Burgund, an Alain, a Taifala, or a Visigoth," wrote Renan. "Every French citizen has forgotten St. Bartholomew's Day and the thirteenth-century massacres in the Midi."

A late entry in France's sixteenth-century Wars of Religion, the St. Bartholomew's Day Massacre saw Catholic mobs slaughter thousands of Calvinist Protestants. But French citizens no more call that day to mind than do American citizens remember how their Puritan ancestors used to hang Quakers on the Boston Common or, for that matter, the history of nineteenth-century Indian wars.

INDIAN REMOVAL FULLY ACCOMPLISHED. When I was a child, we had cereal boxes from the backs of which could be cut cardboard figures of cowboys and Indians. Nightmares then disturbed my sleep, a chaos of cardboard bodies clashing and threatening, their very flatness adding to the horror.

Grandfather and Grandmother owned a cabin on Ten Mile Lake, in northern Minnesota, where we sometimes spent part of the summer. Grandmother once gave me a model canoe, perhaps sixteen inches long and fashioned from birch bark strapped to a bentwood frame. Perhaps it was Ojibwa, perhaps an antique, or perhaps made for the tourist trade; I never knew. And I never to my knowledge met an Indian during our summers at the lake.

At home in Connecticut, I took Grandmother's gift to school to display in the glass case outside our classroom. My teacher Mrs. Swenson inspected my offering and gave her critique: I had misspelled "canoe."

We went on a hike and got lost. I was nine, we were living in rural northeast Connecticut, and we were trying to find Hatchet Pond, a popular excursion site in the nineteenth century (or so we were told by one of our aged neighbors) because around the pond lay the remains of Indian villages and graveyards. In my mind's eye, I can see them still, deep in the shaded pine forest, dark grave mounds with rotted wooden markers. My mind, however, is the only place these graves appear, for in fact we never found them. Nor did we find the pond, despite hiking for hours and Father at one point sending me up a tree in a fruitless attempt to spot it.

My main memory of this adventure is not, however, any details of forest or pond but rather that my brother and I had loaded our backpacks with comic books to read when we pitched our tents that night and Father's amused disgust at how shallow were his children. My favorite comics: *Superman* and *Scrooge McDuck*.

Such is the full account of the Indians of my childhood.

DAWN, NOVEMBER 29, 1864, COLORADO TERRITORY. Two white men came running from the Indian lodges as Colonel John Chivington and his cavalry descended on the Cheyenne and Arapaho encampment at Sand Creek. First the interpreter John Smith ran out with his hands raised, but he retreated when the soldiers shot at him. Then Private Lowderbuck came out with a white flag, but he got the same welcome. Chivington's cavalry of about seven hundred met a similar number of Indians, but only a fraction of these were men of fighting age. "Hundreds of women and children were coming toward us and getting on their knees for mercy," reported Captain Silas Soule, who had refused to join in the attack. "I tell you," he wrote to a fellow officer, "it was hard to see little children on their knees have their brains beat out by men professing to be civilized."

Soule witnessed one soldier sever a woman's arm with a hatchet, then dash her brains out. Another woman hanged herself in a low-roofed lodge, holding up her knees so she might choke to death. Another "was cut open and a child taken out of her, and scalped." Another knelt with her two children "begging for their lives of a dozen soldiers"; when one of these wounded her in the thigh, "she took a knife and cut the throats of both children and then killed herself."

Chiefs Black Kettle and Left Hand had been to Denver earlier that year to meet with Chivington and the territorial governor, John Evans, and to express their desire to live in harmony with the whites. They left with the understanding that they would not be disturbed so long as they flew an American flag. George Bent—whose father was a white trader and mother a Cheyenne and who was living at Sand Creek when Chivington attacked—reported that Black Kettle had the American flag "tied to the end of a long lodgepole and was standing in front of his lodge . . . the flag fluttering in the grey light of the winter dawn." White Antelope "had been telling the Cheyennes for months that the whites were good people and that peace was going to be made." Now, as the cavalry shot him, he "stood in front of his lodge with his arms folded across his breast, singing the death song: 'Nothing lives long, Only the earth and the mountains.'" Left Hand too was shot, "hands folded across his breast . . . saying, 'Soldiers no hurt me—soldiers my friend.'"

Some Indians fought back and some escaped, "but most . . . were run down by horsemen. . . . They were all scalped." Bodies were "horribly mutilated," Soule wrote. Fingers were cut off to get their rings. "White Antelope, War Bonnet and a number of others had Ears and Privates cut off. Squaws' snatches were cut out for trophies." The massacre lasted eight hours, at the end of which Chivington's men burned the camp. For a day afterward, they carried one three-month-old infant around in the feed box of a wagon, then left it on the ground to perish.

"THE VOICES OF CHILDREN . . ." The first memorial to the Sand Creek Massacre appeared in 1950, an obelisk near Chivington, Colorado, bearing a plaque that reads in part, "Many Indians were killed, no prisoners were taken. The white losses were ten killed and thirty-eight wounded. One of the regrettable tragedies in the conquest of the west." Years later, those who were the object of that conquest began to make themselves into the agents of its memory. In 1978, the Cheyenne chief Laird Cometsevah and the Cheyenne Sacred Arrow Keeper conducted a ceremony to reclaim the Sand Creek killing field and make it once again "Cheyenne earth." Later, when the federal government moved to make the site officially "historic," there was considerable disagreement as to the massacre's precise location, but Cometsevah knew exactly where it had taken place because when he and the Arrow Keeper conducted their ritual he had heard "the voices of children, of mothers, crying for help."

For the Cheyenne and Arapaho, a prime motive for memorializing Sand Creek was to respond to those restless dead and give them proper burial. For Gail Ridgely of the Northern Arapaho, whose great-great-grandfather Lame Man survived the massacre, the creation of a national historic site promised to "allow our people to remember their ancestors and help put their suffering to rest."

Ridgely's statement supposes an interesting divide—the memory will endure, the suffering will not—and raises again the question of how traumatic memories get resolved. In the case of Sand Creek, would the creation of a memorial be adequate to the task? Could a "national historic site" serve as the kind of grave marker (something "you can visit but you do not have to") that sufficiently separates past and present to allow a fresh future to unfold?

When I try to enumerate all that needs to be in place for any marker to accomplish such ends, I find myself with a daunting list: it would be good to have truth and justice, of course, but also apology (both declared and acknowledged) or forgiveness (both requested and granted), and reparations for all that was lost, and finally, in this case, the literal burial of the mutilated dead.

TRUTH AND JUSTICE. To begin at the head of this list, there should never have been any doubt about the truth of what happened at Sand Creek, Silas Soule and others having written eyewitness accounts within weeks of the massacre. But from the very first, Chivington and his supporters contested those accounts—to them the engagement had been a glorious battle, not a massacre, and Black Kettle a savage, not a peacemaker—and despite a federal investigation, no one from the Colorado Cavalry was ever brought to trial. The truth teller Soule himself was assassinated: he testified before a military investigation in February 1865, and a few months later, in Denver, two of Chivington's men shot him. For "nearly a century" after that, the historian Ari Kelman tells us, "from the start of the reservation era until relatively recently, Cheyenne and Arapaho people were discouraged, sometimes violently, from telling their Sand Creek stories. Boarding school administrators, Bureau of Indian Affairs officials, and other white authorities believed that keeping alive memories of the massacre preserved links to the past, to a traditional way of life, hindering acculturation."

As for the white population, to this day there are those willing to celebrate Chivington as a hero and to speak of the Sand Creek encampment as "harboring terrorists." For many years, one Jerry Russell of Little Rock, Arkansas, served as national chairman of the Order of the Indian Wars, a group dedicated to preserving the memory of the "soldiers, pioneers and settlers who were the agents of manifest destiny, and who, with unyielding bravery and uncommon sacrifice, helped to tame the New World and build the America that we all cherish beyond description."

Complaining that the National Park Service was wrongly advocating a multicultural agenda, Russell traveled to Colorado in 2003 especially to celebrate Chivington. "Some folks, bleeding hearts from back east, have been calling Sand Creek a massacre for a long time," he declared, but it wasn't a massacre, it was a battle; "battlefields are about honor," and Chivington was an honorable man. The National Park Service's version of events was just "politically correct" history, complained another member of the order. Indians are "always victims. They're always downtrodden, victimized by oppressive power. And there's some truth to that, yeah. But it's an excuse now. Get over it."

In sum, truth and justice have been hard to come by.

AS FOR REPARATIONS AND APOLOGY, these appeared to be in the offing almost immediately after the massacre, when representatives of the U.S. government met with the Cheyenne and Arapaho in the fall of 1865 to sign the Treaty of the Little Arkansas.

Article 6 of that document opens with the United States declaring itself as "being desirous to express its condemnation of, and, as far as may be, [to] repudiate the gross and wanton out-rages perpetrated against certain bands of Cheyenne and Arrapahoe [*sic*] Indians." Noting that "said Indians were at peace with the United States, and under its flag, whose protection they had by lawful authority been promised and induced to seek," the treaty goes on to affirm the government's desire "to make some suitable reparation for the injuries then done," these being mostly land grants (320 acres to Black Kettle, for example) and payment "in United States securities, animals, goods, provisions, or such other useful articles," all as "compensation for property . . . destroyed or taken" by Chivington's troops.

The terms of this treaty have never been honored; until they are, all subsequent expressions of regret have a hollow ring. The Colorado senator Ben Nighthorse Campbell (of Cheyenne descent on his father's side) once announced his support for reparations, and the Kansas senator Sam Brownback once declared, "As a U.S. senator from a Plains state, I deeply apologize, and I'll work to right this wrong. I humbly ask the Native Americans here, and their leaders in particular, to forgive us." But Senator Campbell never followed words with action, saying that to bring the matter before the U.S. Senate would be "a nonstarter," and Senator Brownback's offer "to right this wrong" did not mean making good on the broken promises of the 1865 treaty.

"The Cheyenne will not accept an apology for what happened at Sand Creek for the simple reason that Sand Creek is not over," Laird Cometsevah has said. "The U.S. government still owes the descendants of the massacre. We're not going to accept any apology until Article 6 of the Treaty of the Little Arkansas is completed."

AS FOR ACTUAL AND PROPER BURIAL, the spirits of the Sand Creek dead have good reason to cry out for help. Not only did Chivington's men mutilate the bodies—taking scalps, ears, and genitals for trophies—but some years later General William Tecumseh Sherman and his troops visited the killing fields and gathered more souvenirs. Some of the remains they collected ended up in specimen drawers at the Smithsonian Institution, while others went to the Army Medical Museum in Maryland, where, during the Indian wars, they were used to study the effects of gunshot on the human body. As Steve Brady, head of the Sand Creek Massacre Descendants Committee, once said, "We, the Cheyenne people, were the scientific specimens that improved the U.S. military's killing efficiency, its ordnance."

In 1911, the family of Major Jacob Downing, one of Chivington's fellow officers, made a donation to the Colorado Historical Society, briefly described by its accession label: "Scalp (Cheyenne or Arapaho), Taken from an Indian by a soldier at Sand Creek Massacre, by Jacob Downing Nov. 29, 1864." In the summer of 2008, this and the body parts of five other Sand Creek dead—reclaimed from museums and private collections—were assembled at a National Park Service site near La Junta, Colorado, and then driven to the cemetery established at Sand Creek where Laird Cometsevah had heard the voices of the dead. Beneath an American and a white flag—flying in deliberate echo of those flown in 1864—the gathered descendants prayed in Cheyenne, sang again White Antelope's death song, read aloud Silas Soule's account of the massacre, and then lowered the dead ancestors' remains into sandy graves.

A FAILED EXPERIMENT. Truth, justice, apology, forgiveness, reparations, burial—that list makes for an ambitious preamble to any release from historical trauma. If these notebooks record a thought experiment seeking out places where forgetting is more useful than memory, then here is an instance in which the experiment fails or, at least, where it has yet to be carried to closure. Interring the body parts of six of the mutilated dead seems hardly sufficient to soften the Indians' insistence on the need to keep Sand Creek history alive. "People always say you can't carve things in stone, but we have to. We have to be sure nobody forgets," said Laird Cometsevah during negotiations over the proposed historic site, a sentiment repeated at the dedication of the completed monument: "Now Sand Creek will never be forgotten."

The mutilation of the bodies at Sand Creek was more than trophy hunting; it was an imposition of identity: "You are a conquered people." The cutting of genitalia was an almost literal genocide: these are people who will now not be able to reproduce themselves; the generations will not follow one upon another, the very organs of generation having been cut away and the unborn stripped from their mothers' wombs.

At issue for Native peoples, then, are matters of agency, of cultural and political power. Who's in charge of this story? One of my aphorisms reads, "Nothing can be forgotten that was not first in mind," but I must admit it raises the question of who is forgetting, especially when it comes to cultural memory. If there is a "work of forgetting," it has to involve claiming or creating agency such that you, the people saddled with history, can work on the past rather than have the past work on you. When it comes to collective memory—the kind that calls for a *national* historic site—you can't begin to remember in a way that allows you to forget until the collective itself recognizes and responds to the history at hand. Only then can you both claim an identity as your own and enjoy the privilege of forgetting about it. There is no self-forgetting without self.

AMERICA. Recall Ernest Renan: "The essence of a nation is that all its individuals have many things in common, and also that everyone has forgotten many things." As noted, in one sense, Renan is describing the process by which all abstractions emerge: we select the particulars that count and discard the rest. (Borges's Funes cannot make abstractions, because he has lost his mind's discarding power.) If the goal is to establish a *national* historic site, how then to assemble the abstraction "the United States of America"? Several options come to mind:

- Indians will not forget Sand Creek, and the rest of the nation will not remember it. "America" then does not include the Indians.
- Indians are forced to forget. The story is erased, denied, disputed; its telling is forbidden in the name of assimilation. Indians then become part of an "America" that is a version of Gore Vidal's "United States of Amnesia," a place where the real work of forgetting (the working through of a memory rather than its repression) never gets done. Or it is the "United States of Agnosia," a land that simply does not know its past.
- Indians will not forget, and the rest of the nation joins them in remembering. The Sand Creek Massacre then becomes a thing held "in common," and "America" is understood to be born of blood and cruelty, just as are so many other nations. There is no "American exceptionalism."

FROM THE MUSEUM OF FORGETTING, GALLERY *DAMNATIO MEMORIAE.* "In February 1948, the Communist leader Klement Gottwald stepped out on the balcony of a Baroque palace in Prague to harangue hundreds of thousands of citizens massed in Old Town Square. . . .

"Gottwald was flanked by his comrades, with Clementis standing close to him. It was snowing and cold, and Gottwald was bareheaded. Bursting with solicitude, Clementis took off his fur hat and set it on Gottwald's head.

"The propaganda section made hundreds of thousands of copies of the photograph taken on the balcony where Gottwald, in a fur hat and surrounded by his comrades, spoke to the people. . . . Every child knew that photograph. . . .

"Four years later, Clementis was charged with treason and hanged. The propaganda section immediately made him vanish from history and, of course, from all photographs. Ever since, Gottwald has been alone on the balcony. Where Clementis stood, there is only a bare palace wall. Nothing remains of Clementis but the fur hat on Gottwald's head.

"It is 1971, and Mirek says: The struggle of man against power is the struggle of memory against forgetting," wrote Milan Kundera in *The Book of Laughter and Forgetting.*

THE MEMORY OF DIFFERENCE. It's 1980 and Ronald Reagan kicks off his presidential campaign by telling a cheering crowd at the Neshoba County Fair in Philadelphia, Mississippi, "I believe in states' rights."

It's July 2016 and Donald J. Trump Jr. speaks at the Neshoba County Fair in Philadelphia, Mississippi. "Trump, Trump, Trump," the crowd chants, and "Build that wall." "It's sort of amazing to be on this very stage where Ronald Reagan talked so many years ago," Trump junior says. Asked about the Confederate flag, he says, "I believe in tradition."

It was 1964 and three civil rights workers—Andrew Goodman, Mickey Schwerner, and James Chaney—were murdered by the Ku Klux Klan in Philadelphia, a crime that to this day the State of Mississippi has not prosecuted.

"The struggle of man against power is the struggle of memory against forgetting," wrote Milan Kundera. But such large claims can often be flipped. The Republican Party's "Southern strategy" makes the memory of racial difference its tool. That was 1980, and I say: The struggle against power is the struggle against the memory of difference.

IDENTITY! Cultivating the perception of sameness is key to the forgetting of difference. "Some men have the perception of difference predominant, and are conversant with surfaces and trifles, with coats and watches, and faces and cities. . . . And other men abide by the perception of identity. These are the orientals, the philosophers, the men of faith and divinity," wrote Emerson. The breadth of his reading helped Emerson to this conclusion. He read what was available about Islam, Sufism, and Hinduism and saw how much they had in common with Christianity. "Identity, identity!" he wrote in his journal. "Friend and foe are one stuff, and the stuff is such and so much that the variations of surface are unimportant."

DIFFERENCE, ORGANIZED. Some not only have the perception of difference predominant but make of it a practice. In his copy of Pascal, Henry Adams marked a line that reads, "All men naturally hate one another," Adams himself applying the remark to "politics, as a practice," calling it "the systematic organization of hatreds."

As for the Republicans' "Southern strategy," Garry Wills has noted that, as first elaborated by the party strategist Kevin Phillips, "the plan did not rely merely on Southern racism, but on a deep conviction that, as Phillips put it in a 1968 interview, all politics comes down to 'who hates who.' In that interview, Phillips laid out an elaborate taxonomy of hostilities to be orchestrated by Republicans." Said Phillips, "The more negroes who register as Democrats in the South, the sooner the Negrophobe whites will quit the Democrats and become Republicans. That's where the votes are."

Maybe Ernest Renan's response to the "What is a nation?" question should be replaced by the answer attributed to the Prague-born political scientist Karl Deutsch: "A nation is a group of people united by a mistaken view of the past and a hatred of their neighbors."

THE NEGATIVE NATION. In any event, what "things" does Ernest Renan have in mind when he says that the essence of a nation is that everyone has "forgotten many things"? He gets specific once in regard to France itself: every French citizen "has to have forgotten" the thirteenth-century massacres that took place "in the Midi" (the South of France) and the sixteenth-century St. Bartholomew's Day Massacre.

Both of these belong to Europe's early Wars of Religion, the Roman Catholic Church in each case setting out to suppress, if not wipe out, competing Christian movements. In 1208, Pope Innocent III called for a crusade against a Manichaean sect known as the Cathars. A series of massacres ensued, running from 1209, when the pope's crusaders slaughtered the entire population of Béziers and burned the city to the ground, to 1244, when they besieged the fortress of Montségur and, at the foot of the castle, burned to death several hundred Cathars.

Over three centuries later, the 1572 St. Bartholomew's Day Massacre had actually been preceded by an attempt to end France's ever-recurring sectarian strife. Following years of civil war between Catholics and the Calvinist Protestants known as Huguenots, King Charles IX proposed a marriage between his sister Margaret, a Catholic, and Henry III of Navarre, a Protestant. But Pope Gregory XIII and others condemned the union, and following an assassination attempt on one of the Huguenot leaders, full-scale mob violence broke out in Paris, then spread to a dozen other French cities. The violence lasted several weeks; at least five thousand, perhaps thirty thousand, Protestants died.

In sum, if France is to be a nation, religious difference is what its citizens need to "have already forgotten." In fact,

Renan proposes a kind of *via negativa* of national identity. He carefully goes through all the things that people might use to define nationhood and dismisses each in turn: the essence of a nation is not to be found in religious belief, language, race, "ethnographic politics," economics, military necessity, or even geography ("it is no more soil than it is race which makes a nation").

When he finally comes to nominate nationhood's positive attributes, he offers generalities that leave me skeptical and a bit nervous. A nation is "a soul, a spiritual principle" with "a programme to put into effect," and so on: it's all quite vague and open to interpretation. (Catholics and Cathars alike thought they were defending "a spiritual principle.") I would prefer to forget about the national soul along with all the rest, for it too may contain the seeds of discord. As with the *via negativa* in religious thought, better to stay with erasures. There may well be an "essence of a nation," but as far as possible it should be left unspoken.

SARACENS, AGAIN. In 1933, Onésimo Redondo, Fascist founder of the newspaper *Libertad*, began to stir the antagonisms that would soon fuel the Spanish Civil War: "Marxism, with its Mohammedan utopias . . . , suddenly renews the eclipse of Culture and freedoms like a modern Saracen invasion. . . . This certain danger, of Africanization in the name of Progress, is clearly visible in Spain. We can state categorically that our Marxists are the most African of all Europe. . . . Historically, we are a friction zone between that which is civilized and that which is African, between the Aryan and the Semitic. . . . For this reason, the generations that built the fatherland, those that freed us from being an eternal extension of the dark continent, raised their swords against attack from the south and they never sheathed them."

Spain and Christendom are not only under attack from Saracens, Communists, and Jews, but, in Redondo's most inventive rhetorical trick, they are all in fact black Africans.

THE PACT OF FORGETTING. Nations recovering from civil war or periods of gross human rights abuse typically go through alternating periods of forgetting and remembering. Members of the first generation, those who suffered directly, often exhibit a collective dissociative amnesia. The story is too horrible, too unfitting, and too complicated to be brought to mind, so it isn't.

Spain makes a case in point. The year after the 1975 death of the dictator Franco, the Spaniards adopted a blanket amnesty law, declaring that "as Spain is now heading towards a fully normal democratic state, the moment has come to complete this process by forgetting any discriminatory legacy of the past in the full fraternal harmony of all Spaniards."

There are many kinds of amnesty, one legal scholar having suggested a range that runs from "accountable amnesties"—in which truth is established (those granted amnesty having to openly account for their crimes), archives are opened, killings documented, reparations offered, reconciliation work begun—to the kind of amnesty offered in Spain, "amnesic amnesty," where the absence of all accountability was symbolized by *el pacto del olvido*, Spain's widely accepted informal agreement simply to forget the recent decades of dictatorship.

This Pact of Oblivion held for about twenty years.

"ARRESTED IN BED." Spain's *pacto del olvido* came to a sudden end when a seemingly external event precipitated a case of national recovered memory. In the mid-1990s, activists in Spain began investigating crimes committed in Chile during the dictatorship of Augusto Pinochet (the only head of state to have attended Franco's funeral). In 1998, while Pinochet was traveling in England, a Spanish judge ordered his arrest and extradition to Spain under a legal theory known as "universal jurisdiction." Political parties in Spain, left and right, soon began to argue over what ought to be done with Pinochet, and before long it became clear that the Chilean case was a surrogate for the long-delayed argument over how to remember Franco and the Civil War. Wrote one journalist, Pinochet's arrest was a "vicarious dream of a historical impossibility, that of Franco being arrested in bed."

Dissociative amnesia is a useful defense mechanism in a moment of crisis, but in the long run it is a "dumb forgetting," never working through what has been banished from mind. The post-1998 reengagement with the legacy of the Spanish Civil War began a process that might eventually lead to "smart forgetting," the kind that allows the past to be properly laid to rest, quite literally so in this case: within a few years, the grandchildren of Civil War partisans began to search out the unmarked mass graves of their grandparents, exhume the remains, and give them a proper burial, *un entierro digno.*

The journalist Emilio Silva Barrera's grandfather had been killed in 1936 by the Falangists, his body dumped in a common grave. In 2000, Barrera not only located the site and exhumed and reburied his ancestor's bones, but he also went on to found the Association for the Recovery of Historical Memory, an organization dedicated to excavating mass graves, identifying the dead, and reinterring their remains. In 2004, Spain elected a Socialist prime minister, José Luis Rodríguez Zapatero, also the grandson of a Republican partisan shot by Franco's forces in 1936. His party came to power in part on the promise that it would pass what has come to be called the law for "the recovery of historical memory." In the alternating rhythms of memory and forgetting, it was the second generation after Franco's death that broke the pact of silence that their parents had found necessary to make the transition to democracy.

FROM THE MUSEUM OF FORGETTING, GALLERY *DAMNATIO MEMORIAE* (FRANCO).

JULY 8, 2003: A STATUE OF THE SPANISH DICTATOR FRANCISCO FRANCO BEING REMOVED FROM ITS PLINTH IN THE NORTHWESTERN VILLAGE OF PONTEAREAS, FOLLOWING A VOTE BY THE VILLAGE COUNCIL

"They all were Lorca": A monument erected in the killing fields north of Granada, Spain, where García Lorca's body is among the thousands lying in unmarked graves

THE UNMARKED GRAVE. But after a civil war not everyone will agree on what constitutes proper burial. Take the case of Federico García Lorca. In August 1936, Franco's Black Squadron militia executed the poet and three other men in the dry hills northeast of Granada. Lorca's leftist sympathies were not all that attracted his assassins. "We left him in a ditch and I fired two shots into his arse for being a queer," one of them later explained.

Several efforts have been made to find where Lorca lies buried, all of them opposed by the García Lorca family. "It would be a desecration," his nephew Manuel Fernández-Montesinos has said, explaining that the presumed site has become "a sacred place." People go there to reflect or to recite García Lorca's poems "because his character, his work, his life, or his tragedy moves them." As for remembering what happened, digging up his bones would add nothing; everyone already knows "that Franco and his cohorts were murderers" who made Spain "the asshole of the world for forty years."

Unfortunately, not all Spaniards agree with that assertion, there being no settled way to tell the story of the Civil War even today. Three versions compete: either a reactionary military overthrew a modern democracy; or else a law-and-order military saved the nation from anarchy; or else, finally, both sides were crazy extremists, both committed atrocities, and it would be best to forget the whole thing. Spanish law allows immunity from prosecution in cases of mental illness, so this third way of framing the conflict was popular during the transition with its "pact of forgetting" and its amnesic amnesty. "The whole of Spain lost its head," the newspapers said. "We must take into account the collective insanity." "Spaniards . . . ceased to be themselves."

A gravestone can be a sort of punctuation mark at the end of a story, but it matters first of all to get the story straight. In line with the family's resistance to finding Lorca's bones, one activist group in Spain has opposed all exhumations, saying that recovering individual corpses only obscures the story of mass murder, acting out a "second killing" of the victims. That way of speaking echoes a point made in the context of the Dee-Moore murder narrative. Following a remark by Jacques Lacan ("the symbol first manifests itself as the killing of the thing"), I suggested that a grave marker is the symbol that recognizes the mortality of whatever has happened and that "forgetting is the erasing angel that murders particularity so that concepts can be born, so that time can flow again."

Fair enough, but what happens when no one can agree on what concept should be born? If a nation is a place where "everyone has forgotten many things," what happens to the concept "Spain" when no one can agree on which "things" to forget? In a sense, the 2007 Law of Historical Memory itself forced such questions to the surface: even as it facilitated the search for common graves, it explicitly declined to nominate a common history of the war, guaranteeing instead each individual's or group's right to remember the past in their own way.

With that allowed individualization comes the problem of how to move from the cure of one person's trauma to the cure of collective trauma. One person may finally make up his or her mind to punctuate the past with a gravestone, but collectives are made of many minds, and many minds are often at odds. One strand of the García Lorca family's resistance to exhumation speaks directly to this problem of scale. Even if the bones of the dead are not hopelessly mixed together, to separate them out one by one is to atomize what were in fact collective and political murders. It is estimated that two thousand or more bodies lie in the killing fields outside Granada.

"There is a part of me that wants to know where Lorca's body is," says the poet's niece Laura García Lorca, "but I realize that it would end up becoming a spectacle, a shameless media show," with his bones and skull displayed on YouTube. What then should be done at the presumed site of his murder? "Protect it," she says. "That site is a cemetery. . . . They should place a plaque or a rock there with the names of all those that are known. The fact that Federico García Lorca is one of all those victims, not distinguished, not singled out, is a way for the rest to be remembered."

And could a marker with two thousand names become the accepted symbol of a properly buried past? In 2009, in the city of Granada, on the plastered brick of a cemetery wall, the Association for the Recovery of Historical Memory placed a plaque dedicated to the thousand or more "victims of Francoism who were shot at this wall." Within a few months, someone had pried the plaque from the masonry and spirited it away.

CHARACTERISTIC AMNESIAS. Benedict Anderson, reflecting on Ernest Renan's essay about nationhood, finds a bizarre paradox in the claim that "every French citizen" must have forgotten the long-ago massacres of Cathars and Huguenots. Given that Renan never bothers to explain those events, his "readers were being told to 'have already forgotten' what Renan's own words assumed that they naturally remembered!"

For Anderson, the paradox arises because Renan has taken battles fought long before France itself existed and wrapped them up in present-day Frenchness. Much could be said about the not-French complexity of premodern European wars. The slain thirteenth-century Cathars, for example, "spoke Provençal or Catalan, and . . . their murderers came from many parts of Western Europe." The St. Bartholomew's Day Massacre might have started in Paris, but its players included a Spanish king and an Italian pope. Renan, however, never addresses such details, preferring to cast the conflicts as having been "fratricidal wars between—who else?—*fellow Frenchmen.*"

In Anderson's reading, to claim "the reassurance of fratricide" is a rhetorical trick typical of the nation-making imagination. In the 1860s, the United States split into two independent sovereignties (the Confederate States of America had its own president, its own army, its own currency, and so on), but the Civil War is never figured as such but rather as a misunderstanding between brothers who later joined hands across the bloody chasm.

Such "striking nineteenth-century imaginings of fraternity," Anderson writes, indicate that nationalism in Renan's day "represented a new form of consciousness," that "all profound changes of consciousness . . . bring with them characteristic amnesias," and finally that "out of such oblivions . . . spring narratives." These narratives frame past differences as little more than family quarrels; they remember the abstraction but not the details, the Union but not the blue and the gray, France but not Catholics and Protestants. In short, the fraternal claim allows the national story to be surrounded by a handy moat of oblivion.

POSTWAR. After World War II, it turned out to be almost impossible to differentiate and judge who was guilty of war crimes, who had collaborated with the enemy, and who had simply stood by doing nothing when good conscience should have called for action. In France, for example, the government itself had collaborated with the Germans: Should everyone who worked for the government have been held to account? As distasteful as it might have been, many nations quickly turned their backs on the past. "We have the strength to forget," proclaimed an Italian newspaper the day that Hitler died, "forget as soon as possible!" In Germany in 1949, the freshly elected chancellor, Konrad Adenauer, dispensed with the Nazis: "The government . . . , in the belief that many have subjectively atoned for a guilt that was not heavy, is determined, where it appears acceptable to do so, to put the past behind us." Comments Tony Judt, whose book *Postwar* contains these examples, "Without such collective amnesia, Europe's astonishing post-war recovery would not have been possible."

NUMBERED. The documentary film *Numbered* follows several Israelis who have had their survivor relatives' concentration camp numbers tattooed on their arms. Ten of these tattooed descendants interviewed by *The New York Times* described their motives: they wanted an intimate, enduring connection to the survivors; they wanted to embody the command "Never forget."

"All my generation knows nothing about the Holocaust," said one young woman. "You talk with people and they think it's like the Exodus from Egypt, ancient history." A cashier in a minimart in Jerusalem, she is often asked about the number on her arm. One police officer told her, "God creates the forgetfulness so we can forget." She replied, "Because of people like you who want to forget this, we will have it again." The first time she showed the tattoo—number 157622—to the grandfather who bore the original, he bent and kissed it.

~~AMALEK.~~ The linguistic philosopher J. L. Austin of Oxford once asserted in a lecture that there are many languages in which a double negative makes a positive but none in which a double positive makes a negative, to which the Columbia philosopher Sidney Morgenbesser, sitting in the audience, sarcastically replied, "Yeah, yeah."

The Bible tells us that the Amalekite tribes harassed the Hebrews without provocation. "Remember what Amalek did to you on the way as you came out of Egypt, how he attacked you . . . when you were faint and weary, and cut off your tail, those who were lagging behind you, and he did not fear God."

In this way, Amalek brought down a curse. "Therefore . . . you shall blot out the memory of Amalek from under heaven," the Lord tells the Jews, "you shall not forget." "Write this as a memorial in a book and recite it in the ears of Joshua, that I will utterly blot out the memory of Amalek from under heaven."

At first this seems a contradiction—you must remember to forget—but it is better described as an emphatic, a version of the dismissive double positive: "Yeah, yeah, I'll forget you." It's a case of forgetting as an aid to memory, an early iteration of the command "Never forget." After all, thousands of years have passed and the memory of "what Amalek did . . . as you came out of Egypt" endures. A friend tells me of a modern custom in his Jewish community. When one receives the gift of a new pen, the first thing to do is to write that name, then cross it out: ~~Amalek~~.

"ALL BURNED OUT." "Auschwitz and everything bound up with it . . . is the greatest trauma for the people of Europe since the Crucifixion," wrote Imre Kertész, decades before he was awarded the Nobel Prize in Literature. A survivor himself, Kertész returned to the topic in his 2002 Nobel lecture: "What I discovered in Auschwitz is the human condition, the end point of a great adventure, where the European traveler arrived after his two-thousand-year-old moral and cultural history. . . . Since Auschwitz we are more alone. . . . We must create our values ourselves, day by day, with that persistent though invisible ethical work that will give them life, and perhaps turn them into the foundation of a new European culture."

The following year, Kertész gave the opening speech at an exhibition recording the wartime crimes of the German armed forces. He addressed himself to the survivor's ambivalent relationship to memory, wondering, as he leafed through the exhibition catalog, "Had I forgotten, by any chance, that I myself was a participant in and survivor of these horrors . . . ? If I had not exactly forgotten, once I had transmuted it into words it had all burned out and somehow come to rest within me. Only grudgingly do I surrender that peace of mind."

Kertész had not ignored the past—he had written a cluster of novels about the camps, most famously *Fatelessness*—but notice that writing the Holocaust is its own *holocaustum*, a ritual burning of the thing that "somehow" yields "peace of mind," temporary though it may be.

TROUBLES WITH "NEVER FORGET." "I think that there is an element akin to forgiveness in the sheer passing of time, in the changing of the guards, the young taking over from the old," writes Ruth Kluger, herself a Holocaust survivor. "I think of redemption as closely linked to the flow of time. We speak of the virtues of memory, but forgetfulness has its own virtue."

Kluger describes the proliferation of Holocaust memorials as a "memorial cult" that "seeks to inflict certain aspects of history and their presumed lessons on our children," adding that "its favorite mantra, 'Let us remember, so the same thing doesn't happen again,' is unconvincing. A remembered massacre may serve as a deterrent, but it may also serve as a model for the next massacre. We cannot impose the contents of our minds on our grandchildren, who will remember what they need to remember and forget the rest."

Elie Wiesel once declared the Holocaust to be "the ultimate event, the ultimate mystery, never to be comprehended or transmitted," a framing that lifts its terror out of history and out of politics. Once any great evil becomes transcendent, it joins the immortals of old to stand free from human cause and effect. To be sure, evil itself is an "ultimate mystery," but the Holocaust is but one of its incarnations. To sacralize it only makes it harder to recognize others when they return in new and unexpected forms.

"The same thing doesn't happen twice," Kluger points out. "Every event, like every human being and even every dog, is unique. . . . In our hearts we all know that some aspects of the Shoah have been repeated elsewhere, today and yesterday, and will return in new guise tomorrow." As for "the various Shoah museums," they "tell you what you ought to think. . . . They impede the critical faculty."

THE SAME SUBSTANCE. In 1946, when Juan Perón became president of Argentina, Jorge Luis Borges found himself "promoted" from his position in a municipal library to a post as inspector of poultry and rabbits at the Buenos Aires municipal market. Years later, in the last interview before his death, Borges was asked if he had forgiven the Peronists. "Forgotten, not forgiven," he said. "Forgetting is the only form of forgiveness; it's the only vengeance and the only punishment too. Because if my counterparts see that I'm still thinking about them, in some ways I become their slave, and if I forget them I don't. I think that forgiveness and vengeance are two words for the same substance, which is oblivion."

KOSOVO AND CHOSEN TRAUMA. For hundreds of years, beginning in the late twelfth century, Eastern Orthodox Christian Serbs dominated a huge part of southeastern Europe. In the summer of 1389, however, at the Field of Blackbirds in Kosovo, an army of Muslim Turks defeated Serbian forces led by the feudal lord Lazar Hrebeljanović. Within decades, the Ottoman Empire had fully absorbed its conquered foe. Its rule would continue for four hundred years.

For the Serbs, Lazar's death and the day of the Battle of Kosovo—June 28—have ever since stood for what has been called a "chosen trauma," that is to say, an identity-informing ancestral calamity whose memory mixes actual history with passionate feeling and fantasized grievance and hope.

Lazar's body and severed head—central emblems of that trauma and of all later Serbian resistance—were interred after the battle, at the Serbian monastery of Ravanica. The monks there canonized their hero and, as Ottoman rule expanded in later years, carried his remains into exile to a monastery on Mount Fruška Gora, northwest of Belgrade. As for the symbolically charged date of the battle, it was no accident that the precipitating event of World War I, the 1914 assassination of Archduke Francis Ferdinand, was carried out on June 28. That was, after all, the 525th anniversary of the Battle of Kosovo, and what an insult, then, that a representative of Austria-Hungary, the very heir of Ottoman oppression, dared to enter Serbian Sarajevo.

And flash forward to the late twentieth century, when Yugoslavia began to break into its constituent territories, thereby surfacing long-dormant ethnic conflicts, especially in Bosnia-Herzegovina, whose primary ethnic groups—Muslim

Bosniaks, Roman Catholic Croats, and Eastern Orthodox Serbs—were soon at odds. During the Communist era, these groups had lived in relative, if imposed, harmony (marriages were often mixed; few Muslims attended prayers), but as Bosnia moved toward statehood, the Serbian population—about a third of the whole—feared it would become a second-class minority, and in the spring of 1992, Serbian armed forces began to massacre their Muslim neighbors.

The seeds of that exercise in ethnic cleansing had been planted several years earlier, when Slobodan Milošević, Serbian politician and skilled apologist for the memory of difference, helped organize a series of celebrations in honor of the six hundredth anniversary of the Battle of Kosovo. On June 28, 1988, a year prior to the actual anniversary, Milošević arranged for Lazar's "exiled" body to be returned to the monastery in Ravanica, the relic case containing his bones being paraded through every Serbian village and town, mourned along the way by black-clad throngs of wailing Serbs.

The speech that Milošević gave a year later on the actual six hundredth anniversary included calls for tolerance ("Long live peace and brotherhood among peoples!"), but more often it recalled the ancient conflict ("Let the memory of Kosovo heroism live forever!"), a theme strongly reinforced by the stage-craft of the event: the celebratory crowd had gathered on the very Field of Blackbirds where the original battle had been waged, Milošević himself descending on the site in a helicopter as if the sainted prince Lazar were at last returning from on high. All of that, plus the podium's backdrop prominently displaying the dates 1389 and 1989, called to mind not so much brotherhood as the ancient animosity between Christians and

Muslims, one whose time-collapsed modern iteration was highlighted by Milošević's constant references to dignity and humiliation, freedom and vassalage, motherland and treason, bravery and suffering, pride and shame. "The Kosovo heroism has been inspiring our creativity for six centuries," he declared, "and has been feeding our pride and does not allow us to forget that at one time we were an army great, brave, and proud, one of the few that remained undefeated when losing."

I assume that that odd last phrase is not a mistranslation but rather Milošević's invocation of the remarkable way in which the Serbs have imagined Lazar's defeat as a victory. Legend has it that before the Battle of Kosovo a gray falcon brought Lazar a message from the Virgin Mary giving him a choice: either win the battle and have a kingdom on earth or lose it and have one in heaven. A Serbian ballad has Lazar explaining why he chose death: "The earthly kingdom is of short duration / And the Heavenly is from now to eternity." Thus does a lost cause's apparent humiliation get turned on its head and become proof of the highest of ideals. "Even though we have lost our kingdom," sing the Serbs, "let us not lose our souls."

Positing that eternal kingdom has the imaginative effect of collapsing durational time. If an atemporal ideal lies hidden in Lazar's defeat, then 1389 and 1914 and 1989 are all one and the same, and the chosen trauma may work its magic at any time, its bound-up energy always available to fuel a present fire.

Vamik Volkan, the psychiatrist who gave us the term "chosen trauma," has noted that "the idea that [the Serbs] could change their minds and choose a kingdom on earth was not articulated until the awakening of nationalism in Europe in the nineteenth century." Prompted by that awakening, Ernest Renan's 1882 "What Is a Nation?" warned against the very confusion of nationality and ethnicity that brought civil war to Bosnia: "Ethnographic politics is anything but certain. . . . For everyone, it is better to forget."

Or not, if a chosen trauma's wound is given over to the task of preserving identity by way of mourning without end. Mourning that *does* end, by contrast, promises to convert what has been lost into a memory, and given six hundred years, most memories fade. "Fixed ideas" is what Pierre Janet once called those memories impervious to time; such atemporal artifacts are like blood clots lodged in the flow of time, something the years can neither expel nor dissolve.

In the 1990s, the Serbian genocidal campaign drove hundreds of thousands of Muslims and ethnic Croats from their villages, looting their homes and demolishing mosques and churches. Serbian fighters raped thousands upon thousands of women and, in the town of Srebrenica, massacred more than eight thousand Muslim men and boys.

The Unforgotten, destroyer of nations.

FURIES BECOME EUMENIDES. Aeschylus's play *The Eumenides* is a guidebook for the conversion of the unforgettable into the forgotten. As the drama opens, we find Orestes, "his hands dripping blood," seeking to purify himself at Apollo's altar. In order to avenge the murder of his father, Agamemnon, he has murdered his mother, Clytemnestra, whose ghost has now summoned up the Furies, charging them to "never forget" her anguish. Dog-headed, snake-haired, bat-winged, these ancient embodiments of blood vengeance harry Orestes without respite, crowding around the altar, black and repulsive with rasping breath and oozing eyes. On Apollo's urging, Orestes flees to Athens, but like hunting dogs quickened with the scent of blood, the Furies swiftly follow: "He's wounded— / go for the fawn, my hounds, the splash of blood, / hunt him, rake him down."

In Athens, Orestes shelters at the Areopagus, a rocky outcropping beneath the Acropolis. There he seeks the protection of Athena, who must find a way to resolve the until-now-insoluble conflicts that have long defined the house of Atreus (the conflict in Orestes's case being that between the absolute obligation to avenge his father's murder and the absolute prohibition on matricide). Athena herself feels the stuckness such choices produce. Should she embrace the Furies or expel them? "A crisis either way," she declares. "It defeats me."

Defeats her . . . until she converts contradiction into dialogue, creating an institution—trial by jury—that henceforth replaces the single-minded bloodlust of simple revenge. She appoints twelve citizens as "judges of manslaughter," swears them in, summons witnesses, gathers evidence, and, when the jury's ballots are tied, casts a deciding vote to set Orestes free.

Older than the Olympian gods, the Furies embody the most ancient habit of extralegal vengeance (ancient but also ever present: think vigilantes, think lynch mobs). As one scholar has noted, the Furies "never suffer from forgetfulness, since they somehow predate time," a useful point of origin for eternal powers but also, in this case, a problematic one, the problem with eternals being that, well, they don't change, and change is what the house of Atreus so desperately needs, some way to escape the chain of killings that has left Orestes with those bloody hands.

What is needed is a change in guilt's relationship to time, and in that line what Athena establishes is not just a trial but procedures for its conduct, what we'd now call due process, and justice with due process is a time-based art. What the goddess accomplishes is not only the conversion of Justice-by-Blood-Vengeance into Justice-by-Trial but, to say it in terms of memory, the conversion of the atemporal Furies into temporal beings who must allow for futures that do not repeat the past. Athena draws the eternal impulse toward retribution into time, and in time, things will change.

When they lose their case against Orestes, the Furies fall into wild confusion, threatening to destroy the land, to poison the soil and blast the city, leaf and child. "The bloody tide comes hurling, all mankind destroyed." They don't just declare this curse; they declare it twice, frozen in their rage. But Athena has a way to soften them; she offers them honors and new offices, converting these ancient powers into protectors of the city and of justice reimagined. "Let me persuade you," she says,

> The lethal spell of your voice, never cast it
> down on the land and blight its harvest home. . . .
> The land is rich, and more, when its first fruits,
> offered for heirs and the marriage rites, are yours
> to hold forever, you will praise my words.

That's a change of diet for the old vengeance seekers. "Give me blood for blood!" their leader had cried earlier, addressing Orestes: "Out of your living marrow I will drain / my red libation, out of your veins I suck my food." Aeschylus's plot replaces that cannibalism with the first fruits of the harvest and, consequently, transforms the Furies into spirits of regeneration. It is therefore on this occasion that they are first called Eumenides, "the gracious" or "kindly ones," fertility spirits who will, if honored, ensure that the land and its people flourish.

As for the saga of the house of Atreus, the conversion of the Unforgettables bespeaks its final chapter. There is no follow-on tale of the next generation carrying on the blood vendetta. It's over.

"FORGET THE ALAMO" is the final line of John Sayles's movie *Lone Star*, spoken by the Chicana history teacher, Pilar. Counterpoint to that ending is an earlier scene in which the town school board has a big fight over how to teach history. Do the children really need to know that Texas was originally a slave state? Why do the teachers insist on "tearing down the memory of people who fought and died for this land"? "I'm sure they've got their own account of the Alamo on the other side, but we're not on the other side."

Pilar is in love with Sam, the Anglo sheriff, and in the final scene she has just found out that they are in fact half siblings, Sam's father having had a long affair with Pilar's mother. Sam meanwhile is trying to find out if his father, Buddy Deeds, killed the former sheriff, a murderous and racist fellow named Charlie Wade. By the end of the movie Sam has solved the mystery, but rather than prosecute the men who committed that long-ago crime, he lets it drop. He uncovers a true story, then chooses to forget it.

That sequence could be called the first moral of the story: truth has to precede forgetting. A second moral: truth is rarely simple. Many strands made Texas what it is today, and many strands led up to the killing of Charlie Wade.

Still, the end of the movie steps away from all such complexity. Justice doesn't follow truth. Tribal politics, happy to ignore "the other side" of the Alamo story, remains in place. The lovers will "start from scratch," says Pilar. "All that other stuff, all that history: to hell with it, right? Forget the Alamo." It's an American ending, a Lone Star ending with the kind of individualist forgetting that cannot possibly scale. We get private romance but no model of how to study the nation to forget the nation.

FORGETTING HISTORY can't be a private affair. Frederick Douglass, taken up by the white abolitionists in the North, found himself surprised when, in fact, it turned out that they had their own brand of racism. At first he had been happily oblivious: "For a time I was made to forget that my skin was dark and my hair crisped."

Yes, it is important to forget the memory of difference, but that's hard to do if those around you won't. Richard Rodriguez writes that his friend Darrell says he's black because "that is what the white cop sees when he looks at me." The forgetting of difference must be a collective art.

THOMAS MOORE AT HOME. In the summer of 2007, a jury in Mississippi declared the Ku Klux Klan member James Ford Seale guilty for his part in the 1964 murder of Henry Dee and Charles Moore. After the verdict came down, Moore's older brother, Thomas, long instrumental in reopening the decades-old "cold case," addressed a crowd from the courthouse steps in Jackson: "I want the world to know that Mississippi spoke tonight. The jury is from Mississippi, and I hope that every citizen of Mississippi and Franklin County can rest tonight with the veil of shame off their eyes. I now feel that Mississippi is my home, something I wouldn't have owned up even as of last night."

What is home? In this case, it is a place that has at least three elements: truth, justice, and—most important—shared understanding. The truth about the Dee-Moore murders had not been public knowledge until the trial; Seale's conviction brought a modicum of justice, however long delayed. But what also mattered to Moore was that the jury was "from Mississippi." The overcoming of difference is a collective art, and "home" in this case is where your sense of truth and justice is held in mind by the surrounding community.

AND YET THERE ARE DEGREES OF JUSTICE. David Ridgen's *Reconciliation in Mississippi* video contains a brief exchange between Thomas Moore and the Klansman Charles Marcus Edwards, the import of which eluded me for a time.

The men begin to speak about how the boys were beaten, Edwards saying that he and another man tied them to a tree while James Ford Seale held a gun on them. Moore replies, "I try to think that the shock and that they was on the, uh, how bad they were beaten up I don't know, but just the fact that, I know . . ."

Moore, I now see, has tried to imagine what it felt like to be his brother on that day, and as if to retrospectively protect him, he has "tried to think" that his brother went into shock and did not fully feel the beating. But Moore—usually so eloquent to my ear—fumbles for words as he approaches the unspeakable.

At this point, Edwards interrupts: "They got a pretty good whuppin' but . . . they was nowhere near dead nor nothing like that."

Edwards has not "tried to think" about the boys' suffering, has not brought it to mind. To distance himself from his deeds, he diminishes the torture by speaking as if there were acceptable degrees of whipping and acceptable degrees of being near death.

And when I speak of degrees of justice, I'm thinking that successful convictions like that of James Ford Seale can have the unwanted effect of detracting from any fuller reckoning with the history of racial violence. In this case, the truth is now established, yes, but only one of the killers was punished, and the killings of Dee and Moore were but two out of thousands.

SUCCESSFUL MONUMENTS BECOME INVISIBLE. I once worked at a hospital in Stockbridge, Massachusetts. At the center of town stands a tall brownstone obelisk dedicated to those "who died for their country in the great war of the rebellion." A bronze eagle sits on top, a small cannon at the base. On the sides are inscribed the names of the dead and of the Civil War battlefields where they fought: Gettysburg, Wilderness, Spotsylvania, Antietam . . .

I once asked my colleagues at the hospital if they knew what the monument stood for. Only one man did, and he knew because his brother-in-law from the South had pointed it out to him. For everyone else, and for northerners in general, the Civil War belongs to time out of mind.

"It is possible that there is no other memory than the memory of wounds," wrote Czesław Miłosz. In the South, the wounds of the Civil War are still felt; in the North, less so.

A STRUGGLE FOR NATIONAL REMEMBERING. In 2015, the Equal Justice Initiative of Montgomery, Alabama, released an inventory of about four thousand victims of "racial terror lynching" that had taken place in a dozen southern states from the Compromise of 1877 (the end of Reconstruction and beginning of Jim Crow) up to 1950. That's a little more than one lynching a week for three-quarters of a century. The "great migration" of African Americans from the South to cities in the North, the report argues, should not be thought of simply as a movement of people seeking jobs: those migrants were refugees fleeing terrorism.

The Equal Justice Initiative subsequently built a memorial to that terror. Sitting on a six-acre site overlooking Montgomery, the National Memorial for Peace and Justice contains 805 rusting steel columns, one for every county where a lynching occurred, each one inscribed with the names of the victims and each one hanging from the ceiling like a body hanging from a tree.

There are in fact two columns for every county, one present at the memorial and a second on offer to any county whose residents wish to claim and install it locally as a memorial to their past. If those monuments are ever to become invisible to the local citizens, it will only be by virtue of a fresh victory in a very old culture war, one that began around 1877 with its own "characteristic amnesia" as to the meaning of the Civil War.

A WAR OF NATIONAL FORGETTING. With the 1865 end of the U.S. Civil War came calls on both sides to forget the conflict as soon as possible. Speaking in Richmond, Virginia, in 1867, New York's Horace Greeley called on his mixed-race audience "to forget the years of slavery, and secession, and civil war now happily past . . . forget that some of you have been masters, others slaves—some for disunion, others against it—and remember only that you are Virginians, and all now and henceforth freemen."

Two years later, the Confederate general Robert E. Lee struck the same note. Declining an invitation to a Gettysburg memorial, Lee declared it "wiser . . . not to keep open the sores of war, but to follow the examples of those nations who endeavored to obliterate the marks of civil strife and commit to oblivion the feelings it engendered."

Fine, but such entreaties leave many questions unanswered. Who exactly forgets? What will they commit to oblivion, and what will they preserve? And what story will remain once that sorting is done?

THE WHITE SHEET OF OBLIVION. The most deeply contested national election in U.S. history was finally settled by the Compromise of 1877, which awarded Rutherford B. Hayes the presidency in exchange for complete withdrawal of all federal troops from the South. That marked the end of Reconstruction and the beginning of a homegrown form of apartheid known as Jim Crow.

On May 30 of that year, a certain Roger A. Pryor—former Confederate general and now a lawyer in Brooklyn—gave a Decoration Day speech that amounts to a proclamation of victory in the remembrance of the Lost Cause and the forgetting of the promise of emancipation.

The "Lost Cause": the phrase refers in general to a set of claims about the Old South and the Civil War (that slaves were happy, that they joined their masters in fighting the Yankees, that the South itself would soon have freed them, that an avaricious industrial North destroyed a genteel, organic civilization), but in specific the phrase refers to the claimed autonomy of individual states, their freedom from federal interference. Slavery "was the occasion not the cause of secession," Pryor told his audience. "For the cause of secession you must look beyond" slavery to the "usurpation of Federal power on the sovereign rights of the States."

By Pryor's reading, neither the federal government nor the states had any role to play when it came to slavery because the fate of those in bondage belonged to God, not to politics. "Slavery fell not by any effort of man's will, but by the immediate intervention and act of the Almighty himself." Abolition was a divine adjustment of human history, and as such, it was as pleasing to the South as to the North. "In the anthem of praise ascending to Heaven for the emancipation of four million human beings, the voice of the Confederate soldier mingles its note of devout gratulation."

That is the only reference to emancipation in Pryor's speech, and what it actually does is shift the focus away from those millions freed and onto the gratulating Confederates, men now ready to forget the conflict and reunite with their siblings in blue. "Hands once red with fraternal blood are this day clasped in pledge and proclamation of a restored and perpetual brotherhood."

In Pryor's telling, that brotherhood is white. His speech has nothing more to say about African Americans nor about the Reconstruction project of bringing full citizenship to the formerly enslaved. Instead, he frames Reconstruction as "an expedient devised to balk the ambition of the white race," an ambition that the removal of federal troops has at last set free.

Pryor calls the Compromise of 1877 an "act of concession and conciliation." What did it concede? It conceded the supposedly lost cause, the sovereignty by which states manage their own affairs, especially in regard to the civil rights of blacks. In 1865, the South surrendered to the North at the courthouse in Appomattox; in 1877, the North surrendered to the South, nationwide. Henceforth any story claiming abolition as the cause of the war shall be forgotten. "It behooves both [sides] to drop the veil of oblivion" over continued animosities. With the compromise in place, "from our bosoms every vindictive and uncharitable recollection of the unhappy conflict is banished never to return."

"YOU MUST REALIZE THE TRUTH." After the Civil War, Frederick Douglass spent years disputing men like Roger A. Pryor who offered white reconciliation at the expense of black liberty. Douglass's speeches always call for remembrance and dispute the Lost Cause narrative point by point. Disgusted by the "hand clasping across the bloody chasm business," Douglass called out all who, "in the name of patriotism," ask us "to remember with equal admiration those who struck at the nation's life, and those who struck to save it—those who fought for slavery and those who fought for liberty and justice." Union and Confederacy were not each correct and honorable in their own way. "May my tongue cleave to the roof of my mouth if I forget the difference between the parties to that . . . bloody conflict."

In 1884, Douglass spoke in Syracuse, New York, on the occasion of the thirty-third anniversary of the "Jerry Rescue," Jerry having been a fugitive slave captured in Syracuse and then rescued by abolitionists and transported to Canada. Douglass's speech asks his audience to remember back three decades to the days of the Fugitive Slave Law and the resistance to its enforcement. "You must know," he says, about that infamous law. "You must know" how the North helped enforce it. "You must realize the truth" of that history if you are to appreciate the heroism of those who rescued Jerry.

"We are often asked and exhorted . . . to forget the past," Douglass says. "I differ entirely. . . . If we forget the errors and evils of the past, we must also forget the intelligence, the courage and the moral heroism by which they were combatted and overthrown, and thus lose a vast motive power and inspiration to high and virtuous endeavor."

It is that "motive power" that Douglass would revive in the age of Jim Crow, and to that end he summons up the spirits of the men who rescued Jerry. "I see . . . , I see," he keeps saying: "I see, in the front rank, the majestic form of Gerrit Smith." "I see the amiable face of Samuel J. May." "I see the rugged features and hear the rushing eloquence of Beriah Green." On and on until over a dozen have been called and the past brought to life in the present.

Where memory is the action of telling a story and forgetting is closure (premature or earned, as the case may be), Douglass rightly refuses the reconciliation of white brotherhood. "The past is in some sense the mirror in which we may discern the future with its improved features," and those features are not yet realized. The year is 1884, and Jim Crow is in full swing. (At least fifty-one black Americans were lynched that year, and fifty-three in 1883, and forty-nine in 1882. . . .) Recalling the Jerry Rescue is a case of memory, not forgetting, offering the liquefaction of time: the triumph of the Lost Cause is a false burial; the story of liberation is unfinished and must go on.

The American people are "destitute of political memory," Douglass once said. "We are more likely to forget too soon, than to remember too long, the history of the American conflict with slavery."

PEACE. NOTHING. In *Race and Reunion: The Civil War in American Memory*, David W. Blight repeatedly cites the question that Frederick Douglass asked in regard to reconciliation: "If war among the whites brought peace and liberty to the blacks, what will peace among the whites bring?"

As if in answer, Edwin Lawrence Godkin, founder and editor in chief of *The Nation*, wrote—a month after the Compromise of 1877—that now the "negro will disappear from the field of national politics. Henceforth, the nation as a nation, will have nothing to do with him."

SEPARATE WATER CLOSETS. In this War of National Forgetting, the main rhetorical trick of all Lost Cause orators was to focus on the sincerity, valor, and devotion of individual soldiers, North and South, and so to say nothing about slavery and emancipation. Almost exactly fifty years after the Battle of Gettysburg, on July 4, 1913, the newly elected president, Woodrow Wilson, addressed a gathering of veterans from both sides—"these gallant men in blue and gray"—telling them that "in their presence it were an impertinence to discourse upon how the battle went, how it ended, what it signified!"

Having dispensed with the war's meaning—"our battles [are] long past, the quarrel forgotten"—Wilson declared that what ought to be remembered was "the splendid valor, the manly devotion of the men then arrayed against one another, now grasping hands and smiling into each other's eyes." Those hands and eyes were white, needless to say, the reunion being a segregated affair, with blacks present only as workers hired to distribute blankets.

Nor was segregation limited to that Gettysburg reunion. The year 1913 marks the moment when the federal government began to promote the kind of racial apartheid long left to the states. A senator from Mississippi nicely summarized the assumption of federal policy: "There are no inalienable human rights . . . involved in the question of having separate rooms and separate desks and separate water closets for the two races."

Nineteen thirteen was the year the Treasury Department ordered its architects to design separate toilet facilities in all federal buildings south of the Mason-Dixon Line. And it was the year when, of the seven black clerks who worked in the

Washington, D.C., post office, six ended up in the dead letter office, their desks segregated behind a row of lockers. The seventh remained in the chief inspector's office, his desk surrounded by screens.

"MEMORIAL DAY, 1898. 'ONE DECORATION WILL DO FOR BOTH THIS YEAR'"; FROM THE CHICAGO *INTER OCEAN*, MAY 30, 1898

THE AGONISTIC THIRD. In order for two opposed parties to forget their differences, it helps to have some third thing they can agree upon, something standing apart but belonging to both. After a civil war, that third thing might be a common civic ideal—universal suffrage, say, or due process of law. In the case of the American Civil War, two shared "thirds" appeared in the service of reconciliation: white supremacy and foreign wars. The 1898 Spanish-American War nicely combined both of these, as in this contemporary cartoon showing Yankee and Confederate wrapped in the national flag and united by the sight of Cuba burning in the distance.

WHAT IS AMERICA? If this book is a thought experiment seeking to nominate places where forgetting is better than remembering, then in this case (as with the Sand Creek Massacre case) the experiment fails. If national identity presumes collective forgetting, then the struggle over how to remember the Civil War poses a question: What form shall the abstraction "the United States of America" take? Several options come to mind.

- Following Frederick Douglass, African Americans will not forget the promise of emancipation and, following Pryor, Godkin, Wilson, and so on, the rest of the nation will not remember it. Where the latter group dominates, "America" does not include African Americans.
- Everyone forgets what the war was about, even African Americans. (The old find memory too painful; the young aren't interested.) "America" then is the United States of Amnesia.
- Blacks and whites alike remember the history of slavery, the Civil War's emancipationist cause, the failure of Reconstruction, the rise of Jim Crow, the terrors of lynching, the unending struggle for civil rights. All of this becomes something held "in common," and—in a kind of national kenosis, a giving up of pride—"America" is understood to be a nation born in a bloody and ongoing struggle for equality.
- This common understanding leads, over time, to a proper burial of the past. Americans study the nation to forget the nation. The history is documented, taught, and agreed upon; reparations are paid; apologies are made and

accepted. Monuments to Confederate heroes are moved to museums. Monuments to victims of racial violence and to civil rights heroes get erected, but citizens become so intimate with what these memorials stand for that they fade into the background, as forgotten as the Yankee-Pennamite Wars. "America" lives steeped in history but not in the past.

THE AGONISTIC THIRD, AGAIN. In 2003, there was an unusually cordial meeting of officers from the Colorado National Guard—the heirs, in a sense, of Colonel John Chivington's militia—and Native descendants of the Sand Creek Massacre. The officers were visiting Sand Creek as part of a study of military history and invited the Indians to join them. There were some testy moments—this was the occasion, for example, when Laird Cometsevah said that there could be no apology until the 1865 treaty had been honored—but on the whole the gathering was amicable for the simple reason that the guardsmen and many of the Indian descendants had all served in the military, were "brothers in arms," and could joke and reminisce about that shared background.

In my account of the reconciliation between Thomas Moore and the Klansman Charles Marcus Edwards, I noted that the two men managed to find a common language in Jesus's gospel of forgiveness, a way of speaking that allowed them to transcend their differences, to step beyond themselves into something other than opposition. When the Colorado National Guard met the descendants at Sand Creek, one of the Cheyenne arrived wearing the emblems indicating his service in Vietnam; another had fought in World War II and entertained the guardsmen with stories of his exploits. In this case, military service, preceding and exterior to the Sand Creek meeting, gave the men a way to speak beyond any potential antagonism. But of course to speak of mutual enemies is a displacement of antagonism rather than its transcendence.

And transcendence is what is needed for the kind of forgetting that amounts to freedom from history. At the time of the establishment of the Sand Creek Massacre National Historic Site, it was not clear where descendants from both sides of the conflict might find a higher "third" sufficient to achieve that freedom.

THE SKULL OF LITTLE CROW. If, in the psychology of individuals, unresolved traumatic memories present themselves symptomatically (as obsessions, acting out, self-mutilation, nightmares, flashbacks, fainting spells . . .) does something similar hold for the psychology of nations? Does unexamined history reappear in some form of collective acting out, nightmare, flashback, and so on? If so, then forced forgetting doesn't resolve or transcend a violent past but obliges it to live on by displacement.

Such is the import of the way the Indian wars appear in Robert Bly's Vietnam-era poetry. Vietnamese peasants "are dying because gold deposits have been found among the Shoshoni Indians," reads a typical line. In the same vein, I remember Bly at an antiwar poetry reading saying something like "We are killing men with black hair because the Minnesota Historical Society owns the scalp of Little Crow."

Little Crow was a Dakota Sioux, one of the leaders of the Sioux Rebellion of 1862. A decade before that date, the Sioux had entered into a treaty with the U.S. government in which they agreed to settle along the Minnesota River in exchange for land, annuities, and certain other goods. The U.S. Senate then reneged on this deal, whereupon the Sioux tried to drive European settlers out of Minnesota.

This rebellion failed, and a year later Little Crow was shot by a farmer while foraging for berries near Hutchinson, Minnesota. The farmer took the body into town, where the townspeople mutilated it, dragging it through the streets with firecrackers stuck in the ears and dogs picking at the head. The farmer scalped him, there being a bounty on the Sioux at that time and a double bounty for Little Crow. When I was a student at the University of Minnesota in the 1960s, Little Crow's scalp and skull belonged to the Minnesota Historical Society.

Bly's point, and mine, is that violence denied and repressed doesn't disappear; it repeats. If "America" is a nation created by organized forgetting, then by this logic its foundational violence will always be with us, exported perhaps to foreign shores but "American" nonetheless. The proper burial of Little Crow's remains could be thought of as an act of foreign policy.

AMNESTY, AMNESIC OR MEMORABLE. Amnesty is judicial forgetting: the law agrees that it will not remember the crime. Memory may persist in other realms—people may talk, books may be written—but nothing will happen in the courts of law. In the courts, amnesty is forgetting as nonaction.

Amnesties often appear when nations are recovering from civil war or periods of gross human rights abuse. Broadly speaking, such transitional amnesties take two forms, the amnesic and the memorable. Amnesic amnesties are above all self-serving: the generals who started the war or the race baiters who organized the genocide simply decree that their crimes will not be punished. There is no public discussion, no search for truth, no input from the victims, no naming of perpetrators, no reparations on offer, no apologies made, no forgiveness sought. The legal scholar Ronald C. Slye nominates the Chilean dictator Augusto Pinochet's 1978 Amnesty Law as a good example of such an amnesic decree. The law the Spaniards passed after the death of Franco is another.

At the other end of the spectrum are memorable amnesties—memorable because legal forgetting here insists on memory work as its precondition. Memorable amnesties study the crime to forget the crime. The governing laws are created democratically, not by fiat. They mandate a public search for truth, calling on all who seek amnesty to fully describe their crimes and to submit to questions and challenges from their victims. Victims for their part may be accorded reparations. Above all, memorable amnesties are designed to enable transition to a new government that will be protective of human rights. "Accountable" is the designation Slye gives to the amnesties that I am calling memorable, and the amnesty that South Africa offered in the 1990s to the criminal perpetrators of apartheid is, he suggests, "the only one to date that comes close to qualifying" as accountable.

COLD FORGETTING. In the case of South Africa's Truth and Reconciliation Commission (TRC), in order to be considered for amnesty, perpetrators had to fully disclose all the facts relevant to their case; they had to demonstrate that their crimes were politically motivated; and they had to show their crimes to be proportional to the ends being sought. (Killing a child, for example, could never be held to be proportional to any political aim.)

Applicants were *not* required to indicate remorse or regret, nor to apologize or make atonement.

The commission might well have been named Truth and Reconciliation, but there is in fact no way to mandate that the latter follow from the former. Reconciliation is often the last in a sequence: first, a full telling of the truth, then repentance and apology, then forgiveness, and finally, sometimes, reconciliation. But only the first of these can be mandated and adjudicated. Perpetrators can be called to tell what happened and then judged as to the veracity and fullness of the account.

As for repentance, forgiveness, and all the rest, a full public account prepares the ground for these, whereupon they either happen or they don't. The grant of amnesty carries no guarantee; amnesty is, therefore, a cold forgetting, expedient and instrumental, structural and abstract. It exists to serve the state.

THE WHY NOT BAR BOMBING. In my own reading about the work of the TRC, I always find myself drawn to those moving accounts in which the players reach the commission's ideal end, reconciliation. To the degree that such stories are about forgetting, it usually entails the willing erasure of apartheid's presumption of racial difference. Amnesty, however, is a forgetting of a different order, as should become apparent if we look at two cases where the fruit of reconciliation never appeared, where difference remains despite the promise of judicial oblivion.

Take the case of Robert McBride, an operative in the military wing of the African National Congress (ANC). "All my life I'd been categorized in racial terms—either 'black' or 'colored' or, even worse, 'non-white,'" McBride has said. But when he joined the African National Congress, these race names dropped away: "I became a South African . . . , a South African freedom fighter." As such, between 1985 and 1994 he participated in more than a dozen acts of sabotage, resistance, and terror directed against the South African state and its security forces.

In his 1999 petition for amnesty, he publicly described in detail how he and his fellow militants planted bombs to destroy oil pipelines, electrical substations, storage tanks, and power lines. They threw grenades into the homes of white politicians, injuring at least two. They attacked a hospital to free a captured comrade, McBride himself killing a black police officer during the raid. Most egregiously, McBride organized and executed the bombing of the Why Not Bar in Durban, a nightspot that the ANC believed to be frequented by South African security forces. The car bomb he detonated—over a hundred pounds of shrapnel-laced explosives—killed three women outright and injured scores of others, none of whom, as it turned out, had any clear connection to the security apparatus.

The TRC's inquiry into these events addressed itself in each case to the mandated conditions for amnesty. As regards the political ends, the amnesty committee's decision variously lists these as "to cause economic sabotage," "for propaganda," to "attack security personnel," "to commemorate the Sharpeville Massacre," to commemorate the Soweto Youth Uprising, to "demonstrate the [ANC's] military power," to resist captivity "in any way" (thus the hospital raid), and always to undermine faith in the government and destabilize the apartheid state.

In my reading of the decision, I find "proportionality" to be the most perplexing category, especially in regard to the attacks that killed or injured civilians. When a hand grenade thrown into a policeman's home wounds the man's wife, to what end is that injury proportional? When a car bomb kills three women bystanders, how is that proportional to the stated goal of attacking the security forces, let alone to commemorating the Soweto Youth Uprising?

The amnesty committee grounds its response to such questions in the acknowledged rules of engagement on both sides of the conflict. It set the stage on the opening pages of its response to McBride's petition:

> The advent of the system of apartheid met with resistance from those who were the victims thereof. . . . With the passage of time, the effect of apartheid became harsher and was met with increased resistance. Eventually the

> ANC took the drastic step of employing armed options. . . . MK [the military arm] was consequently established and thereafter armed attacks on South African governmental institutions followed and later the policy of avoiding civilians was relaxed.

That policy was relaxed, in fact, in response to a similar relaxation on the part of the South African state. The date of the Why Not Bar bombing—June 14, 1986—seems to indicate that it was meant to mark the one-year anniversary of the South African Defense Forces' June 14, 1985, raid on an ANC base in Gaborone, Botswana, an attack that killed five ANC activists but also seven civilians, including women and children.

Whatever the case, in the committee's report on McBride's petition one phrase repeats: "The policy of avoiding civilians was relaxed." Relaxed consciously, it would seem, for when McBride had traveled to Botswana for training, he "received political instruction regarding the morality of the plan"; it was "explained to him that civilian risk was secondary," that South African security personnel "could no longer hide behind civilians," they themselves having repeatedly ignored such risks "in protecting the apartheid machinery."

Of interest as well is at least one exception to the "somewhat relaxed" policy regarding civilians. McBride and his team had at first considered bombing an apartment block housing many South African police, but they "abandoned the idea because of the possibility of killing little children." The ANC's rules of engagement regarding civilians had indeed been relaxed, but they had not been eliminated. As cold-blooded as they may be, distinctions were being made.

The amnesty committee's report on McBride's petition recounts the details of more than a dozen acts of terror or sabotage and finds that in each case the motive was political, the means were proportional to the ends, and the truth was being told. In 2001, McBride was granted amnesty for his crimes.

THE CRADOCK FOUR. Take the case of Eric Taylor, a white South African security officer who, in the summer of 1985, helped murder the black activist Matthew Goniwe and three of his companions. Formerly a high school teacher in the town of Cradock, Goniwe was the organizer of the regional anti-apartheid United Democratic Front and the local Cradock Residents Association, these in turn being involved in school boycotts, rent boycotts, and other acts of resistance.

Eric Taylor and his fellow security officers later pointed to somewhat cryptic commands from their superiors ("do what is best for the country," "make a plan") as having instructed them to assassinate Goniwe and thereby put an end to "the unrest situation in the Eastern Cape."

Whatever the case, one night Taylor, two other white security officers, and several of their black collaborators waited along the Port Elizabeth national road for the car in which they knew Goniwe and his friends were traveling. They stopped the car, killed the four occupants, and burned the bodies, the plan being to make the murders look like the result of a vigilante attack.

An officer named Gerhardus Lotz killed Matthew Goniwe. Taylor himself killed one of the other men, Fort Calata: "I hit Mr. Calata from behind with this heavy iron object approximately where the head joins the neck. He fell to the ground. Then the other black members stabbed him with knives." They poured gasoline over the bodies, and by Taylor's admission, he "set both these bodies alight." Then he went home. "I can remember at home I just had the opportunity to shower, dress and I returned back to my office at the security branch."

Ten years later, Eric Taylor and his co-conspirators applied to the TRC for amnesty. After more than a week of testimony and cross-examination, the amnesty committee refused their request, finding itself unpersuaded as to the political nature of the crime, the proportionality of the actions, and the truth of the account.

Two details stand out, especially as regards proportionality and truth. The killers claimed that their political aim was to calm "the unrest situation," but of course the killing of the Cradock Four did just the opposite. (A huge demonstration marked their funeral, for example.) As the commission pointed out in a sobering admission of how things actually worked under apartheid, if one wanted to quell unrest, there were "legal mechanisms" at hand: "At the discretion of . . . the South African Police . . . , citizens could be and indeed many were incarcerated without trial for reasons related to alleged political activities." "Any of the deceased could have been removed from their position of perceived power to cause the unrest, by invoking the appropriate laws or regulations."

Moreover, the killers had trouble explaining why the other three men had to be killed if the goal was to neutralize Goniwe. The killers could, perhaps, have claimed that the other three were unfortunate bystanders whose deaths were sadly unavoidable. But they didn't, choosing instead to present the others as known actors, just as troublesome to the state as the organizer Goniwe.

That was not the case, as became clear at a striking turning point in the hearing. On the eighth day of testimony, the lawyer representing the victims' families read into the record "a report made by the South African police in Port Elizabeth" that describes one of the victims, Sicelo Mhlauli, as "unknown" to the police. Declared the lawyer with theatrical thunder, "Now, Mr. Taylor, it is my sad duty to tell you that the documents emanating from your office . . . indicate that you are deliberately committing perjury!"

The committee agreed. Of Sicelo Mhlauli, that most innocent victim, they write in their final report, "He could hardly have been regarded as a threat to the law and order in the Eastern Cape. . . . The applicants failed to provide any convincing factual basis for concluding that he was a leader required to be assassinated. His elevation to political leadership and therefore a candidate for assassination seems to us to be a mendacious, convenient and opportunistic way of explaining his murder."

In sum, the committee ruled that the crimes of Eric Taylor and his co-conspirators were in no way proportional to the declared political ends and that they had not told the truth.

"Their lack of explanation surrounding the order, planning and execution of these offences does not lend itself to a favorable credibility finding. . . . We do not believe the versions of the applicants. . . . Consequently the applications of Taylor [et al.] . . . for amnesty in respect to the murders . . . are REFUSED."

"MY PARENTS," "MY CHILD." Under the TRC guidelines, as noted earlier, applicants for amnesty were *not* required to indicate remorse or regret, nor to apologize or make atonement. And yet there were times when the amnesty hearings did in fact prepare the ground for such hoped-for ends. There is, for example, the story of Amy Biehl, a white American Fulbright exchange student and anti-apartheid activist, stoned and stabbed to death by a mob in August 1993, whose repentant killers faced the TRC and whose parents met, worked with, and forgave them. Biehl's mother calls the men her sons. She takes them shopping. She hired them into leadership positions at the memorial Amy Biehl Foundation.

Or take the case of Thapelo Mbelo, a black former police collaborator who once helped his bosses lure seven young black activists to their deaths. As part of his petition for amnesty, Mbelo asked to meet with and apologize to the mothers of his victims. The enraged mothers refused his apology and berated him: he had betrayed his own blood; he was a wolf in sheep's clothing; he'd left their families destitute, the grandchildren orphaned and impoverished. . . .

Helpless before this pain and anger, Mbelo sat in silence, his face twitching. Finally, he addressed the women in a formula native to the Xhosa language—"I ask your forgiveness, my parents"—words that called upon a preexisting ethic of familial care and prompted one mother to answer on the same terms: "My son, you are the same age as my son, Christopher. I want to tell you today, that I as Christopher's mother, I forgive you, my son. I forgive you. Yes, I have forgiven. Yes, I'm at peace. Go well, my child."

Or take the case of the white police commander Brian

Mitchell, who ordered an attack on a terrorist hideout in the village of Trust Feed, only to find out that he'd targeted the wrong house and killed eleven innocent people. "I was in absolute shock as I walked through the house. . . . Blood was everywhere and the bodies of women and children lay where they had fallen." Mitchell was tried, convicted of murder, and sentenced to death; later, his sentence was commuted, opening the way for him to apply for amnesty.

The petition eventually granted, Mitchell returned to Trust Feed to seek forgiveness from surviving family members. The villagers, however, refused to absolve him, and for the next year he found himself unable to move on, deeply depressed. Then came a telephone call, asking that he return to Trust Feed for a day of reconciliation: the son of one of the victims had had a dream in which his murdered mother told him, "You must forgive my killer and not seek revenge."

COLD-BLOODED. I have presented the McBride and Taylor cases in contrast to heartwarming tales of reconciliation because, absent a happy ending, each leaves us with the foundational kernel of the TRC's work, a transactional exchange of amnesty for truth. (Yes, Taylor was not amnestied, but the process itself did the needed work: at the end of the day, the Cradock Four widows knew the true story of their husbands' murders, and so did the South African public.)

Apology and forgiveness played no real role in either case. No white mother ever called Robert McBride "my son"; no widowed mother from Cradock ever went shopping with Eric Taylor. Both McBride and Taylor offered apologies to the families of their victims, but neither of them met any acceptance.

At his amnesty hearing, McBride read from a prepared statement, saying, "I particularly want to speak to the families of the people whose deaths I caused. I'm truly sorry for causing the deaths of your loved ones. I had nothing personal against them. It was in a quest for my own freedom . . . that I brought about the deaths of your loved ones. For this I am sorry." The sister of one of the women killed by McBride spoke on behalf of the relatives, and she would have none of it. "He came across as very arrogant," she said. "Mr. McBride is a cold-blooded murderer."

Eric Taylor's story is the same. He met with the families before his amnesty hearing, but the meeting did not go well, because he didn't want to tell his story in full until the amnesty committee met. "I'm not going to absolve him," Matthew Goniwe's widow later said. "If he wants to feel lighter, I'm not the person who's going to do that. No. I refuse to do that."

In short, these cases give us amnesty in its minimal state, a cold forgetting, instrumental and expedient, there to serve the state, the new South Africa that the architects of the TRC hoped would emerge once the truth about the political past had been held in the public mind fully enough to be dropped.

"THE TRUTH COMMISSION MICROPHONE WITH ITS LITTLE RED LIGHT." It is not hard to find fault with the TRC. To begin with, it was powerless to address the structural inequalities left by apartheid, the great divisions in wealth, education, employment, life expectancy, and landownership. (Whites, little more than a tenth of the population, owned almost 90 percent of the land and virtually all natural resources.) The form of the TRC hearings, in fact, with its focus on individual violations of human rights, sidestepped structural inequality and questions of collective responsibility, the ANC's earlier, radical critique of the system giving way to milder language of apology and forgiveness. The hearings offered up a single, Christian-inflected narrative in regard to change; the banners read "Reconciliation, Healing Our Past," not "Justice, an Equal Future." Finally, the national government that emerged after the transition never followed through on many TRC recommendations (failing, for example, to prosecute all those who chose not to apply for amnesty).

None of the many complaints about the TRC, however, undermine my own high regard. What were the alternatives? South Africa had been at war with itself for over a decade. The task was to manage a peaceful transition, not to engage in the kind of rigorous search for justice that's as likely to perpetuate a civil war as end it. It was the outgoing National Party that insisted on amnesty provisions as a precondition to the transition, while the incoming ANC insisted on a public accounting of human rights abuses. The TRC has to be seen as a compromise cobbled together under such specific historical circumstances. It was almost a laboratory for testing if a new nation could be created along the lines that Ernest Renan once suggested: its "essence" to be "that all its individuals have many things in common, and also that everyone has forgotten many things"—in this case, the common things being simultaneously the things forgotten by virtue of amnesty.

"For me," wrote the South African poet and journalist Antjie Krog, "the Truth Commission microphone with its little red light was the ultimate symbol of the whole process: here the marginalized voice speaks to the public ear, the unspeakable is spoken. . . . The personal story brought from the innermost of the individual binds us anew to the collective." The founding document of that new collective is not its constitution so much as the many-thousand-page final report of the TRC, a history simultaneously shared and amnestied so that it might, in the fullness of time, be like one of those old war monuments so well-known as to be invisible, or like a grave marker that the survivors may visit, although they do not have to.

"NEIGHBORS BECOME PLAYFUL." Vamik Volkan, the psychiatrist who gave us the idea of "chosen trauma," has long worked with contending ethnic, religious, or national groups—Arabs and Israelis, Serbs and Bosniaks, Turks and Greeks, Estonians and Russians—and at the end of one of his books he lists a set of questions the work gives rise to:

- How can the symbols of chosen traumas be made dormant so that they no longer inflame?
- How can group members "adaptively mourn" so that their losses no longer give rise to anger, humiliation, and a desire for revenge?
- How can a preoccupation with minor differences between neighbors become playful?
- And how can major differences be accepted without being contaminated with racism?

If the struggle against power is the struggle to forget our differences, then these questions suggest a curriculum for a large-group *ars oblivionis*, an art for loosening the hand of collective thought. In Mississippi, long after the murders of Goodman, Schwerner, and Chaney, black and white citizens convened the Philadelphia Coalition to work together to face the divide between them. Imagine a presidential candidate who would visit Philadelphia, Mississippi, not to speak of states' rights but to sit with the coalition and participate in the work of reconciliation. Imagine domestic nation building.

"FORGETTING IS THE SHEARS with which you cut away what you cannot use, doing it under the supreme direction of memory. Forgetting and remembering are thus identical arts, and the artistic achievement of this identity is the Archimedean point from which one lifts the whole world. When we say that we *consign* something to oblivion, we suggest simultaneously that it is to be forgotten and yet also remembered," says Søren Kierkegaard.

"It's a fascinating choice of metaphor," comments a literary friend, adding that he was especially struck by the word "consign": "'To consign' something etymologically descends from the Latin *consignāre*, to mark with a seal, and therein is the paradox: 'I have marked, that is, singled out, this thing to be forgotten. I will know it is to be forgotten by this mark.' I suppose that this paradox describes accurately the kind of stance to the past that makes reconciliation possible: it is necessary to forget *and* remember at the same time."

Lee Mingwei, *Guernica in Sand*

FROM THE MUSEUM OF FORGETTING. The artist Lee Mingwei says of his ephemeral installation *Guernica in Sand*, "I used Picasso's *Guernica* as the departure point for a different view of the damage done when human beings are victimized. Instead of simply being critical of what happened in the Basque town of Guernica in 1937, I wanted to use the concept of impermanence as a lens for focusing on such violent events in terms of the ongoing phenomena of destruction and creation. . . . My goal was to draw attention to the creative power of transformation rather than to the pain caused by clinging to things as they are.

"I began the project by creating the majority of a sand-painting version of *Guernica* before the exhibition opened. I then created the remainder of the piece within one day, midway through the exhibition. This performance started at sunrise and concluded at sunset. Throughout this day, one person at a time was allowed to walk (ideally barefoot) on the sand-painting, effacing it at the same time I was creating it. Visitors were allowed to view this process of simultaneous creation and destruction from the vantage point of a small island constructed above the sand-painting. At sunset on that day, four participants were invited to sweep the sand toward the middle of the installation, and the project was then left in this condition until the exhibition closed."

NOTEBOOK IV

CREATION

"To Forget Its Creator Is One of the Functions of a Creation"

The Aphorisms

Abstraction is oblivion by design.

Writing damages forgetfulness.

The ashes do not remember the firewood.

Artificial memory demands artificial forgetting.

Forgetting is radical nonaction.

The laws of habit govern the laws of memory.

Forgetting is a formalist art.

Insomnia: the too-much-memory disease.

"The now that remains creates eternity."

ANTI-MNEMONICS. Umberto Eco writes that "once as a joke some friends and I invented advertisements for university positions in nonexistent disciplines," one of these being an *ars oblivionalis*, as opposed to the ancient arts of memory. Eco tells the story in an essay meant to prove that from a semiotician's point of view no such art could possibly exist.

Others would disagree. At one point in the *Biographia Literaria*, Coleridge complains about the habit of reading periodicals, suggesting that it should rightly be added to the "catalogue of Anti-Mnemonics," a list of practices that weaken the memory, which he had found in the work of a Muslim scholar. These include "throwing to the ground lice picked from the hair, without crushing them; eating of unripe fruit; gazing on the clouds, and (*in genere*) on movable things suspended in the air; riding among a multitude of camels; frequent laughter . . . ; the habit of reading tomb-stones in church-yards, &c."

"CROTHF DELETOK." In fact, the *ars oblivionalis* (or *oblivionis*, as most would have it) not only exists; it's more easily mastered than any of the old arts of memory, now happily forgotten. Take, for example, Robert Richardson's description of the nineteenth-century method for remembering historical dates as offered by a certain Richard Grey:

> Grey used a table of numbers with letter equivalents. To remember a given date, one made up a new word, beginning with letters designed to recall the desired event, and ending with a date coded in letters. . . . To remember that the creation of the world came in 4004, one remembered the word 'crothf,' 'cr' being a tag for Creation, 'othf' standing for 4004. . . . [*Th* = 1,000; *o* being four times that, and *f* being the simple 4.] To remember the dates for Creation, the Deluge, the call of Abraham, the Exodus, and the foundation of Solomon's temple, one memorized the line "Crothf Deletok Abaneb Exasna Tembybe."

MOVING PICTURES. In 1917, a group of Dadaists living in New York—Marcel Duchamp and Henri-Pierre Roché, from France, and the American studio artist Beatrice Wood (the "Mama of Dada")—published a short-lived journal, *The Blind Man*, whose second issue comments on Duchamp's having submitted a urinal, credited to R. Mutt and titled *Fountain*, for an exhibition of the Society of Independent Artists:

> They say any artist paying six dollars may exhibit.
> Mr. Richard Mutt sent in a fountain. Without discussion this article disappeared and never was exhibited. What were the grounds for refusing Mr. Mutt's fountain:—
>
> 1. Some contended it was immoral, vulgar.
> 2. Others, it was plagiarism, a plain piece of plumbing.
>
> Now Mr. Mutt's fountain is not immoral, that is absurd, no more than a bath tub is immoral. It is a fixture that you see every day in plumbers' show windows.
>
> Whether Mr. Mutt with his own hands made the fountain or not has no importance. He CHOSE it. He took an ordinary article of life, placed it so that its useful significance disappeared under the new title and point of view—created a new thought for that object.

Question: How does one create "a new thought" for any object? Answer: Move it around. And therein lies a problem with the "place system," that old technique of artificial memory in which an image is committed to memory (committed!—as if to prison) by fixing it in a specific location. The whole apparatus freezes meaning, solidifies it, produces durable, fixed ideas, useful in the short term, to be sure, but what happens to those ideas when they are in need of change? Just to take the "Virtues and Vices" images that Giotto painted in the Arena Chapel in Padua: What if, as the centuries unfold, it turns out that the sword by which Fortitude is figured has outlived its usefulness? What if questions arise as to why Giotto painted Inconstancy as a woman?

Move it around: Duchamp's life coincided with the birth of "motion pictures," a technology that he imported into the plastic arts as a key element of a new *ars oblivionis* for old ideas.

DISTANCE. The painter Brice Marden sometimes draws with a long stick or branch dipped in ink, distancing himself from the work and deliberately interfering with his control of the stroke. Says Marden, "The works start out with observation and then automatic reaction, and then I back off, so there's a layering of different ways of drawing. . . . It's the opposite of knowing yourself through analysis. It's more like knowing yourself by forgetting yourself, learning not to be so involved with yourself."

How to forget yourself: use a long stick.

"THORNY." Jeffrey Eugenides, interviewed by Terry Gross on *Fresh Air*, explains that Mitchell Grammaticus, a character in his novel *The Marriage Plot*, spends time in India, as he himself had done. Gross says that it seems to her "it would probably be very helpful to have authentic memories to draw from."

"It's not that helpful," says Eugenides. "I'm not really an autobiographical writer. . . . When I actually write about myself, I get very confused. And with Mitchell, I wrote that chapter many times. It was the slowest and the hardest to write. The problem was that I remembered too much, and I put in every person that I remembered in Calcutta and everything I saw and every amazing sight in Calcutta.

"And suddenly I had a hundred pages of this thorny fiction, and I had to pare away so much of the autobiography to finally find the proper shape for Mitchell's story, and it just took forever, and I never knew where the spine of the story was."

REVISION BY FORGETTING. "The supreme achievement of memory . . . is the masterly use it makes of innate harmonies when gathering to its fold the suspended and wandering tonalities of the past," says Vladimir Nabokov.

Myself, when writing poems, I practice revision by forgetting. I write a draft of the poem, and then another and another, allowing the versions to pile up in a jumble—lines I am attached to, although they don't belong, lines that fit but go flat in the middle, words replaced and then reinserted, promising developments that never delivered—it all sits there, a shapeless pile, clammy with fatigue.

Then I set the mess aside and ignore it for at least one day. Then I write the poem from memory. Great chunks will have fallen into oblivion, while others will have returned clarified from the pool. The double goddess attends, erasing as she records, drawing shape from shapelessness, dropping the discord to reveal the harmony.

LOUISE BOURGEOIS, *ODE À L'OUBLI* (ODE TO FORGETTING) (2002); UNIQUE FABRIC BOOK OF THIRTY-TWO EMBROIDERED AND COLLAGED PAGES; LITHOGRAPHED COVER AND TEXT, 11" × 13"

FROM THE MUSEUM OF FORGETTING. Louise Bourgeois—eighty years after her father abandoned the family to enlist in World War I, seventy years after he abandoned them again, taking young Louise's English tutor as his mistress ("the trauma of abandonment . . . has remained active ever since"), twenty years after the death of her husband, and just a few years after the death of one of her three sons—made this large, unique fabric book using for pages the linen hand towels embroidered with the initials LBG for Louise Bourgeois Goldwater, her married name, each page collaged with designs cut from fragments of clothing and household items, some as old as the memories of trauma themselves.

Bourgeois has said that every day you must accept the past and abandon it, and "if you can't accept it, then you have to do sculpture. . . . If your need is to refuse to abandon the past, then you have to recreate it. Which is what I have been doing." Except, as the title implies, in the case of *Ode à l'oubli,* for here the process of making designs out of old cloth is intended to put the past to rest.

Abstraction was, for Bourgeois, an *ars oblivionis.* To calm and relieve her insomnia (the too-much-memory disease!), she used to draw repeated, simple lines across sheets of paper. With *Ode à l'oubli* she takes a near century of memories ("You can . . . remember your life by the shape, weight, color, and smell of those clothes in your closet") and converts them into grids and circles, pyramids, starbursts, and waves ("strong emotion . . . held in a kind of formal restraint"). True, there is one oddly soiled page. In red letters it reads, "The / return / of / the / repressed," and a long brown stain runs across the page between the last two words. And yet, if we take the book as a whole, that unyielding stain is ten square inches of the Unforgettable in over four thousand square inches of oblivion-by-design.

"LOOK AT A COCA-COLA BOTTLE." At one point in *Notes and Projects for the Large Glass*, Marcel Duchamp reflects on inventing new languages as a way of getting to some sort of primary experience. In this context, he addresses the way in which memory abstracts and so impedes perception. Note 31 reads, "To lose the possibility of recognizing 2 similar objects (2 colors, 2 laces, 2 hats, 2 forms whatsoever). To reach the impossibility of sufficient visual memory, to transfer from one like object to another the memory imprint—Same possibility with sounds; with brain facts."

John Cage was struck by Duchamp's notion. In a 1984 interview (cited in Notebook I), Cage remarked that, for him, to repeat a phrase in music moves him "toward my taste and memory," exactly what he wanted "to become free of." He then repeated Duchamp's "beautiful statement" about the memory imprint, explaining that from Duchamp's "visual point of view" it meant "to look at a Coca-Cola bottle without the feeling that you've ever seen one before, as though you're looking at it for the very first time. That's what I'd like to find with sounds—to play them and hear them as if you've never heard them before."

TRANSFER, TRANSFERENCE. When Duchamp writes of how we "transfer from one like object to another the memory imprint," we might note the verb "transfer" and bring to it the memory imprint of Freud's idea of transference. The patient unconsciously projects the memory of other people onto the analyst, whereupon, to rewrite Duchamp, the goal becomes "to lose the possibility of recognizing 2 similar persons (2 lovers, 2 parents, 2 enemies, 2 people whomsoever). To reach the impossibility of sufficient emotional memory, to transfer from one like person to another the memory imprint." Psychotherapeutic work includes becoming conscious of memory's transfer habit and dropping it so as to experience more directly not just the therapist but any other person.

AGNES MARTIN, *THE TREE* (1964); OIL, PENCIL, CANVAS, 72" × 72"

FROM THE MUSEUM OF FORGETTING. How did Agnes Martin begin a painting? She would sit and wait for something to come to mind. Once, early in her career, she was thinking of "the innocence of trees" and "a grid came into [her] mind. It looked like innocence." From then on, her paintings were all variations on the grid.

She imagined the mind as operating either by intellect or by inspiration. Intellect is problematic. It's "the servant of ego" (and "everybody's born 100 percent ego; after that it's just adjustment"). Intellect "does all the conquering." It struggles with facts, discovering first one and then another until finally making a deduction. "But in my opinion that is just guesswork, so completely inaccurate." It's "never going to find the truth about life."

"I gave up facts entirely in order to have an empty mind for inspiration to come into. . . . You have to practice quiet, empty mind. I gave up the intellect entirely. I had a hard time giving up evolution and the atomic theory but I managed it. . . . And I never have any ideas myself. I'm very careful not to have ideas."

OF THE PAINTER who figures largely in Marcel Proust's novel, the narrator says, "The effort made by Elstir, when seeing reality, to rid himself of all the ideas the mind contains, to make himself ignorant in order to paint, to forget everything for the sake of his own integrity . . . , was especially admirable in a man whose own mind was exceptionally cultivated."

Elaine de Kooning, *Frank O'Hara* (1962);
oil on canvas, 93" × 42" (detail)

FROM THE MUSEUM OF FORGETTING, GALLERY OF ERASURES. "Frank was standing there," says Elaine de Kooning. "First I painted the whole structure of his face; then I wiped out the face, and when the face was gone, it was more Frank than when the face was there."

HAPPY AND FORGETFUL HERDS. Says Nietzsche, freely translated: Consider the herd grazing in front of you. These animals know nothing of yesterday or today, but leap about, eat, rest, digest, and leap again, and so from morning to night and from day to day, their likes and dislikes closely tied to the peg of the moment, they are neither melancholy nor bored. It upsets a man to see this, for while his humanity makes him proud, the animal's contentment makes him jealous.

One day the man may ask the beast, "Why do you not talk to me of your happiness, but only gaze in silence?" The beast wants to answer and say, "That's because I so quickly forget what I wanted to say!" But this it also forgets. It does not speak, and the man is left to wonder.

SADDLED WITH HISTORY. But Nietzsche is wrong to say the grazing herd so easily forgets. True, as far as we know, animals don't remember the way that we remember, but if that's the case, then neither do they forget. The pastured herd ruminates on grass, not on yesterday's weather, let alone its childhood. Agnosia is not amnesia. *Nothing can be forgotten that was not first in mind.*

Animals need no art of forgetting nor, of course, any art of memory. And the mid-nineteenth-century German "science" of memory was the true target of Nietzsche's essay that opens with the oblivious cattle. "The Use and Abuse of History for Life" is the nominal title, but it might more properly be called "The Use and Abuse of History *Departments*," for Nietzsche reserved his scorn for academics who had saddled German youth with a "science of history" that stifled all emerging life and left the young feeling they were living "in the fifth act of the tragedy," as if they were to be the proof of Hesiod's prophecy "that men would one day be born with grey hair."

As antidote, Nietzsche recommended an "unhistorical" frame of mind figured as a fertile clouding of temporal categories, a "living whirlpool in a dead sea of night and forgetting" that could become the "cradle of deeds." "The man of action . . . forgets a great deal to do one thing."

ROBERT SMITHSON, *NON-SITE (PALISADES-EDGEWATER, N.J.)* (1968); PAINTED ALUMINUM, TRAPROCK, AND WALL TEXT WITH MAP, DIMENSIONS VARIABLE

I am a Modern artist dying of Modernism.
—ROBERT SMITHSON

FROM THE MUSEUM OF FORGETTING. With its simple piles of traprock and its date of 1968, this installation is in part Robert Smithson's response to the emotive "action painting" of the 1950s. At the same time, by calling the work a "non-site" and by putting a little map on the wall, Smithson indicates that the true site of the work is not in the gallery or the museum but on the Palisades, along the Hudson River in New Jersey. In setting up the contrast between the cultural non-site and the geological true-site, Smithson opens an inquiry into how we think of time. New Jersey traprock is a Triassic diabase intrusion laid down over 200 million years ago, a span of time within which the era of abstract expressionism and the year 1968 are vanishing markers.

Geological time offered Smithson refuge from the time of art history. Absent such sanctuary, he believed, artists too often find themselves submerged in a historical narrative written by the critics and museums, not by artists. "The remnants of art history," he wrote, float "in [a] temporal river," and "the deeper an artist sinks into [that] time stream the more it becomes *oblivion*." Better to forget about art history than to drown in its so-recent waters and be yourself forgotten.

As for how to avoid the oblivion of history, Smithson's advice was to "remain close to the temporal surfaces." At first this might seem to mean that the artists should focus on the present moment, not on geological time, but in fact these two are one and the same. For Smithson, attending to temporal surfaces did not mean exploring the daily news: "The 'present' . . . must instead explore the pre- and post-historic mind; it must go into the places where remote futures meet remote pasts." The cleavage planes of traprock are at once instant and primordial; in neither register do they have much to do with memories of human culture.

NIETZSCHE BROUGHT MACHISMO to forgetting. Historical study produces "a race of eunuchs." *"The weak are completely extinguished by it."* Better, then, to wear the "cloak of the unhistorical" and enter its "mysterious circle of mist." Better, then, to protect the *pure will*, the *highest strength*, the *rarest minds*, the *active and powerful man* who *fights the great fight* on a *solitary height*.

Nietzsche made forgetting a part of the hero's journey.

FÜHRERPARKPLATZ, FROM THE MUSEUM OF FORGETTING, GALLERY *DAMNATIO MEMORIAE.* Except for an information board installed in 2006, no memorial marks the underground hideout where Adolf Hitler took his own life in April 1945. The Führerbunker, with its warren of rooms and tunnels, its bomb-proof walls and eleven-foot-thick ceiling, has been filled in, sealed up, and abandoned. A recent visitor to the site found it occupied by a Chinese restaurant and a parking lot.

Even empty plinths, like those scattered around Russia where statues of Lenin used to stand, cannot but call the past to mind. A parking lot, not so much. It comes close to what the Irish activist Edna Longley suggested in hopes of under-cutting the Northern Irish obsession with commemoration: "We should erect a statue to Amnesia and forget where we put it."

CONTRARY WATERS OF MEMORY. In 1908, the German city of Kassel commissioned a fountain to stand in the town square. Paid for by the entrepreneur Sigmund Aschrott and designed by the local architect Karl Roth, what became known as the Aschrott Fountain stood as a tall, neo-Gothic pyramid rising from a round reflecting pool.

Thirty years later, the Nazis decided that the fountain was Jewish and destroyed it. Over three thousand of Kassel's Jews eventually died in the camps. In later years, citizens dealt with the fountain's history by planting its remains with flowers and saying that, as best they could remember, the original had been destroyed by Allied bombers.

In the 1980s, following a call for the fountain to be restored, the artist Horst Hoheisel proposed a "negative-form" monument, "a mirror image of the old one," he explained, to be sunk beneath the square where the original stood. Hoheisel turned what was once a tall pyramid into a deep funnel "into whose darkness water runs down."

During construction, a white concrete version of the original pyramid stood upright in the square. This was then inverted and buried so that now whoever comes upon the site is met by water flowing from eight narrow channels into the center, where it pours into the underground hollow of a now-invisible structure. "The sunken fountain is not the memorial at all," Hoheisel says. "It is only history turned into a pedestal, an invitation to passersby who stand upon it to search for the memorial in their own heads."

Monuments often become invisible, marking the end of something so that everyone can turn away from the past. An intentionally invisible monument, however, is harder to ignore. Just as the biblical command that the Jews "blot out the memory of Amalek" in fact enlists forgetting as an aid to memory, so the counter-memorials that have arisen in postwar Germany enlist physical erasures as aids to mental presence. Citizens are asked to bear in mind what conventional memorials might lead them to forget.

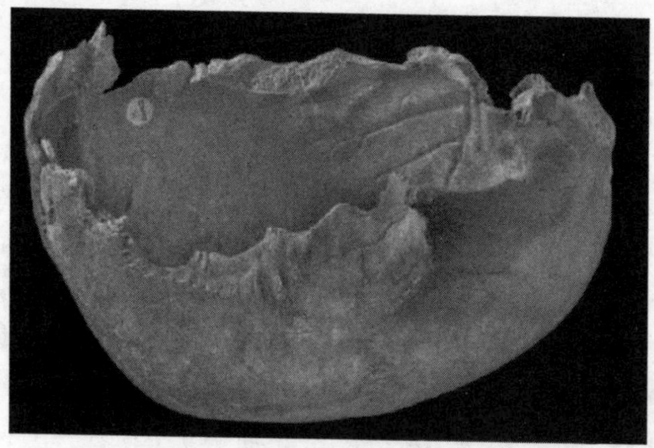

HUMAN SKULL CUP UNCOVERED IN GOUGH'S CAVE, SOMERSET, ENGLAND

FROM THE MUSEUM OF FORGETTING (PROPOSAL FOR AN AMERICAN APARTHEID MEMORIAL). Given that, as in the case of the murders of Henry Dee and Charles Moore, members of the Ku Klux Klan would not drink from the Mississippi River for fear that it flowed with "water off a dead Negro";

And given the ancient and widespread belief in rivers whose "waters of forgetfulness" carry the dissolved memories of the dead;

And given that these dissolved memories are not lost but bubble to the surface at certain sacred springs;

And given the surmise that in Norse mythology Mímir's Spring contained a skull from which Odin drank the waters of ancestral knowledge;

And given that Henry Dee's skull is but one of many that lie still unrecovered in the Mississippi River;

And given that skull cups have long been used as drinking vessels as, for example, the fifteen-thousand-year-old cup found in a cave in Somerset, England, or the cup upon which Lord Byron inscribed a poem to "rhyme and revel with the dead";

A memorial having the following form is proposed:

On the Natchez high bluff, on the eastern shore of the Mississippi River, will stand a pavilion dedicated to the memory of African Americans murdered during the centuries of American apartheid. The pavilion will contain the names and stories of all whose deaths have been documented, including the four thousand victims of racial terror lynching recorded by the Equal Justice Initiative and the 350 racially motivated killings investigated by the Civil Rights and Restorative Justice Project at Northeastern University.

Visitors to this pavilion will be assigned a victim's name at random and taught the details of the case.

From the center of the pavilion, a spiral staircase will descend to a level below the river. The names of the many thousands dead will be inscribed on the walls of the descending shaft, and visitors will drag their hands across these names as they go such that the inscriptions will be fully erased in three or four centuries.

At the bottom of the stair, in the center of the spiral, will lie a pool fed by a spring of Mississippi River water. Skull cups cast in bronze will lie on the surrounding shelves and visitors will take a cup, say aloud the name that they carried in mind as they descended, dip the cup, and drink.

After returning the cups to their shelves, visitors will enter a tunnel that lets them travel beneath the Mississippi, out to the western shore.

ORAL AMNESIA. In Africa in the early twentieth century, the British took to writing things down that had previously lived only in oral traditions, passed from generation to generation through spoken memory. It must have seemed a useful contribution, but as the years went by, the written record proved to be problematic: fixed accounts turned out to potentially conflict with the useful ways in which an oral culture adjusts itself over time so that stories from the past are always in accord with current conditions.

A case in point concerns the state of Gonja, in northern Ghana. Around 1900, the British recorded an origin myth: the state had been founded in ancient times by a man who came in search of gold, conquered the indigenous peoples, and enthroned his seven sons as rulers of seven divisional chiefdoms. Sixty years later, when the anthropologist Jack Goody visited, the story had changed. Two of the divisional chiefdoms had disappeared in the intervening decades, one incorporated into its neighbor and the other erased by altered boundaries. Now when the origin myth was told, the founder was credited with only five sons. The other two were simply forgotten.

We may think of myth as representing things from the primeval past, but a case like this shows that it is sometimes better to say that myth offers a map of present conditions, giving them authority by framing them as primeval. In an oral culture, each generation is free to reimagine its heritage in a form that matches the past to the present. Comments Goody, “Whatever parts of it have ceased to be of contemporary relevance are likely to be eliminated by the process of forgetting.” This is “structural amnesia”: as the shape of things changes (five chiefdoms, not seven), what no longer fits is simply dropped. Happily mingling memory and forgetting, the oral mode allows for ongoing flexibility. The past never seems far from the present. The world has always been as it is now.

NEW PLATO. It was Plato's opinion that "no serious man will ever think of writing about serious realities for the general public," a position he defended in the *Phaedrus* by commenting on a story out of Egypt concerning a god named Theuth who invented the art of writing and offered it as a gift to King Thamus, saying, "Here, O king, is a branch of learning that will make the people of Egypt wiser and improve their memories; my discovery provides a recipe for memory and wisdom."

No, it doesn't, replied King Thamus. "If men learn this, it will implant forgetfulness in their souls; they will cease to exercise memory because they rely on that which is written, calling things to mind no longer from within themselves, but by means of external marks. It is not true wisdom that you offer but only its semblance."

Fair enough, but with the flexibility of oral cultures in mind, we can add a parallel critique. "If men learn this," King Thamus might have said, "it will strip forgetfulness from their souls. Relying on writing, they will cease to exercise imagination, calling things to mind no longer from the quick of present attention but from a past frozen in ink. What you have discovered is a recipe not for the mastery of living speech but for dead speech to master the living."

Writing damages forgetfulness.

AN ARTIFICE OF FORGETTING. Before the widespread use of written records, legal arguments concerning past events could be settled through an appeal to "living memory." In England in 1127, for example, a dispute arose as to which of two churches was entitled to customs dues from the port of Sandwich. The case was decided by having "twenty-four mature, wise seniors" swear on a Bible and then testify as to their recollection of the matter, the accepted understanding being that "legal memory" extended only to times that could be recalled by living persons, any prior period being "time out of mind" or "time immemorial," terms indicating the temporal limit—a century, perhaps, but not much more—beyond which the law could not reach.

As in oral societies, where forgetting the past enables present change, so too in the early Middle Ages, where "remembered truth was . . . flexible and up to date," as M. T. Clanchy writes, "because no ancient custom could be proved to be older than the memory of the oldest living wise man. There was no conflict . . . between ancient precedents and present practice." Customary law, another scholar notes, "quietly passes over obsolete laws, which sink into oblivion, and die peacefully, but the law itself remains young, always in the belief that it is old."

As for what happens when the past doesn't die peacefully, when legal memory subsists in writing rather than in mind, the decades surrounding the year 1200 provide an interesting case. In England, these were the years when the archbishop of Canterbury modernized the Charter Roll by insisting that henceforth all land transactions be recorded in writing. This "turning point in the history of keeping records" changed the nature of legal memory going forward, of course, but because it was new it also marked a great divide in the history of law: the new record keeping was still powerless to extend legal memory backward into the centuries *before* the archbishop got busy writing everything down. Everything before about 1190 was still "time out of mind."

It took several decades for there to be any formal acknowledgment of this divide, but it came finally in 1275 with the Statute of Westminster, the first ever "statute of limitation," which announced that whenever arguments about landownership arose, no action could be taken if the origins of the dispute predated 1189, the first year of the reign of Richard I. On one side of the year 1189 lay the period of legal memory; on the other side lay time immemorial, the period of legal oblivion.

Simply put, the spread of written records as an artifice of memory called for a corresponding artifice of forgetting, what we now know as statutes of limitations.

CHANSON FIXE. Radovan Karadžić, war criminal of the Bosnian war, who "wagged the stick of genocide at the Bosnian Muslims," as Aleksandar Hemon has put it, was well versed in traditional Serbian epic poetry and an accomplished player of the single-stringed Balkan gusle. In performance, he used to model himself on a Christian bishop, the hero of a nineteenth-century epic, who preached against the Ottoman Empire and argued for the total extermination of Muslims. Karadžić "believed that he was the one to finish the job" that the bishop started. "He was to be the hero in an epic poem that would be sung by a distant future generation."

After the war, Karadžić went into hiding in Belgrade, though in fact he could be found in a certain bar offering up his gusle-accompanied epics, praising the legendary bishop as a model for his own genocidal actions. "Hundreds of thousands died," writes Hemon, "millions . . . were displaced, untold numbers of people paid in pain for his induction into the pantheon of Serbian epic poetry."

The poem Karadžić sang was part of "the socialist cannon" in Tito's Yugoslavia; all schoolchildren were obliged to learn it. Let's not overstate the flexibility of the oral; yes, it can change with the times, but it can also pass a code of ethnic difference down through the centuries. That said, what Karadžić sang was no oral epic. It was a text unchanged since its first publication in 1847, an unforgotten song ready to hand whenever it came time to reanimate a murderous division between Christians and Muslims.

FORGETTING FOR ETERNITY. My favorite part of Saint Augustine's *Confessions* is not that famous moment when he asks the Lord to relieve him of his lusts, but not just yet ("Just a little longer, please"), nor the amusing end of the chapter on memory, where he's mystified by the fact that he still dreams about sex. No, it's the end of the chapter on time and eternity, where he describes the reciting of a psalm as a way of explaining his ideas about both of those mysteries. He has by then spent many pages driving himself nuts trying to figure out what time is. ("My mind is on fire to solve this very intricate enigma.") He has decided that the past and future don't exist: "How can they 'be' when the past is not now present and the future is not yet present?" As for the present itself, it "flies so quickly from future into past that it is an interval with no duration."

He moves then to thinking of these temporal categories as existing not by themselves but as human mind-states, all of them taking place in that fleeting present. His boyhood lies in the past, but when he recalls it, he is "looking on its image in present time." To speak of time with any exactness, we need to say that "there are three times: a present of things past, a present of things present, a present of things to come." And we have a name for each of these: "The present considering the past is the memory, the present considering the present is immediate awareness, the present considering the future is expectation."

And time? Time is the experience of simultaneously holding two of these states in mind. When we do so, the mind gets stretched out just as the body gets stretched when touching two separate spots in space. Augustine's name for this mental stretching is "distension," a term he probably borrowed from

Plotinus, who also speaks of time as a "spreading out (*diastasis*) of life." Says Augustine, "I have come to think that time is simply a distension. But of what is it a distension? I do not know, but it would be surprising if it is not that of the mind itself."

All this given, Augustine illustrates this idea by asking that we imagine him reciting a psalm: "Before I begin, my expectation is directed towards the whole. But when I have begun, the verses from it which I take into the past become the object of my memory. The life of this act of mine is stretched two ways, into my memory, because of the words I have already said, and into my expectation, because of those which I am about to say. But my attention is on what is present: by that the future is transferred to become the past."

Note that he begins with something he calls "the whole." If he says he's going to recite Psalm 23, his auditors and he imagine a single thing with that name, a unity all of whose parts exist simultaneously—until, that is, he begins to recite, whereupon the psalm becomes temporal, its parts disposed successively.

Augustine uses the spoken psalm not only to illustrate mental distension but also to describe human life: spoken word by word, the psalm is a unity broken into pieces, and "the same is true . . . of the entire life of an individual person, where all actions are parts of a whole, and it is true of the total history of 'the sons of men,' where all human lives are but parts."

He finds this temporal successiveness painful and confusing. It's a kind of disintegration. "I am scattered in times whose order I do not understand. The storms of incoherent events tear to pieces my thoughts, the inmost entrails of my soul." He longs for "that day when, purified and molten by the fire" of God's love, he will "flow together" and be made whole again.

And how might that happen? With the help of Jesus Christ, the mediator between temporal beings and the atemporal God. A verse in Saint Paul's Letter to the Philippians suggests a path. "I want to know Christ," Paul writes. "Not that I have . . . arrived at my goal, but I press on that I might apprehend him in whom also I am apprehended. . . . Forgetting the past and moving toward the things which are before me, I press on toward the goal."

There are two time frames in that verse: the past, which is to be forgotten, and "what is ahead," a future in Christ. When Augustine cites this verse, however, he adjusts that second time frame to distinguish the earthbound future from the heavenly one. He needs to do so because he is thinking of distension, especially of the human mind that dwells in memory and earthly expectation, and he needs to be quit of both of these if he is to be quit of time.

Thus in Augustine we get Saint Paul amended with what I here italicize: God has upheld him through Jesus Christ, "so 'I might apprehend him in whom also I am apprehended,' and leaving behind the old days I might be gathered to follow the One, 'forgetting the past' and moving *not toward those future things which are transitory* but to 'the things which are before' me."

The path to salvation demands letting go of all transitory things, both past and future. This is the great double forgetting that, for Saint Augustine, promises to open the door to eternity.

THE TIME TO WAKE UP. The Buddhists suggest a similar double forgetting, though without a savior and without talk of eternity. In a discourse on time, the thirteenth-century Zen master Dogen writes,

> Firewood becomes ash, and it does not become firewood again. Yet, do not suppose that the ash is future and the firewood past. You should understand that firewood abides in the phenomenal expression of firewood, which fully includes past and future and is independent of past and future. Ash abides in the phenomenal expression of ash, which fully includes future and past. Just as firewood does not become firewood again after it is ash, you do not return to birth after death. . . .
>
> Birth is an expression complete this moment. Death is an expression complete this moment. They are like winter and spring. You do not call winter the beginning of spring, nor summer the end of spring.

I find that intriguing but enigmatic. Dogen's discourses on the Buddha Way are as dense as dried bricks of black tea; I suspect that only the waters of constant practice can soften them. Still, in this case it seems to me that Dogen is addressing something like Augustine's idea of distension. If we look at firewood and think about how it will someday become ashes, we are entertaining two mental time frames, present and future. Likewise, if we look at ashes and remember their former state as firewood. In both cases, the mind must leave the present moment, and the present, the Buddhists say, is the cutting edge of practice, the only time available for becoming an awakened being.

REMEMBERING FORGETFULNESS IN MASSACHUSETTS. In his journal, Henry D. Thoreau once wrote out a complicated dream that ends with him walking in a meadow with his friend Bronson Alcott. They fall to speaking lines of poetry to each other:

> I quoted one which in my waking hours I have no knowledge of, but in my dream it was familiar enough. I only know that those which I quoted expressed regret, and were like the following, though they were not these, *viz.*:
>
> "The short parenthesis of life was sweet," "The remembrance of youth is a sigh," etc.
>
> It had the word "memory" in it!! And then again the instant that I awoke, methought I was a musical instrument from which I heard a strain die out—a bugle, or a clarionet, or a flute. My body was the organ and channel of melody, as a flute is of the music that is breathed through it. . . . I awoke, therefore, to an infinite regret—to find myself, not the thoroughfare of glorious and world-stirring inspirations, but a scuttle full of dirt.

Thinking back on what might have induced this dream, Thoreau remembers that he had been reading a book about the Northmen, the night before, one that must have summoned to mind a desired if unobtainable life, for as he read, he felt "a fertile regret" and derived "an inexpressible satisfaction" from that feeling.

Here "memory" seems to be the name of the faculty of mind that, if purified, might know what we do not know, and might express itself in poetry or music. But it is not quite available, at least not in daylight. Each of us has had the experience of being on the verge of uttering a thought, then being distracted and forgetting what we had to say, then being madly haunted by the ghost of what was so clearly present a moment ago. Imagine living a life suffused with that feeling. Imagine having the sense that you have come here to say something, only to find it has slipped your mind. Worse yet, imagine such is the case but that you do not even feel the loss.

Thoreau finds his regret satisfying and fertile because it indicates some loss is felt and thus implies there was something to be lost. Forgetting is the warrant of that knowledge. His "fertile sadness," as he elsewhere calls it, contains a sort of backward promise, a hope that arises because something has been taken away. The literary critic Barbara Johnson writes that it was Thoreau's great gift to wake us to "our own lost losses." Not losses simply—we all have those—but the losses we are not even aware of. If we are ever to recover them, remembering that we have forgotten is the first step.

"IF THE VERY SOUL IS NO LONGER THINKING ABOUT ITSELF." In the middle of his chapter on memory, Augustine finds himself deeply puzzled over the fact that he remembers forgetfulness. How can that be? If forgetfulness is a loss of memory, how could it be present in the memory? Could memory be recalling something that it never contained?—no, that's "quite absurd." Maybe what's remembered is the image of forgetfulness, not the thing itself, but that doesn't make sense either: we remember a city like Carthage by way of images impressed on the mind, but forgetfulness doesn't leave images; it deletes them.

Still, "it is certain to me that I remember forgetfulness," writes Augustine, even though he finds that fact "incomprehensible and inexplicable."

Be that as it may, by the end of the chapter, I myself get a glimmer of what he might eventually have understood about this puzzle. It helps to note, first of all, that Augustine was influenced by Plato's ideas about recollection. He had found things hidden in his memory that did not come from any worldly experience. How did they get there? "I do not know how. . . . They were there even before I had learnt them. . . . They were already in the memory, but so remote and pushed into the background, as if in most secret caverns, that unless they were dug out by someone drawing attention to them, perhaps I could not have thought of them."

Second, God is *not* one of those things hidden in the memory. True, Augustine remembers his conversion—"Since the day I learnt of you, I have never forgotten you"—but recalling that day is not the same as having found God in the memory to begin with. He conducted a thorough interior search, plumbing "the very seat of my mind, which is located in the memory," and did not find God. No, "you were not already in my memory before I learnt of you."

In this regard, Augustine is not a Neoplatonist, for in Plato all the eternals are in the mind, albeit forgotten and in need of recovery. Not so with Augustine; with Augustine, awareness of God enters the mind from outside. And how does that happen?

By indirection. By attending to something other than God, something that *is* found in the memory, and by so doing, preparing there a receptive ground. As a young man, Augustine had read a philosophical dialogue by Cicero that spoke of "the happy life," something that apparently could be "dug out by someone drawing attention to" it, for, unlike the divinity, "the happy life is found in the memory and is recognized when the words are uttered."

In Cicero, carnal pleasures are not the source of the "happy life"; the source is the search for truth. Without trying to say exactly what such a search entails, we can more simply notice what it is that Augustine does, which is to slowly divest himself of things he takes to be false, as if clearing an interior space so that something of a different order might enter. Most obviously, he struggles to leave behind the pleasures of the flesh, but that is not all.

In a less striking but more telling move, when he turns toward the church, he abandons public teaching. In Carthage, in Milan, and in Rome, Augustine had earned his living as a teacher of rhetoric, but as he turned toward the priesthood, he decided "quietly to retire from my post as a salesman of words in the markets of rhetoric. I did not wish my pupils, who were giving their minds . . . to frenzied lies and lawcourt squabbles, to buy from my mouth weapons for their madness." The search for the happy life amounts not just to dissolving the "glue of lust" but to a more subtle emptying out, a kenosis, a purging of images and even a quitting of "the noise of . . . human speech where a sentence has both a beginning and an end."

So much, then, for the old arts of memory with their word tricks and picture galleries. Contrast the origin story that the rhetoricians tell—how Simonides remembered the place of each dinner guest crushed by a fallen roof—with the scene in which Augustine has taken a house in Ostia, on the Tiber, to care for his dying mother. The two of them meditate together on the passage in Philippians that counsels "forgetting the past" (the same passage Augustine later amended to also include forgetting transitory "future things"). Theirs was an art of temporal erasure, not of memory. Plotinus, another of Augustine's guides in these matters, wrote of "the higher soul," the one that "flies from multiplicity": "The more it presses on towards the heights the more it will forget . . . , so that if anyone said that the good soul was forgetful, it would be correct."

With the necessary temporal distension, word by word now, let us revisit that paradoxical phrase "remembering forgetfulness." "Remembering" denotes a capacity to know, to be aware; "forgetfulness" implies the absence of memory's usual content, all the stuff the rhetoricians urged their students to acquire. Images are absent, and so are words in all their successivity. It is as if to say "I am aware of something that cannot be described" or "I have an intimation of something whose content cannot be imagined, whose being is not spread out in time." Augustine complains, "I find my own self hard to grasp," but that may be because what he's seeking is not himself at all but an awareness of what is the case, once the self gets out of the way.

In that house at Ostia on the Tiber, Augustine and his mother said to themselves, "If . . . the tumult of the flesh has fallen silent, if the images of earth, water, and air are quiescent, if the heavens themselves are shut out and the very soul itself is making no sound and is surpassing itself by no longer thinking about itself, if all dreams and visions in the imagination are excluded, if all language and every sign and everything transitory is silent . . . , then. . . ."

DAN FLAVIN, *"MONUMENT" I FOR V. TATLIN* (1964); FLUORESCENT LIGHTS AND METAL FIXTURES, 8' × 24"

FROM THE MUSEUM OF FORGETTING. Robert Smithson's essay on his "minimalist" contemporaries, "Entropy and the New Monuments," took as its point of departure this installation by Dan Flavin and led to his declaration that "instead of causing us to remember the past like the old monuments, the new monuments seem to cause us to forget the future."

To forget the future reverses a long-standing American habit of mind. Said Benjamin Franklin regarding the Pennsylvania governor Sir William Keith, whose false promises had sent young Franklin to London, "He wish'd to please everybody; and, having little to give, he gave *expectations.*" Said Emerson, "Our American literature and spiritual history are . . . in the *optative* mood" (the "if only" mood). Since the nation's birth, Americans have chosen to live in a wished-for future, an ever-moving temporal and spatial frontier.

But the date of Smithson's essay is 1966, and hopeful expectation has lost its charm. It's the age of nuclear weapons, suburban sprawl, and, writes Smithson, the kind of false advertising that claims that "soap is 99.44% pure, beer has more spirit in it, and dog food is ideal." The created landscape is the opposite of promissory: New Jersey is a "destroyed California, a derelict California," and his walking tour of Passaic reveals buildings that "don't *fall* into ruin *after* they are built but rather *rise* into ruin before they are built."

Where minimalist artists make monuments, they do so to "neutralize the myth of progress." Their works "are not built for the ages, but rather against the ages." Forget about things getting better, they say. Forget about the atomic age, forget about the New Frontier.

HABIT VERSUS REBIRTH. Outside my study window stands an ugly nest of power lines. I see it all the time, so I hardly notice it. Nearby, the wild beauty of an ancient elm with its break-dance branches—that too can elude me. Were I traveling in a foreign country, however, little would have such invisibility. Strange lands leave the traveler by turns enlivened and anxious, alert and weary, every unknown thing demanding attention. Once, the day after a night flight to Amsterdam, every touch of beauty—a small Vermeer in the Rijksmuseum, the reedy flutes of Peruvian street musicians—found me in unguarded tears. On the other hand, once in a rented apartment in Rome the staircases terrified me; steep black iron affairs like fire escapes with uneven risers and no handrails, they had me mentally mapping a route to the hospital in the sure event of a bloody tumble. A few weeks later, though, my constant climbing up and down having worn my fear away, the stairs had become nothing but stairs.

Such is one of Marcel Proust's great themes, the trade-off between the delight or anxiety of fresh perception and the comfort or dullness of the habitual. Habit's first duty is to help us feel at home in our surroundings, a virtue Proust readily acknowledges, calling habit "that skillful, slow-moving housekeeper" whom we are glad to have with us, "for without habit our mind . . . would be powerless to make a lodging habitable." By the same token, Proust acknowledges that the sudden loss of a habitual surrounding can be terrifying.

But on the whole, he is a declared enemy of habit. Its comforts anesthetize and stupefy, its "annihilating force" suppresses original perception, its "second nature" keeps us from knowing our first, its very competence lulls our faculties into dormancy, it puts beauty beyond our grasp, it renders speech vapid and cliché-ridden, it "cuts away the taproot" that gives significance to thought, and finally, by softening all discomfort, it stands in the way of the very suffering that our growth requires.

No wonder, then, that when Proust's narrator, Marcel, eats that famous madeleine and finds himself reborn, he pauses to note that he did so "contrary to my habit," and no wonder that the forgetting of habits of mind figures so largely in the many volumes of *In Search of Lost Time.*

HABIT VERSUS THE TREASURE CHEST OF OBLIVION. Says Proust's lovelorn narrator, Marcel, "One day in Balbec I overheard a stranger mention, as I walked past him on the esplanade, 'the head of the Ministry of Posts.'" The remark gives him "a sharp stab of pain" because it reproduces a phrase once overheard in a conversation between his first sweetheart, Gilberte, and her father, a conversation he had forgotten, "had never given another thought to."

He goes on: "The memories of love are no exception to the general laws of memory, which in turn are governed by the still more general laws of Habit. And as Habit weakens everything, what best reminds us of a person is precisely what we had forgotten (because it was of no importance, and we therefore left it in full possession of its strength). That is why the better part of our memories exists outside us, in a wind-swept rain, in the smell of an unaired room or of the first crackling brushwood fire in a cold grate: wherever, in short, we happen upon what our mind, having no use for it, had rejected, the last treasure that the past has in store, the richest, that which, when all our flow of tears seems to have dried at the source, can make us weep again.

"Outside us? Inside us, rather, but hidden from our eyes in an oblivion more or less prolonged. . . . The broad daylight of habitual memory gradually fades our images of the past, wears them away until nothing remains of them and the past becomes irrecoverable . . . were it not that a few words (such as this 'head of the Ministry of Posts') had been carefully locked away in oblivion."

SECOND NATURE VERSUS A SECOND NAÏVETÉ. So the first thing one needs to know about memory and forgetting in Proust is that memory is subordinate to habit. The second thing is that for Proust there are two kinds of memory, the voluntary and the involuntary. The former is "the memory of intelligence." Responsive to our will, it gives "information . . . about the past," something "quite dead." Involuntary memory, on the other hand, comes unbidden, by chance, and full of life.

Proust's narrator, Marcel, connects involuntary memory to "the Celtic belief that the souls of those we have lost are held captive in some inferior being, in an animal, in a plant, in some inanimate object, effectively lost to us until the day (which for many never comes) when we happen to pass close to the tree, come into possession of the object that is their prison. Then they quiver, they call out to us, and as soon as we have recognized them, the spell is broken. Delivered by us, they have overcome death and they return to live with us."

In the course of *In Search of Lost Time*, the first thing that calls out to Marcel in this manner is a spoonful of herb tea holding a softened bit of "one of those squat, plump cakes called *petites madeleines*." No sooner has he tasted the tea-soaked cake than a scene from his childhood comes to mind, the Sunday morning ritual of tea and cake at the home of his aunt Léonie.

That moment of accidental recollection comes after a long account of how, as a child, he used to suffer when his mother failed to come and kiss him good night. Of interest, then, is how trivial seems the contrasting memory of drinking tea with his aunt.

That apparent triviality also marks the other cases of "involuntary memory" in Proust's novel. Each blessed recollection arises from the most mundane of prompting perceptions: the musty smell of a public lavatory in the Champs-Élysées, the buttons of his boots as he bends to undo them, some uneven flagstones in a courtyard in Paris, the sound of a spoon struck against a plate, the starchy feel of a napkin against his mouth.

Each of these past moments contains one of those "souls we have lost," its liveliness protected from the deadening force of mental habit by a guardian forgetfulness. Each, that is to say, has been forgotten in the etymological sense of having been hidden in the mind (*lethe* related to *letho*, "I am hidden") until such time as it is called from hiding to offer up something the narrator calls an essence or a truth (*aletheia*). These essences or truths are not so much in the memories themselves as in the uncanny coincidence of past and present that points to something exclusive to neither and therefore lying outside time.

"YES, YES, YES." In the days when I was writing about Proust, I had a dream in which I am a young Jewish boy living among gentiles. People seem nice enough, but there is anti-Semitism in the air, and I am silently making preparations to flee. It seems I have with me a baby elephant that I decide to leave behind—he can fend for himself, I reckon—though before I go, I fill a tub with water; it's for him to drink, but in fact he climbs into the tub, and I set to work soaping and washing his back.

I wrote this dream down in my journal but found myself, an aging gentile, wholly unable to explain its meaning or origins. Later that same day I happened to revisit a website where I'd recently listened to an old folk song, "Keep It Clean." Suddenly I realized that a bit of my dream must have come from a fragment of that song that begins, "If you want to hear that old elephant laugh, / Take him down to the river, wash his yes yes yes. . . . / Take soap and water / For to keep it clean."

In the second volume of Proust's novel, young Marcel is enchanted by the early morning sight of a peasant girl walking down a line of train cars offering coffee and milk to the passengers. Musing on why the sight strikes him so directly, he notes that he has been traveling, and therefore "my habits . . . for once were missing, and all my faculties came hurrying to take their place." A dream like mine implies that all our faculties are *always* present, always on duty, even though their gleanings don't always find their way into the watchtower brain with its spinning lights. Sometimes, however, as in this case, they make their way into the weavings of the night brain and even, assuming they survive the "state-transition amnesia" of waking, present themselves to the baffled morning.

When I wrote out my dream, I hadn't remembered that folk song, but then again the I-that-dreams hadn't forgotten it. "Remembered"/"forgotten": the terms are so binary! What name shall we give these little elephants of mental life, these traces of perception that are present but not present, noticed but not noticed? The "unthought known," say some psychologists; the fruits of "pure memory," says the philosopher Henri Bergson, or of "extreme inattention," says Samuel Beckett. They are like letters received but not yet opened, their content available to the invisible weaver of dreams because never exposed to the domesticating force of habitual thought.

THE REQUIRED GAP. Late in the novel, having found himself blessed by a whole series of involuntary memories, Marcel explains their necessary dependence on forgetfulness: "If, thanks to forgetfulness, the returning memory can throw no bridge, form no connecting link between itself and the present moment, if it has kept its distance, its isolation in the depths of a valley or on the highest peak of a mountain, then it can suddenly make us breathe a new air . . . , that purer air . . . which could induce so profound a sensation of renewal only if it had been breathed before, since the true paradise is the paradise that we have lost."

NUNC FLUENS FACIT TEMPUS; / Nunc stans facit aeternitatum. "The now that passes creates time; / The now that remains creates eternity." With this couplet the Roman philosopher Boethius helpfully suggests we should think of the present moment, the "now," as having two varieties. That surely is the case in Proust. "There had been reborn in me a veritable moment of the past," Marcel says after a flash of involuntary memory, a statement that makes most sense if we think of a moment truly "reborn" as belonging to a "now" that remains, not one "of the past." The taste of lime-blossom tea reproduces in Marcel a moment from his childhood that isn't exactly a "memory," because with it a self that had seemed "past" comes to life in the present. The time assumed to separate one "now" from another turns out not to exist, its absence revealing something extra-temporal, something belonging to "the now that remains."

If the present moment has two forms in Proust, so does the human self. The self of "the now that passes" is discontinuous, scattered in time (distended, Saint Augustine would say), so much so that the narrator suggests each iteration ought to "bear a different name from the preceding one," today's self having only a vague sense of yesterday's pleasures and pains. "What we suppose to be our love or our jealousy is never a single, continuous indivisible passion. It is composed of an infinity of successive loves, of different jealousies, each of which is ephemeral."

In contrast, there is something Proust calls "our true self" (*notre vrai moi*), a being revealed in the time collapse of involuntary memory. Past, present, and future: none of the various stations of time can sustain that self. "In the observation of the present . . . the senses cannot feed it," nor can "consideration of a past," nor can "the anticipation of a future." But "let a noise or a scent, once heard or once smelt, be heard or smelt again in the present and at the same time in the past . . . , and immediately the permanent and habitually concealed essence of things is liberated and our true self . . . is awakened."

It's worth flagging two phrases in that declaration: "at the same time": that is, these impressions are simultaneous, not successive; "habitually concealed essence": that is, true being emerges when the habits of mind usually obscuring it are suspended. The revelation of the true self requires this double forgetting—of habits of mind and of the time that would otherwise separate the present from the past.

I did see some of the women again, grown old . . . ,
wandering, desperately searching for heaven
knows what in the Virgilian groves.
—SWANN'S WAY

MAKING TIME. Not all moments of involuntary memory lead to paradise in Proust. Take the case of Charles Swann, the love-crossed hero of *Swann's Way.* Swann has a love affair with Odette, but her affections eventually fade, something Swann most fully realizes when he finds himself moved by a passage of music reminiscent of the days when he was loved. As with Marcel's madeleine, the music prompts an involuntary memory—"the forgotten refrain of happiness"—but in this case the juxtaposition of past and present reveals time's progress (from love to not-love), whereas Marcel's most typically reveal time's collapse (madeleine to madeleine).

Typically but not always, for Marcel also has moments of involuntary but time-marked memory, upsetting recollections that reveal how greatly things have changed. That overheard remark about "the head of the Ministry of Posts" gives him a stab of pain because Gilberte is no longer his sweetheart. More striking still is the scene in which Marcel, revisiting the seaside resort of Balbec, bends to unbutton his boots and suddenly recalls the time when his grandmother had helped him with that simple task. With that memory, he finally knows fully that his grandmother has died, and he weeps.

Such are the "nows" that pass. Odette's love has passed, Gilberte's love has passed, his grandmother's life has passed. The forgetting that has held each of these facts at bay might best be described as a species of dissociative amnesia. "That didn't happen!" the mind declares, walling itself off from the painful real, refusing its proper burial. But then an apparently trivial trigger—a snatch of music, an overheard remark, a simple gesture—eludes the guardian amnesia, and of a sudden comes the understanding that the "now" of the past has truly passed, the memory recovered from the far side of oblivion revealing the self to be contingent, mortal, a creature of time.

James Turrell, *Roden Crater* (1975–);
Painted Desert region, northern Arizona

FROM THE MUSEUM OF FORGETTING. A series of tunnels, rooms, and apertures carved into a volcanic cinder cone, James Turrell's *Roden Crater* offers a staged environment for the perception and contemplation of astronomical light.

Prior to his 1975 acquisition of the crater, Turrell had visited archaeological sites in Mexico and Central America and found that he was always attracted to spaces that no longer served any civic or religious purpose. The structures abandoned at Palenque, Uxmal, Chichén Itzá, Copán, or Tikal have all been "emptied of their use" by the passage of time. And yet they continue to have presence. "I'm interested in public places that are devoid of their function," says Turrell. "The impact of the space of the Gothic cathedral, for example, and the light within it, is much more interesting to me than the rhetoric that is spoken there."

The length of time needed to strip Mayan buildings of their purpose gets radically expanded by the temporal setting of *Roden Crater*. The volcanic cone itself is at least 400,000 years old; it rises from a Late Triassic plateau 225 million years old. Ancient, yes, but just a gateway to even more inhuman spans of time. "I wanted the stage set of geological time," says Turrell, "so you're out of the time set of the construction of mankind" and "on the way to astronomical time," the time of the four-billion-year-old sun, of light echoing still from the edges of the thirteen-billion-year-old universe.

To the degree that our minds can entertain such vast reaches of time, the things of human memory become vanishingly small. The Orphic burials in southern Italy are small, and Italy is small. The birth of Jesus and the flight into Egypt are small, and Egypt is small. The former lives of the Buddha as recounted in the Pali canon are small. The Battle of Kosovo, the slave trade, Indian removal, the descendants of Andrew Hyde, psychoanalytic theory, Guernica, the hurricane of '38 . . . Human history fades before the incandescent flash of a meteor over *Roden Crater*; it vanishes in the sheen of unknowing that is the light of distant stars.

IT MUST HAVE BEEN THANKSGIVING or some such holiday, because I have shown up at my brother's house to find Mother and Father waiting. Mother stands in the front hall bearing her old smile of greeting, overlaid now with a touch of anxiety because, I realize, she doesn't remember my name. "Lewis is here!" I call out, as if such announcements were our custom. I don't want to embarrass her. "Lewis is here!"

THE UNPAID BILL. Sometime in the 1920s in Berlin, a certain Dr. Kurt Lewin noticed that the waiters were very good at remembering the particulars of his restaurant bill—until the bill was paid. Soon settled, soon forgotten. Lewin wondered if he hadn't stumbled upon a fact of mental life, that the finished task drops into oblivion more easily than the unfinished.

In 1927, a colleague of Lewin's, Bluma Zeigarnik, designed a study that appeared to show that Lewin had observed a specific example of the general case, now called the Zeigarnik effect. "Unfinished tasks are remembered approximately twice as well as completed ones," she concluded. That was her finding with adults; with children, the effect was stronger: not only did they remember tasks they'd been forced to leave unfinished, but "not infrequently they would beg to continue the interrupted tasks even two or three days after the experiment was over."

Zeigarnik's explanation of the effect seems a touch obvious (each task brings a "quasi-need for completion" or a "tension system which tends toward resolution," and memory endures when these are not discharged), but her conclusions are clear: "Strong needs, impatience to gratify them, a childlike and natural approach—the more there is of these, the more will unfinished tasks enjoy in memory a special advantage." On the other hand, memory of a completed task—even if driven by need, impatience, or childlike enthusiasm—soon disappears. Pay your bill and the waiter moves on.

ZEIGARNIK AND HISTORY. Pay your bill and the waiter moves on. Or, win your war, erect a few statues, and everyone moves on. It is the battle lost, not the battle won, that clings to the mind. What never found satisfying closure becomes the opening chapter of a story that cannot be forgotten. The seceding states' "Lost Cause" makes for a durable tale precisely because the Confederacy was defeated. So too with the Battle of Kosovo and its unforgettable hero, the martyred lord Lazar Hrebeljanović. The Virgin Mary sent a gray falcon to give Lazar a choice; by now no one would know his name had he chosen to win the battle rather than ascend to heaven immediately. But loss is what he chose, and therefore neither the assassin of Archduke Ferdinand nor the apologists for the Bosnian war had to strike any new sparks to set a dormant enmity aflame.

ZEIGARNIKING HEMINGWAY. When Ernest Hemingway's wife lost a suitcase containing the only copies of many of his stories, he found he was unable to re-create them. They were done and gone. A character in a posthumously published short story, "The Strange Country," explains:

> "Some of the stories had been about boxing, and some about baseball and others about horse racing. They were the things I had known best and had been closest to and several were about the first war. Writing them I had felt all the emotion I had to feel about those things and I had put it all in and all the knowledge of them that I could express and I had rewritten and rewritten until it was all in them and all gone out of me.
>
> "Because I had worked on newspapers since I was very young I could never remember anything once I had written it down; as each day you wiped your memory clear with writing as you might wipe a blackboard clear with a sponge or a wet rag."

SEX VERSUS NONSENSE. Modern studies of the Zeigarnik effect have been inconclusive, leading some now to think it does not exist. To my mind, however, the studies have been poorly designed. Typically, undergraduate test subjects are either interrupted or not while doing the most banal of tasks: rearranging letters in nonsense syllables, remembering strings of consonants, or solving anagrams ("ibrd" should be "bird"—that sort of thing). Not surprisingly, the results have been mixed. Subjects interrupted while solving anagrams, for example, had no better memory of what they were doing than students allowed to finish.

I wish they'd take two groups of undergraduates and interrupt half of them while they were cashing a paycheck or making love. Memories of emotional states are processed by the amygdalae, and I bet those nonsense syllables never light up those organs. Desire seeks completion and unrequited desire does not easily abandon the search. Money or sex, a war against the infidels or a pilgrimage to the promised land: should the finish line be reached, the memory thins out, but the unfinished hangs around for years, for decades, for generations. In fact, time itself may be a creation of all the undone stuff that clings to the mind. Past, present, and future do not exist, argued Saint Augustine; what does exist are temporal states that stretch out the mind, and from the distended mind arise the sleepless nights, the years, the decades. . . .

FREE FORGETTING. Why might we repeatedly read a classic work of literature, or go to a play we've seen before, or listen again to a familiar symphony? After all, at a certain point we know what will happen. The first time through *Swann's Way*, it is a surprise that Swann marries Odette, and such unexpected turns are part of the novel's pleasures. Why read the book a second time?

Such is the puzzle posed in an essay by Edward Cone, the American composer and music theorist, and Cone has an answer that he illustrates with what seems a particularly pointed case, that of mystery stories. The first time we read of Sherlock Holmes and "The Adventure of the Speckled Band," we may wonder, as does Holmes, if the "band" isn't a band of gypsies, but by the end of the story the "band" turns out to be a spotted swamp adder, "the deadliest snake in India." A surprise, surely, and a satisfying one, but only on a first reading. Why ever go back?

Cone's real interest is music, and the Holmes example is but an introduction to "a full-fledged mystery story" in a composition by Brahms. The first time we listen to Intermezzo, op. 118, no. 1, we may be puzzled as to the tonic. Is the key the F major suggested by the opening? Or the C major of the first cadence? No—it's A minor! A surprise on a first hearing, but not so forever after. Why go back again and again?

Cone's response outlines the growing intimacy we get from repeated exposure to such classics. In a First Reading (or Hearing), we are naïve, misled sometimes, confused, astonished, impressed. . . . In a Second Reading, obscurity and surprise disappear, and we can attend to how the thing is made. "Mystery and suspense are banished from this reading, which admits of no emotional involvement on the part of the reader—except perhaps that resulting from his admiration of the writer's technique." No longer confined to the temporal sequence of events, we come to see the atemporal structure. The Second Reading "treats the story, not as a work of art that owes its effect to progress through time, but as an object abstracted . . . , a static art-object that can be contemplated timelessly." In "The Adventure of the Speckled Band," we are told who the killer is halfway through the story, even before we've come to the scene of the crime; on a First Reading, we might not believe what we're told—it's too obvious! Only on a Second Reading can we see the complexity of Arthur Conan Doyle's design, how he plays with our expectations.

The insights of a Second Reading open the way for a play of memory and forgetting in all later readings. The Third Reading, like the First, experiences the work as a thing in time, one element following upon another from start to finish, but now, enlightened by the atemporal Second Reading, the naïve pleasures of the First are replaced by "informed appreciation." At the same time, however, "this reading requires an intentional 'forgetting.' For . . . one must concentrate on each event as it comes, trying to suppress from consciousness those elements meant to be concealed until some later point in the story." The pattern discovered in the Second Reading "still exerts its control, but it must do so invisibly and silently. To be sure, it can never really be forgotten, but in the Third Reading it must remain hidden."

"Forgetting" here means the kind of mental sequestering I earlier described in regard to forgetting the future ("forget about going to Carthage next year," "forget about using the car tonight"). Let us now call this "free forgetting" (or "free dissociation") to underline the presence of choice. In this game of mental hide-and-seek, the forgotten pattern of the Second Reading is hidden and revealed at will. To play that game is one of the joys of any art worthy of repeated visits. On a Third Reading of Swann's first night of intimacy with Odette, knowing from the First the depths of her duplicity, we take pleasure in Proust's skill at simultaneously concealing and revealing the larger story.

As with free association, free forgetting and free remembering are marks of a nimble mind, and as such, Cone's model of moving at will among distinct temporal registers while reading (or listening, or being) offers a nice way to imagine creative and spiritual self-forgetfulness, for in these too, consciousness is nimble, free to quit the self and free to return, confined not by pride or shame or dementia.

MR. FORSTER FORGETS. E. M. Forster opens an essay on "anonymity" by pointing out that we know absolutely nothing about the author of the ballad "Sir Patrick Spens" but we know a great deal about the author of *The Rime of the Ancient Mariner*. We know Samuel Taylor Coleridge "ran away from Cambridge; he enlisted as a Dragoon under the name of Trooper Comberback, but fell so constantly from his horse that it had to be withdrawn from beneath him permanently; he was employed instead upon matters relating to sanitation; he married Southey's sister, and gave lectures; he become stout, pious and dishonest, took opium and died."

Much can be said about one author and nothing at all about the other. So what? What difference does the difference make?

None, really, says Forster. There's always *information* to be had about the circumstances of a work of art, but that isn't what makes it art. Whoever offers information—"he married Southey's sister"—ought to sign his name to the account so as to be held responsible for its veracity. But worldly facts are not what matter in art. "While we are reading *The Ancient Mariner* we forget our astronomy and geography and daily ethics. Do we not also forget the author? Does not Samuel Taylor Coleridge, lecturer, opium eater, and dragoon, disappear along with the rest of the world of information . . . ? While we read *The Ancient Mariner* a change takes place in it. It becomes anonymous, like the *Ballad of Sir Patrick Spens*."

Such is Forster's idea: "All literature tends towards a condition of anonymity." It "wants not to be signed." Literature is a living thing distinct from the living person who made it. "To forget its Creator is one of the functions of a Creation."

As for interest in the author's personality, that is a modern concern and tends to simplify what is in fact complex. "Each human mind has two personalities, one on the surface, one deeper down." The latter is "a very queer affair"; there is "something general about it," and into it a man must dip his bucket occasionally if he wishes to make "first-class work." The "lower personality" is "the force that makes for anonymity," for what is found there is not the stuff of dinner parties, sanitation work, or military service. All such matters of individual identity drop away in deep-bucket labors. "The poet wrote the poem no doubt, but he forgot himself while he wrote it, and we forget him while we read."

Forster offers, by way of counterpoint, "two writers who are not first class," Charles Lamb and Robert Louis Stevenson. Such men "always write with their surface-personalities and never let down buckets into their underworld." They "append their names in full to every sentence they write." True artists, on the other hand (Dante, Shakespeare), invite us to attend not to themselves but to the "world they have created" and to become "in a sense co-partners in it." Coleridge may not be Shakespeare, but he too invites us to be co-partners in his world, and as we read, "we forget for ten minutes his name and our own." "This temporary forgetfulness, this momentary and mutual anonymity," Forster argues, "is surely evidence of good stuff."

AMBITION. Ewan MacColl was a British singer-songwriter, leader of the 1950s British folk revival, and author of "The First Time Ever I Saw Your Face." According to his wife, Peggy Seeger, his one great ambition was to write a song "that would sink so deep into the memory of a nation that they would forget who made it up—and he did just that."

You can tell anything but on condition that you never say: I.
—Marcel Proust to André Gide

Promise me one thing: from now on, never write I *any more. . . . In art, you see, there is no first person.*
—Oscar Wilde to André Gide

FORGET MARRIAGE. Behind much self-forgetting lies some species of idealism. In his essay on anonymity, E. M. Forster imagines that the writers found in the so-called Greek Anthology were after "the poem, not the poet," and that "by continuous rehandling"—writing the same lyric over and over in slightly changed language—"the perfect expression natural to the poem may be attained." And when he says that the deep personality is common, not individual—it's inside Coleridge, but it isn't his—he adds that "the mystic will assert that the common quality is God." And the mark of the deeper self in art is "something general . . . , namely beauty."

As I say, idealism lies beyond the forgotten, surface self: beauty, "perfect expression," a "natural" thing, a thing the mystics know.

When I read Forster's essay carefully, I begin to wonder if ideal self-forgetting in this case doesn't also contain a hidden challenge. Is it significant that the essay makes several passing references to marriage? It's not just that Coleridge "married Southey's sister" (though even that is a bit odd—he could have given us her name), but among the questions asked of the surface person we find not only "What is his name?" and "Where did he live?" but "Was he married?" And, conversely, in the deep self, where "there are no names," there is also "no marrying or giving in marriage."

We're reading an essay, not a novel, so it may be less a violation of Forster's aesthetic to bring the life to bear on the work and say that for a closeted gay novelist writing in 1925 (and faced, for example, with the option of taking on that old story, that cultural habit of mind, the marriage plot) to consign conventional marriage to the surface is to suggest that in the deep personality, marriage is something more than his readers know. "Only connect." Forget the marriage plot. Think of love.

PLOTLESS. Montaigne, in his essay "On Books," complains that in his day the authors of comedies "use three or four plots from Terence or Plautus" or pile up "five or six stories from Boccaccio" to make one new play. And why? Because they cannot support themselves "by their own graces" and therefore lean on borrowed plots. The opposite is the case with a great poet like Horace: "The perfections and beauties of his style of expression make us lose our appetite for his subject. His distinction and elegance hold us throughout; he is everywhere so delightful . . . , and so fills our soul with his charms, that we forget those of his plot."

In a true work of narrative art, plot is what Alfred Hitchcock called a MacGuffin. The plot of *Citizen Kane* concerns a reporter's attempt to solve the mystery of a tycoon's dying word, "Rosebud," a mystery that is at last resolved in the movie's closing shot. But plot is not what has made *Citizen Kane* endure. After the first viewing, you can forget it; the film that Orson Welles made stays with us, and can be watched again and again, because of "the perfections and beauties of his style of expression."

Christian Marclay made a twenty-four-hour-long montage of scenes from the movies, each brief clip containing an image of, or reference to, a particular time of day, the film as a whole being shown so that screen time is synchronized with actual time. If you are sitting in the theater at 3:14 p.m., the scene playing on the screen will contain a clock or wristwatch showing that exact time. What is surprising is how not boring is *The Clock*, not boring because almost all the scenes are little gems of cinematic style, gems supported "by their own graces."

Thousands of scenes go by, none of them offering the plot they once inhabited; the pleasures of cinema are not at all diluted by that absence, not diluted because plot is a forgettable MacGuffin.

The *ars oblivionis* is a formalist art.

MEANINGLESS. "The chief use of the 'meaning' of a poem, in the ordinary sense, may be . . . to satisfy one habit of the reader, to keep his mind diverted and quiet, while the poem does its work upon him: much as the imaginary burglar is always provided with a bit of nice meat for the house-dog. This is an ordinary situation of which I approve," says T. S. Eliot.

Non-site, Amarillo Sand: The End of Biological Time (no date); sand, commercial sandbox (10' × 10'), and map. Collection of the author's mind

FROM THE MUSEUM OF FORGETTING. The sand in this installation comes from the site, seventeen miles northwest of Amarillo, Texas, where Robert Smithson died in a plane crash, July 20, 1973. He was at the time searching for a location for what became, after his death, the earthwork known as *Amarillo Ramp*. Of such searches, Smithson once said, "When I get to a site that strikes the kind of timeless chord, I use it. The site selection is by chance. There is no willful choice. A site at zero degree, where the material strikes the mind, where absences become apparent, appeals to me, where the disintegrating of space and time seems very apparent. Sort of an end of selfhood—the ego vanishes for a while."

"INSTRUCTIONS FOR THE COOK." Zen master Eihei Dogen, the man whose writings include the aphorism "to study the self is to forget the self," was born in Japan in the year A.D. 1200. He entered a monastery when he was about thirteen, eventually working with a teacher who had been to China and knew the lineage of Chinese Zen. In 1223, Dogen himself traveled to China. The journey was rough, and Dogen got sick, so he stayed onboard to recover after reaching the port.

One day, the cook from a local monastery came to the ship to buy Japanese mushrooms for a noodle soup he was going to make for the monks. The man was old, he had walked a dozen miles to make his purchase, and ahead of him lay a long return journey. Dogen suggested he spend the night; surely his kitchen duties could wait. "Why don't you study the words of the ancient masters rather than troubling yourself by being the cook?" Dogen asked.

The man laughed. "Good man from a foreign country, you do not yet understand practice or know the meaning of the words of ancient masters."

Dogen felt ashamed. "What are words? What is practice?" he asked.

"If you penetrate your questions, you can't fail to become a person of understanding," the cook replied. "The sun will soon be down. I must hurry." And he left.

The revelation for Dogen was that Buddhist practice does not consist in studying the sutras and staying up all night enjoying subtle points of doctrine. Every mindful action is practice—walking a long distance, making noodle soup, buying mushrooms.

Dogen's later discourse, "Instructions for the Cook,"

clarifies the lesson. Every action can express the Buddha Way, no matter how ordinary. To be a monastery cook "is a buddha's practice." All that's needed is the presence of the Way-seeking mind—the one that does not make a drama out of its likes and dislikes or amuse itself with words. "Do not arouse disdainful mind when you prepare a broth of wild grasses; do not arouse joyful mind when you prepare a fine cream soup. . . . If this is not yet clear to you it is because your thoughts run around like a wild horse and your feelings jump about like a monkey in the forest."

"DO NOT AROUSE DISDAINFUL MIND." As we have seen in several cases, forgetting can mean nonaction. "We can forget about going to Carthage" means we won't be taking that trip (not that we can't talk and daydream about it), or from ancient Athens to modern South Africa a grant of amnesty means no legal action will be taken (not that people can't think, gossip, and write about the crime in question).

The forgetting that belongs to meditation practice ("study the self to forget the self") entails much more radical nonaction. Meditation typically consists in keeping the attention focused on something simple, like the breath. That turns out to be quite difficult; I can rarely get to ten breaths before my attention wanders. Feelings like a monkey, thoughts like a wild horse: body and mind keep disturbing the concentration. Previously dormant itches flare up and call for immediate scratching; thoughts tumble through the mind. The practice then amounts to returning to the breath rather than scratching or following the thought. Dogen called it *shikantaza*, "just sitting," breathing naturally in an upright posture, and doing nothing with those restless horses and leaping monkeys.

All thoughts and feelings are the seeds of possible actions; when we let them blossom into actual actions (physical or mental), they bear the fruit of individual self. I scratch an itch and now I am a Person-Who-Scratches. I daydream about fixing a leaky faucet or building a walnut bookcase and I am the Handyman. I fret about some stupid remark and I am the Dummy. Following a train of thought or acting on an impulse is the elemental form of self-making. Not acting but instead returning to the breath is the elemental form of self-forgetting.

THE NORTHERNER. All these preoccupations that I carried out of childhood, when I take action in regard to any of them (even in the simplest sense of entertaining them in mind), they become my identity (from classical Latin, *idem*, the same), and with identity comes difference, so much so that even attributes we usually value can become divisive. Thinking of my pride in having worked in the civil rights movement, I was struck by a remark reported in Harry MacLean's book about the Klansman James Ford Seale and the Dee-Moore murder trial. A local citizen notes that he sees no hope of putting Mississippi's past behind it: "It'll go on forever. You guys need Mississippi down on the bottom, just like the whites in Mississippi needed the blacks down on the bottom. Human nature, I guess."

Ouch.

NOTHING EVOLVES. "To forget the self" can mean abandoning one's habits of mind (as in Proust, or as in James Turrell's advice to drop our "prejudicial perception"), the promise being that we might freshly perceive a world otherwise obscured by habit's filters. In actual meditation practice, however, even fresh perception drops away. Returning to the breath doesn't give rise to original theories or works of art. Elizabeth Bishop's "Darwin letter" imagines the young scientist having "a self-forgetful, perfectly useless concentration," but if that state leads Darwin to his idea about the origin of species, then it is not the self-forgetting of Dogen. Had Darwin been a student of Zen, then during his time on the cushion he would have had to return to the breath and forget about his brilliant idea. He might have had to say, as Agnes Martin did, "I had a hard time giving up evolution," but such is the practice of radical nonaction.

CLOSURE. When Odysseus slays the suitors at the end of the *Odyssey*, there is a risk that those killings will trigger yet another round of grief, anger, and revenge. In fact, Eupithes, father of the first man slain, unsheathes his sword and calls for vengeance, saying—in words liable to invoke the Furies—that a "grief that cannot be forgotten" has seized him. At this point, Zeus intervenes: Odysseus has done enough—his honor has been restored, he will be king again—and now "we, for our part, will blot out the memory / of sons and brothers slain. As in the old time / let men of Ithaca henceforth be friends." The needed forgetting is authored by the gods, not by mortals, as if in Homeric times the forgetting of discord were an art as yet foreign to humankind. Note that when Zeus blots out the memory of strife, the story comes to its end. Plots are fueled by memory-as-action; forgetting as nonaction brings the epic to a close.

THE FORGETTABLE LIFE. Plato's "Myth of Er" has it that the souls of the dead get to choose the life they will lead when next reborn. Er witnesses several famous souls making their choices, the last of these being Odysseus: "Now the memory of former sufferings having cured him of all ambition, he looked around for a long time to find the uneventful life of an ordinary man. He had some difficulty in finding this, which was lying about and had been neglected by everybody else; and when he saw it . . . he chose it with joy."

We have no story of this "ordinary man," for his is a life that brings no glory, no *kleos*. It is a forgettable life, not a memorable one. Perhaps the reborn Odysseus, the happily uncelebrated man, still walks among us, living in a manner that leaves no mark on memory.

Forgetfulness . . . is a great aid to interpretation.
—Frank Kermode

TO THE READER. I claim no strong connection between forgetfulness and this book's episodic form, but if there is one, it most likely lies in the way that juxtaposition encourages not just free association but free forgetting. Jumping from one thing to another, the entries decline to declare a train of thought. I realize that putting macho Nietzsche next to Hitler's abandoned bunker, for example, may be thought provoking and that some readers will bridge the gap with their own transitional abstraction. Myself, I leave it alone. Interpretation too readily declared dims the lights of things; holding off allows the elements to glow.

Readers then, as they cross the divide between any two entries, will enjoy or suffer their own level of state-transition amnesia. Some entries will fade immediately, others linger in the mind, and some disappear, only to later return unbidden, involuntary memory having drawn upon its treasure chest of oblivion. The spaces between entries foreground what happens with any book we read: we retain some things as we go along, while others drop away until, finally, out of the keepers and the discards, we extract the unique book of our own engagement. Unless we kill a book by committing it to memory, active imagination ("memory and oblivion, we call that imagination") will make for us the book that is our book. The episodic form acknowledges the collaged afterlife of anything we read—or of any life, for that matter, for we too are discontinuous creatures, scattered in time, the meaning of our existence something we can only imagine.

BIRD BUDDHA. Writes Zen master Dogen, "When a bird flies in the sky, beasts do not even dream of finding or following its trace. . . . However, a bird can see traces of hundreds and thousands of small birds having passed in flocks, or traces of so many lines of large birds having flown south or north. . . . In this way, a bird sees birds' traces. Buddhas are like this."

We moderns—we who remember Darwin—might say yes, a flying bird leaves no trace, but nonetheless, given the primordial history of migration, each bird has an evolved sense of the traceless trace left by its ancestors. It knows which way to fly in each given season.

Not all actions are the same. Returning to the breath, the action of nonaction, is distinct and gives rise to a distinct kind of self—the true self, the Buddhists call it, or simply the Buddha. "Sitting is non-doing," wrote Dogen, and "sitting itself is the practice of the Buddha." The passage in Dogen that begins "To study the Buddha Way is to study the self" ends with a subtle awakening as the body and mind of self drop away: "There is a trace of realization that cannot be grasped. We endlessly express this ungraspable trace of realization." Another translation figures that grasping and not-grasping in terms of forgetting: body and mind fall away, and then "we can forget the mental trace of realization, and show the real signs of forgotten realization continually, moment by moment."

In this practice, that is to say, awakening may well mark the practitioner's mind but not with a mark to be acted upon or remembered. No "I" will claim it as an identity. Nonetheless, it leaves a trace that other birds can see. Dogen noticed how the cook walked back to the monastery with the mushrooms.

THE TRACELESS TRACE. Alberto Caeiro was one of the many pseudonyms of the Portuguese poet Fernando Pessoa. Here is a poem written under that name:

Rather the flight of the bird passing and leaving no trace
Than creatures passing, leaving tracks on the ground.
The bird goes by and forgets, which is as it should be.
The creature, no longer there, and so, perfectly useless,
Shows it was there—also perfectly useless.

Remembering betrays Nature,
Because yesterday's Nature is not Nature.
What's past is nothing and remembering is not seeing.

Fly, bird, fly away; teach me to disappear.

Sources

WHAT THIS IS

3 ***What This Is***: Walter J. Ong, *Orality and Literacy* (New York: Routledge, 2002), 46.

NOTEBOOK I: MYTH

10 ***To the reader***: Aphorism 621, adapted from Friedrich Nietzsche, *Human, All Too Human* (New York: Cambridge University Press, 1996), 196.

11 ***Miraculous***: *Conversing with Cage*, ed. Richard Kostelanetz (New York: Limelight, 1991), 119; John Cage, *Silence* (Middletown, Conn.: Wesleyan University Press, 1961), 136; John Cage, *The Ten Thousand Things* (Pasadena, Calif.: MicroFest Records, 2013). For Dogen, see "Actualizing the Fundamental Point: *Genjō Kōan*," in *Moon in a Dewdrop: Writings of Zen Master Dogen* (San Francisco: North Point Press, 1985), 69–73;

Shohaku Okumura, *Realizing Genjokoan: The Key to Dogen's Shobogenzo* (Boston: Wisdom, 2010), 1–5.

12 ***The twin goddess***: Hesiod, *Theogony* 93–103.

14 ***Gary Snyder***: *Riprap and Cold Mountain Poems* (Berkeley, Calif.: Counterpoint, 2010), 3.

15 ***In the desert***: Paul Bowles, *Travels: Collected Writings, 1950–1993* (New York: Ecco, 2011), 75.

16 ***A story out of Plato***: Plato, *Republic* 614–21.

17 ***"A musical instrument reminding you"***: Plato, *Phaedrus* 248c–d; Plato, *Phaedo* 72–76; Plato, *Philebus* 33c–34c; Plato, *Seventh Letter* 344a–b.

19 ***American epistemology***: Herman Melville, *The Confidence-Man* (New York: Dix, Edwards, 1857), 26–35.

22 ***"The precipitate"***: Ludwig Wittgenstein, *Philosophical Investigations* (New York: Macmillan, 1953), ix; David Markson, *This Is Not a Novel* (Washington, D.C.: Counterpoint, 2001), 1 and 128.

24 ***Speechless***: J. Hackin, *Asiatic Mythology* (New Delhi: Asian Educational Services, 1994), 368.

25 ***Remember who you are***: *Borges at Eighty: Conversations*, ed. Willis Barnstone (Bloomington: Indiana University Press, 1982), 17.

26 ***Against insomnia***: Francis Crick and Graeme Mitchison, "The Function of Dream Sleep," *Nature* 304 (1983): 111–14; Jorge Luis Borges, *Ficciones* (New York: Knopf, 1993), 90.

27 ***State-transition amnesia***: For nepenthe, see Homer, *Odyssey* 4.220–89; for stoned students and "amnesic effect," see James Eric Eich, "The Cue-Dependent Nature of State-Dependent Retrieval," *Memory and Cognition* 8, no. 2 (1980): 157–73.

29 ***Grandma Hyde versus Foucault***: Michel Foucault, "Nietzsche, Genealogy, History," in *Language, Counter-memory, Practice* (Ithaca, N.Y.: Cornell University Press, 1977), 145.

30 ***From the Museum of Forgetting: The Two Waters***: My translation derives from several sources. See especially Richard Janko, "Forgetfulness in the Golden Tablets of Memory," *Classical Quarterly*, n.s., 34, no. 1 (1984): 89–100.

33 ***The Two Waters—an oracle***: Marcel Detienne, *The Masters of Truth in Archaic Greece* (New York: Zone Books, 1996), 63–64, 84; Pausanias, *Description of Greece* 9.39.3–14. See also theoi.com/Khthonios/Trophonios.html.

35 ***Badminton***: Søren Kierkegaard, *Either/Or*, 2 vols. (Princeton, N.J.: Princeton University Press, 1944), 1:241.

37 ***Mímir's skull***: Ovid, *Metamorphosis* 11; Jacqueline Simpson, "Mímir: Two Myths or One?," *Saga-Book of the Viking Society for Northern Research* 16 (1962–65): 41–53, esp. 44–45, 50; Anne Ross, "Severed Heads in Wells: An Aspect of the Well Cult," *Scottish Studies* 6, no. 1 (1962): 31–48, esp. 34, 36, 41; Ralph Metzner, *The Well of Remembrance* (Boston: Shambala, 1994), 219; A. LeRoy Andrews, "Old Norse Notes:

Some Observations on Mímir," *Modern Language Notes* 43, no. 3 (March 1928): 166–71, esp. 168; Snorri Sturluson, *The Prose Edda*, trans. Arthur Gilchrist Brodeur (New York: American-Scandinavian Foundation, 1916), 27, 79–80; Bruce Lincoln, "Waters of Memory, Waters of Forgetfulness," in *Death, War, and Sacrifice* (Chicago: University of Chicago Press, 1991), 54–55; *The Poetic Edda*, trans. Carolyne Larrington (New York: Oxford University Press, 1996), 10. For Byron, see Thomas Medwin, *Conversations of Lord Byron*, 2nd ed. (London: Henry Colburn, 1824), 87–89; "Lines Inscribed upon a Cup Formed from a Skull," in *The Poetical Works of Lord Byron* (London: John Murray, 1868), 539.

38 ***Waters bubble up***: Lincoln, "Waters of Memory, Waters of Forgetfulness," 49–61; *Kausitaki Upanishad* 1.4, in ibid., 52–53; Sturluson, *Gylfaginning* 4, in ibid., 54.

39 ***Two categories***: *Borges at Eighty*, 21.

40 ***No family, no mother***: Roland Barthes, *Camera Lucida*, trans. Richard Howard (New York: Hill and Wang, 1990), 65, 67, 71, 74.

41 ***Forgotten is also true***: Heraclitus, frag. 123. For discussion of this line, see perceiverations.wordpress.com/heraclitus-fragment-123/. Detienne, *Masters of Truth*, 16, 42–43, 52, 81. Homer, *Iliad* 2.591–602.

43 ***The birth of a memory art***: Cicero, *De Oratore* 86.351–54.

45 ***Testes***: *Ad Herennium* 3.22.33–35.

46 ***Drawn down into time***: Detienne, *Masters of Truth*, 51, 109–10.

48 ***Boredom***: Susan P. Montague, conference lecture, trobriandsindepth.com/Trobriand%20CVs/MontagueCV.pdf.

49 ***Liquidation***: Judith Herman, *Trauma and Recovery* (New York: Basic Books, 1992), 195; Pierre Janet, *Psychological Healing*, trans. Eden Paul and Cedar Paul, 2 vols. (New York: Macmillan, 1925), 1:661, 665 (emphasis omitted).

51 ***Sorting the dead***: Virgil, *Aeneid* 6.317–30.

52 ***In Fiji***: Cited by Jane E. Harrison in a book review, *Classical Review* 17, no. 1 (Feb. 1903): 85.

53 ***In Anne Michaels's novel***: *Fugitive Pieces* (New York: Vintage, 1998), 25.

54 ***"Let go"***: www.facebook.com/womanstandsshining/posts/2020234734919981.

55 ***"Teach me I am forgotten"***: Robert D. Richardson Jr., *Emerson: The Mind on Fire* (Berkeley: University of California Press, 1996), 110.

56 ***Blood at the root***: Cicero, *De Oratore*.

57 ***An altar to oblivion***: Plutarch, *Moralia, Volume VIII: Table-Talk, Books 1–6*, trans. P. A. Clement and H. B. Hoffleit, Loeb Classical Library 424 (Cambridge, Mass.: Harvard University Press, 1969), 249. See also Herodotus, *The Persian Wars* 8.55.

58 ***Endless***: *New York Times*, April 14, 2015.

59 ***Mixing myth and history***: Plutarch, *Moralia*.

60 ***The tyranny***: Xenophon, *Hellenica* 2.3.56 and 2.4.20–22.

62 ***The death of Polemarchus***: *Lysias*, trans. W. R. M. Lamb, Loeb Classical Library 244 (Cambridge, Mass.: Harvard University Press, 1930), 233.

63 ***The unforgettable***: Homer, *Odyssey* 14.174; Sophocles, *Electra* 221–24, 1246–50. For "forces of insomnia," see Nicole Loraux, *The Divided City: On Memory and Forgetting in Ancient Athens* (New York: Zone Books, 2006), 163.

65 ***The terms of peace***: Aristotle, *The Athenian Constitution* 38.4, 39.1–5, 40.3. See the version translated by P. J. Rhodes (New York: Penguin Books, 1984), 82–85.

66 ***Forget about it***: Ludwig Wittgenstein, *Philosophical Investigations*, trans. G. E. M. Anscombe (New York: Macmillan, 1953), 16.

67 ***The oath***: Loraux, *Divided City*, 39, 149; Aeschylus, *Eumenides* 382; Adriaan M. Lanni, "Transitional Justice in Ancient Athens: A Case Study," *University of Pennsylvania Journal of International Law* 32 (2010): 569–71.

69 ***"Acts of Oblivion"***: Bernadette A. Meyler, "Forgetting Oblivion: The Demise of the Legislative Pardon" (Cornell Law Faculty Working Papers, paper 83, 2011), 14, 15n, 19–20, 34, scholarship.law.cornell.edu /clsops_paper/83.

70 ***The philtrum***: Louis Ginsberg, *The Legends of the Jews: From the Creation to Jacob* (Philadelphia: Jewish Publication Society of America, 1909), 56–58.

71 ***Babble***: Roman Jakobson, *Child Language, Aphasia, and Phonological Universals* (Paris: Mouton, 1968), 21, 25. For this reference and several others, I am indebted to Daniel Heller-Roazen's *Echolalias: On the Forgetting of Language* (New York: Zone Books, 2005).

NOTEBOOK II: SELF

80 ***The empty studio***: *It Is*, no. 5 (Spring 1960): 37, as cited in *New York School, the First Generation* (Los Angeles: Los Angeles County Museum of Art, 1965), 16.

81 ***The Darwin letter***: Elizabeth Bishop to Anne Stevenson, Jan. 8–20, 1964. See Anne Stevenson, *Elizabeth Bishop* (New York: Twayne, 1966), 66, and Lloyd Schwartz and Sybil P. Estess, eds., *Elizabeth Bishop and Her Art* (Ann Arbor: University of Michigan Press, 1983), 288.

84 ***A short history of habit***: William James, *The Principles of Psychology*, 2 vols. (New York: Henry Holt, 1890), 1:121. Pater's remark is from *Studies in the History of the Renaissance* (1873); Bergson's is from *Matter and Memory* (1896). See David Gross, "Bergson, Proust, and the Revaluation of Memory," *International Philosophical Quarterly* 25 (Dec. 1985): 369–80; Philip Fisher, "The Failure of Habit," in *Uses of Literature*, ed. Monroe Engel (Cambridge, Mass.: Harvard University Press, 1973), 3–18; Marcel Proust, *In Search of Lost Time*, trans. C. K. Scott Moncrieff and Terence Kilmartin, revised by D. J. Enright, 6 vols. (New York: Modern Library, 1992), 1:238.

85 ***From the Museum of Forgetting***: "Francis Picabia," in *Dada in the Collection of the Museum of Modern Art*, ed. Anne Upland et al. (New York: Museum of Modern Art, 2008), 241–45.

87 ***Tribal scars***: For "You have to be somebody . . . ," see Andrew Cohen, "The 1001 Forms of Self-Grasping: An Interview with Jack Engler," *What Is Enlightenment?* 17 (June 30, 2000). See also the discussion of "somebody/nobody" in *Psychoanalysis and Buddhism*, ed. Jeremy D. Safran (Boston: Wisdom, 2003).

92 ***Sweeping the tomb***: My telling of case 5 is indebted to a talk by John Tarrant, Sept. 13, 1992, Oakland, California, online at www.sacred-texts.com/bud/zen/case5trn.txt. See also *The Gateless Barrier*, trans. Robert Aitken (San Francisco: North Point Press, 1991), 38.

94 ***"Ease and cheer"***: Emanuel Lasker, *Lasker's Manual of Chess* (New York: E. P. Dutton, 1927; repr., New York: Dover, 1960), 337.

99 ***Feed on the present***: From a July 3, 2002, dharma talk by Larry Rosenberg to be found online at dharmaseed.org/teacher/106/talk/8736/.

102 ***Changes of identity***: Moses Rischin, *The Promised City: New York's Jews, 1870–1914* (Cambridge, Mass.: Harvard University Press, 1962), 75, translating a passage from George M. Price, *Di Yuden in Amerika* (Odessa, 1891), 6. The Emerson quotation is from "Self-Reliance," the Thoreau from "Walking."

103 ***In Tibet***: Ian Buruma, "Tibet Disenchanted," *New York Review of Books*, July 20, 2000, 24.

104 ***Kenosis***: Philippians 2:4–8.

106 ***Not to be repeated***: Sameer Padania, "Interview: Adam Phillips, on Balance (for *BOMB* magazine)," blog.sameerpadania.com/2010/09/04/adam-phillips-intervie/.

107 ***"Simultaneous composition and decomposition"***: Daniel Heller-Roazen, *Echolalias: On the Forgetting of Language* (New York: Zone Books, 2005), 191–93, citing Abdelfattah Kilito, *The Author and His Doubles*, trans. Michael Cooperson (Syracuse, N.Y.: Syracuse University Press, 2001), 14.

109 ***Refocus***: "Red Sox Start 2nd Half with Big Homestand," Associated Press, July 18, 2013.

110 **Anattā**: The Emerson quotation is from "Self-Reliance."

112 ***Less stress***: Daan Heerma van Voss, "The Day of Forgetting," *New York Times*, May 28, 2014.

113 ***Don't look back***: Jean Starobinski, "The Idea of Nostalgia," *Diogenes* 14, no. 54 (July 1966): 81–103.

114 ***The Lotus Eaters tell their version***: On lotus and the battle with the Ciciones, see Jonathan Shay, *Odysseus in America* (New York: Scribner, 2002), chapter 4. The italicized phrase is from Michel Foucault, "Nietzsche, Genealogy, History," in *Language, Counter-memory, Practice* (Ithaca, N.Y.: Cornell University Press, 1977), 162.

117 ***Nostalgia amused***: Vladimir Nabokov, *Speak, Memory* (New York: Vintage International, 1989), 13, 92–93, 136, 250; Vladimir Nabokov,

Strong Opinions (New York: Vintage International, 1990), 78; Svetlana Boym, *The Future of Nostalgia* (New York: Basic Books, 2001), xviii, 41–50.

119 ***The liquefaction of the fixed idea***: Pierre Janet, *Psychological Healing*, trans. Eden Paul and Cedar Paul, 2 vols. (New York: Macmillan, 1925), 1:661–65. On salutary dissociation, see Philip Bromberg, *Standing in the Spaces* (Hillsdale, N.J.: Analytic Press, 1998), 169–84, 273–75.

121 ***Unless it contemplate***: *The Poems of Emily Dickinson*, ed. R. W. Franklin (Cambridge, Mass.: Harvard University Press, 1999), 587–88.

122 ***"Remembering in a way . . ."***: Sigmund Freud, "Remembering, Repeating, and Working-Through," in *Case History of Schreber, Papers on Technique, and Other Works*, vol. 12 of *The Standard Edition of the Complete Psychological Works of Sigmund Freud* (London: Hogarth Press, 1957–74), 147–57; Adam Phillips, "Freud and the Uses of Forgetting," in *On Flirtation* (Cambridge, Mass.: Harvard University Press, 1994), 22.

123 ***The horse's mouth***: Victor Shklovsky, "Art as Technique," in *Russian Formalist Criticism: Four Essays*, trans. Lee T. Lemon and Marion J. Reis (Lincoln: University of Nebraska Press, 1965), 12–15. See also Marjorie Perloff, "New Thresholds, Old Anatomies: Contemporary Poetry and the Limits of Exegesis," *Iowa Review* 5 (Winter 1974): 88–89.

126 ***No . . . , no . . .*** : Wilfred Bion, *Attention and Interpretation* (London: Maresfield Reprints, 1984), 42; Wilfred Bion, *Second Thoughts* (London: Maresfield Library, 1987), 17–19.

128 ***Sometimes I think it's hopeless***: Tim O'Brien, *The Things They Carried* (Boston: Houghton Mifflin Harcourt, 2009), 72; "After PTSD, More Trauma," *New York Times*, Jan. 18, 2015.

130 ***Achilles and the unforgettable***: Robert Graves, *The Greek Myths*, 2 vols. (New York: George Braziller, 1957), 2:292; *The Greek Questions of Plutarch*, trans. W. R. Halliday (Oxford: Clarendon Press, 1928), 133–37.

131 ***Other bodies (a murder story)***: Epigraphs: Boris Pasternak, *Doctor Zhivago*, trans. Max Hayward and Manya Harari (New York: Random House, 1991), 10; Charles Wright, *Negative Blue: Selected Later Poems* (New York: Farrar, Straus and Giroux, 2000), 13. "Steeped in history but not living in the past" is also the motto of the Royal High School of Bath, England. David Ridgen's films, videos, and podcasts constitute the primary source materials for the Dee and Moore murder case. His multipart podcast can be found on the Canadian Broadcast Corporation website as season 3 of a series called *Someone Knows Something*, cbc.ca/radio/sks/season3. A link on that webpage ("Watch key moments from Dee & Moore") leads to a number of online videos, including that of the 2007 meeting between Thomas Moore and Charles Marcus Edwards, *Reconciliation in Mississippi*. See also Harry N. MacLean, *The Past Is Never Dead: The Trial of James Ford Seale and Mississippi's Struggle for Redemption* (New York: BasicCivitas Books, 2009).

136 ***Sambo Amusement***: On "disturbing the rest of one James Turner," see *Activities of Ku Klux Klan Organizations in the United States*, part 4 of

the *Hearings Before the Committee on Un-American Activities* (Washington, D.C.: U.S. Government Printing Office, 1966), 2945, "Ernest Gilbert Exhibit No. 1," reproducing an article in the *Jackson (Miss.) Clarion-Ledger*, Nov. 16, 1965, titled "Report of Arms Cache False; Officials Begin Probe of Klan."

137 ***On Saturday, May 2, 1964***: Ernest Gilbert was the Klansman who became an FBI informant and, in August 1964, testified in secret as to the details of the murders. The FBI documents recording his testimony can be found at abcnews.go.com/2020/story?id=2826491. Sophocles, *Antigone* 998–1022.

141 ***The second death***: Jacques Lacan, *The Ethics of Psychoanalysis, 1959–1960* (London: Routledge, 1992), 279; Jacques Lacan, *Écrits* (New York: W. W. Norton, 2002), 262–63.

145 ***"My brother's got peace"***: Hannah Arendt, *The Human Condition*, 2nd ed. (Chicago: University of Chicago Press, 1998), 237, 240n, 241; John P. Muller, "Why the Pair Needs the Third," *Journal of the American Academy of Psychoanalysis and Dynamic Psychiatry* 35, no. 2 (2007): 221–41.

154 ***It disappears***: The Chinese character for "forget": Yamada Katsumi and Shindō Hideyuki, *Kanji jigen jiten* [Etymological dictionary of Chinese characters] (Tokyo: Kadokaw Shoten, 1995).

155 ***The work***: Martha Minow, *Between Vengeance and Forgiveness* (Boston: Beacon Press, 1998), 10.

158 ***Into broad daylight***: Robert Storr et al., *Louise Bourgeois* (New York: Phaidon Press, 2003), 22.

159 ***From the Museum of Forgetting: "No image, no object, no focus"***: *James Turrell's Roden Crater*, a film commissioned by the Los Angeles County Museum of Art on the occasion of the exhibition *James Turrell: A Retrospective*, May 2013 through April 2014, online at vimeo.com/67926427; art21.org/texts/james-turrell/interview-james-turrell-live-oak-friends-meeting-house; Lynn M. Herbert, "Spirit and Light and the Immensity Within," in Lynn M. Herbert et al., *James Turrell: Spirit and Light* (Houston: Contemporary Arts Museum, 1988), 11–21.

NOTEBOOK III: NATION

164 ***Ogier the Dane***: George W. Cox, *Popular Romances of the Middle Ages* (London: Longmans, Green, 1871), 348–68.

166 ***Sham grandeurs***: Mark Twain, *Life on the Mississippi* (New York: Harper Bros., 1911), 347.

168 ***"The essence of a nation"***: Ernest Renan, "What Is a Nation?," in *Nation and Narration*, ed. Homi K. Bhabha (London: Routledge, 1990), 11; Walter J. Ong, *Orality and Literacy* (New York: Routledge, 2002), 46.

171 ***Dawn, November 29, 1864***: Ari Kelman, *A Misplaced Massacre: Struggling over the Memory of Sand Creek* (Cambridge, Mass.: Harvard University Press, 2013), is the primary source for material on the Sand

Creek Massacre. See also the letters from Joe Cramer (dated Dec. 19, 1864) and Silas Soule (dated Dec. 14, 1864), online at www.nps.gov/sand/learn/historyculture/upload/Combined-Letters-with-Sign-2.pdf; the National Park Service description of the battle, found at www.nps.gov/sand/learn/historyculture/index.htm; Matt Kelley, "Senator Releases Massacre Letters," Associated Press, Sept. 14, 2000, rebelcherokee.labdiva.com/newsarticle.html.

175 ***Truth and Justice***: On the Order of the Indian Wars, see www.oiwus.org/order.htm.

183 ***From the Museum of Forgetting, Gallery* Damnatio Memoriae**: Milan Kundera, *The Book of Laughter and Forgetting* (New York: HarperPerennial, 1999), 3–4.

185 ***The memory of difference***: Ronald Reagan's Neshoba County Fair speech: neshobademocrat.com/Content/1up-Test/1up-Test/Article/Transcript-of-Ronald-Reagan-s-1980-Neshoba-County-Fair-speech/91/572/15601; and, for a recording of the speech, see www.youtube.com/watch?v=450DA4AZG6U. For Donald Trump Jr., see "Donald Trump Jr. Speaks at Neshoba Fair," *Clarion-Ledger*, July 17, 2016, clarionledger.com/story/news/politics/2016/07/26/trump-neshoba-fair-geoff-pender/87561270/.

188 ***The negative nation***: Renan, "What Is a Nation?," 18–19.

190 ***Saracens, again***: Paul Preston, "The Theorists of Extermination," in *Unearthing Franco's Legacy*, ed. Carlos Jerez-Farrán and Samuel Amago (Notre Dame, Ind.: University of Notre Dame Press, 2010), 58.

191 ***The pact of forgetting***: Royal Decree-Law No. 10/76 of June 30, 1976, cited in Paloma Aguilar, *Memory and Amnesia: The Role of the Spanish Civil War in the Transition to Democracy* (New York: Berghahn Books, 2002), 193n; Ronald C. Slye, "The Legitimacy of Amnesties Under International Law and General Principles of Anglo-American Law: Is a Legitimate Amnesty Possible?," *Virginia Journal of International Law* 43 (2002–3): 240–47.

192 ***"Arrested in bed"***: Madeleine Davis, "Is Spain Recovering Its Memory? Breaking the *Pacto del Olvido*," *Human Rights Quarterly* 27 (2005): 868–69; Carolyn P. Boyd, "The Politics of History and Memory in Democratic Spain," *Annals of the American Academy of Political and Social Science* 617 (May 2008): 143; Jerez-Farrán and Amago, *Unearthing Franco's Legacy*, 327.

195 ***The unmarked grave***: Aguilar, *Memory and Amnesia*, 209, 209n; Anna Anabitare, "Familia de García Lorca se opone a su exhumación," *El Universal*, Aug. 18, 2006, archivo.eluniversal.com.mx/cultura/49661.html; Jon Lee Anderson, "Lorca's Bones," *New Yorker*, June 22, 2009; Boyd, "Politics of History and Memory in Democratic Spain," 146; Ian Gibson, *The Death of Lorca* (Chicago: J. P. O'Hara, 1973), 136; Gina Herrmann, "Mass Graves on Spanish TV: A Tale of Two Documentaries," in Jerez-Farrán and Amago, *Unearthing Franco's Legacy*, 185; Jesús

Ruiz Mantillia, "Las exhumaciones ejemplares son un disparate," *El País*, Aug. 6, 2011, elpais.com/diario/2011/08/06/babelia/1312589561_850215.html.

199 ***Characteristic amnesias***: Benedict Anderson, *Imagined Communities*, rev. ed. (New York: Verso, 1991), 200–204.

201 ***Postwar***: Tony Judt, *Postwar: A History of Europe Since 1945* (New York: Penguin Press, 2005), 61.

202 **Numbered**: Jodi Rudoren, "Proudly Bearing Elders' Scars, Their Skin Says 'Never Forget,'" *New York Times*, Oct. 1, 2012.

203 ***Amalek***: Deuteronomy 25:17–18; Exodus 17:14. Morgenbesser's witticism is repeated by Steven Strogatz in "The Enemy of My Enemy," *New York Times*, Nov. 12, 2013.

204 ***"All burned out"***: Imre Kertész, *Dossier K*, trans. Tim Wilkinson (Brooklyn: Melville House, 2013), 183–84, 190–91, and see nobelprize.org/nobel_prizes/literature/laureates/2002/kertesz-lecture-e.html.

205 ***Troubles with "Never Forget"***: Ruth Kluger, "Forgiving and Remembering," *PMLA* 117, no. 2 (March 2002): 313; Ruth Kluger, *Still Alive* (New York: Feminist Press, 2012), 64, 198; Elie Wiesel, *And the Sea Is Never Full* (New York: Knopf, 2010), 122.

206 ***The same substance***: *Jorge Luis Borges: The Last Interview and Other Conversations* (Brooklyn: Melville House, 2013), unpaginated.

207 ***Kosovo and chosen trauma***: Vamik Volkan, *Bloodlines: From Ethnic Pride to Ethnic Terrorism* (Boulder, Colo.: Westview Press, 1998), 48, 63–65; Robert D. Kaplan, *Balkan Ghosts* (New York: St. Martin's Press, 1993), 38; "Radovan Karadzic, a Bosnian Serb, Is Convicted of Genocide," *New York Times*, March 24, 2016; "Slobodan Milosevic's 1989 St. Vitus Day Speech," slobodan-milosevic.org/spch-kosovo1989.htm (a translation "Compiled by the National Technical Information Service of the Department of Commerce of the U.S"; another translation is available at www.hirhome.com/yugo/bbc_milosevic.htm).

211 ***Furies become Eumenides***: Aeschylus, *Eumenides*; Aeschylus, *The Oresteia*, trans. Robert Fagles (New York: Penguin Books, 1975), 77, 328. For "they somehow predate time," see Marcel Detienne, *The Masters of Truth in Archaic Greece* (New York: Zone Books, 1996), 75.

215 ***Forgetting history***: Frederick Douglass, *My Bondage and My Freedom* (New York: Miller, Orton and Mulligan, 1855), 360; Richard Rodriguez, *Brown: The Last Discovery of America* (New York: Viking, 2002), 136 (emphasis omitted).

216 ***Thomas Moore at home***: Harry N. MacLean, *The Past Is Never Dead: The Trial of James Ford Seale and Mississippi's Struggle for Redemption* (New York: BasicCivitas Books, 2009), 211.

217 ***And yet there are degrees of justice***: David Ridgen's *Reconciliation in Mississippi*: www.cbc.ca/radio/sks/season3/watch-key-moments-from-dee-moore-1.4360198. For more on how individual convictions detract

from a fuller account of racial terror, see Renee C. Romano, *Racial Reckoning: Prosecuting America's Civil Rights Murders* (Cambridge, Mass.: Harvard University Press, 2014).

218 ***Successful monuments become invisible***: Czesław Miłosz, Nobel lecture, Dec. 8, 1980, nobelprize.org/nobel_prizes/literature/laureates/1980/milosz-lecture.html.

219 ***A struggle for national remembering***: *Lynching in America: Confronting the Legacy of Racial Terror* (Montgomery, Ala.: Equal Justice Initiative, 2015); "History of Lynchings in the South Documents Nearly 4,000 Names," *New York Times*, Feb. 10, 2015.

220 ***A war of national forgetting***: David W. Blight, *Race and Reunion: The Civil War in American Memory* (Cambridge, Mass.: Harvard University Press, 2001), 61, 149.

221 ***The white sheet of oblivion***: Roger A. Pryor, "The Soldier, the Friend of Peace and Union," in *The Proceedings on the Evening of Decoration Day, May 30th, 1877, at the Academy of Music, City of Brooklyn, N.Y.* (Brooklyn: Members of the Bar, Eagle Job and Book Printing Department, 1877), 7–28. The American Antiquarian Society in Worcester, Massachusetts, holds a copy of this pamphlet.

223 ***"You must realize the truth"***: Blight, *Race and Reunion*, 106, 127; "Speech at the Thirty-Third Anniversary of the Jerry Rescue," Library of Congress, Douglass Papers, reel 16, online at www.loc.gov/collections/frederick-douglass-papers. Lynching statistics: see the timeline for 1852–80 at www.loc.gov/collections/african-american-perspectives-rare-books/.

225 ***Peace. Nothing***: Blight, *Race and Reunion*, 132, 138.

226 ***Separate water closets***: Woodrow Wilson, "Address at Gettysburg," July 4, 1913, online at www.presidency.ucsb.edu/ws/?pid=65370; Blight, *Race and Reunion*, 386; Joel Williamson, *The Crucible of Race* (New York: Oxford, 1984), 367–71.

228 ***The agonistic third***: *Chicago Inter Ocean*, May 30, 1898, in *Cartoons of the War of 1898 with Spain* (Chicago: Belford, Middlebrook, 1898), 89, and online at nationalhumanitiescenter.org/pds/gilded/empire/text10/twowars.pdf.

231 ***The agonistic third, again***: Kelman, *Misplaced Massacre*, 231.

233 ***The skull of Little Crow***: Robert Bly, *Eating the Honey of Words* (New York: Harper Flamingo, 1999), 12; Robert Bly, *Selected Poems* (New York: Harper and Row, 1986), 75, 84.

235 ***Amnesty, amnesic or memorable***: Slye, "Legitimacy of Amnesties Under International Law and General Principles of Anglo-American Law," 173–247.

238 ***The Why Not Bar bombing***: This and other entries dealing with South Africa's TRC: Both the McBride and the Taylor cases are featured in *Long Night's Journey into Day: South Africa's Search for Truth and Reconciliation*, DVD, directed by Frances Reid and Deborah Hoffmann (San Francisco: California Newsreel, 2000). Transcripts of the amnesty

committee hearings and decisions for both cases can be found by searching the TRC website at justice.gov.za/trc/. For stories of reconciliation, see Pumla Gobodo-Madikizela and Chris Van Der Merwe, eds., *Memory, Narrative, and Forgiveness* (Newcastle, U.K.: Cambridge Scholars, 2009), esp. chapters 7 and 8. The Biehl and Mbelo stories are also featured in the film *Long Night's Journey into Day.*

249 ***"The Truth Commission microphone with its little red light"***: Desmond Tutu, "South Africa's Unfinished Business," *Boston Globe*, April 26, 2014; Antjie Krog, cited in *Looking Back, Reaching Forward: Reflections of the TRC of South Africa*, ed. Charles Villa-Vicencio and Wilhelm Verwoerd (London: Zed Books, 2000), 164.

251 ***"Neighbors become playful"***: Vamik Volkan, *Enemies on the Couch* (Durham, N.C.: Pitchstone, 2013), 225–26.

252 ***"Forgetting is the shears"***: *A Kierkegaard Anthology*, ed. Robert Bretall (Princeton, N.J.: Princeton University Press, 1946), 28; Austin Butler, email to the author.

254 ***From the Museum of Forgetting***: www.leemingwei.com/projects.php#.

NOTEBOOK IV: CREATION

258 ***Anti-mnemonics***: Samuel Taylor Coleridge, *Biographia Literaria*, ed. James Engell and W. Jackson Bate (Princeton, N.J.: Princeton University Press, 1983), 49n. Engell and Bate note that Coleridge misremembers his source; the author was Burhan al-Din, not Averroes. Coleridge gives the phrase about lice in Latin: *"Pedicalos e capillis excerptos in arenam jarere incontusos."*

259 ***"Crothf Deletok"***: Robert D. Richardson Jr., *Emerson: The Mind on Fire* (Berkeley: University of California Press, 1996), 544.

260 ***Moving pictures***: "The Richard Mutt Case," *Blind Man*, no. 2 (May 1917): 5.

262 ***Distance***: Cited by the curator Regine Basha in *Diary of à Human Hand* (Montreal: Galerie du Centre des Arts Saidye Bronfman, 1995), 16, giving her source as a catalog: Brenda Richardson, *Brice Marden—Cold Mountain* (Houston, Tex.: Houston Fine Art Press, 1992).

263 ***"Thorny"***: *Fresh Air*, Oct. 11, 2011, www.npr.org/templates/transcript/transcript.php?storyId=140949453.

264 ***Revision by forgetting***: Vladimir Nabokov, *Speak, Memory* (New York: Vintage International, 1989), 170.

265 ***From the Museum of Forgetting***: Louise Bourgeois, *Trauma of Abandonment*, unique fabric book in the collection of the Museum of Modern Art, New York, www.moma.org/collection_lb/browse_results.php?object_id=173172; Louise Bourgeois, *Album* (New York: Peter Blum, 1994); Louise Bourgeois, *The Insomnia Drawings*, 2 vols. (Zurich: Daros, 2000); Deborah Wye, "Louise Bourgeois (American, born France 1911)," in *Modern Women: Women Artists at the Museum of Modern Art*, ed. Cornelia Butler and Alexandra Schwartz (New York: Museum of Modern Art, 2010), 275.

267 ***"Look at a Coca-Cola bottle"***: Marcel Duchamp, *Notes and Projects for the Large Glass* (London: Thames and Hudson, 1969), 70–72; *Conversing with Cage*, ed. Richard Kostelanetz (New York: Limelight, 1991), 52, 222.

269 ***From the Museum of Forgetting***: *With my Back to the World*, DVD, produced and directed by Mary Lance (Corrales, N.M.: New Deal Films, 2002).

271 ***Of the painter***: Marcel Proust, *In Search of Lost Time*, trans. C. K. Scott Moncrieff and Terence Kilmartin, revised by D. J. Enright, 6 vols. (New York: Modern Library, 1992), 2:572–73. All references to Proust refer to this Modern Library edition. My own translations usually start with Moncrieff's, but I often refer as well to the six volumes translated (one volume each) by Lydia Davis, James Grieve, Mark Treharne, John Sturrock, Carol Clark and Peter Collier, and Ian Patterson (London: Penguin Press, 2002) and to the original French as it appears in the editions from Gallimard in Paris.

272 ***From the Museum of Forgetting, Gallery of Erasures***: Russell Ferguson, *In Memory of My Feelings: Frank O'Hara and American Art* (Los Angeles: Museum of Contemporary Art, 1999), 89.

273 ***Happy and forgetful herds***: Adapted from Friedrich Nietzsche, *The Use and Abuse of History*, trans. Adrian Collins (New York: Macmillan, 1957), 5, and from the online translation by Ian Johnston: johnstonia texts.x10host.com/nietzsche/historyhtml.html.

274 ***Saddled with history***. Ibid.; Glenn W. Most, "On the Use and Abuse of Ancient Greece for Life," *Cultura Tedesca* 20 (2000): 11–12, 44.

275 ***From the Museum of Forgetting***: Cited in Thomas Crow, *No Idols* (Sydney: University of Sydney, 2017), 88; Robert Smithson, *The Collected Writings*, ed. Jack Flam (Berkeley: University of California Press, 1996), 113.

277 ***Nietzsche brought machismo***: The italicized phrases all come from Nietzsche, *Use and Abuse of History*.

278 ***Führerparkplatz, from the Museum of Forgetting***: seanmunger.com /2014/01/16/reluctantly-remembered-the-strange-historical-odyssey-of -the-fuhrerbunker/; theguardian.com/books/2006/oct/14/featuresreviews .guardianreview26.

279 ***Contrary waters of memory***: James E. Young, "Memory and Countermemory," *Harvard Design Magazine*, no. 9 (Fall 1999), harvarddesign magazine.org/issues/9/memory-and-counter-memory.

281 ***From the Museum of Forgetting (proposal for an American Apartheid Memorial)***: For skull cups, see www.ncbi.nlm.nih.gov/pmc/articles /PMC3040189/ and Thomas Medwin, *Conversations of Lord Byron* (London: Henry Colburn, 1825), 70–71.

283 ***Oral amnesia***: Jack Goody and Ian Watt, "The Consequences of Literacy," in *Literacy in Traditional Societies*, ed. Jack Goody (Cambridge, U.K.: Cambridge University Press, 1968), 30, 33. See also David Henige, "'The Disease of Writing': Ganda and Nyoro Kinglists in a Newly

Literate World," in *The African Past Speaks*, ed. Joseph C. Miller (Hamden, Conn.: Archon, 1980), 240–61; Walter J. Ong, *Orality and Literacy* (New York: Routledge, 2002), 46–49.

285 ***New Plato***: Plato, *Seventh Letter* 344c; Plato, *Phaedrus* 274c–275b.

286 ***An artifice of forgetting***: M. T. Clanchy, *From Memory to Written Record: England, 1066–1307* (Cambridge, Mass.: Harvard University Press, 1979), 27, 123, 233; Fritz Kern, *Kingship and Law in the Middle Ages* (Oxford: B. Blackwell, 1948), 179.

288 **Chanson fixe**: Aleksandar Hemon, *The Book of My Lives* (New York: Farrar, Straus and Giroux, 2013), 75–79.

289 ***Forgetting for eternity***: Saint Augustine, *Confessions*, trans. Henry Chadwick (New York: Oxford University Press, 1998), 141, 203, and book 11, "Time and Eternity"; Philippians 3:10–14 (the Revised Standard Version adjusted to fit Augustine's version).

292 ***The time to wake up***: Dogen, *Moon in a Dewdrop: Writings of Zen Master Dogen* (San Francisco: North Point Press, 1985), 70–71.

293 ***Remembering forgetfulness in Massachusetts***: *The Essays of Henry D. Thoreau*, ed. Lewis Hyde (New York: North Point Press, 2002), xxii–xxiii.

295 ***"If the very soul is no longer thinking about itself"***: Augustine, *Confessions*, xiii–xiv, 38–39, 155–56, 171–72, and book 10, "Memory"; Plotinus, *Ennead*, trans. A. H. Armstrong, Loeb Classical Library 440 (Cambridge, Mass.: Harvard University Press, 1969), 135.

299 ***From the Museum of Forgetting***: Robert Smithson, "The Monuments of Passaic," *Artforum*, Dec. 1967, 26–27; Smithson, *Collected Writings*, 72, 298.

301 ***Habit versus rebirth***: Proust, *In Search of Lost Time*, 1:8–9; 2:141, 319; 4:208; 5:564–65, 732–33.

303 ***Habit versus the treasure chest of oblivion***: Ibid., 2:300–301.

304 ***Second nature versus a second naïveté***: Ibid., 2:59.

306 ***"Yes, yes, yes"***: Willie Watson, "Keep It Clean," youtube.com/watch?v=ohhmJGDVrxA; earlier version by Charley Jordan, youtube.com/watch?v=bjYz80E94VA&list=RDEMIhJlIjNxBzQRuFEdaMWPwQ&index=3; Proust, *In Search of Lost Time*, 2:319; Christopher Bollas, *The Shadow of the Object: Psychoanalysis of the Unthought Known* (London: Free Association Books, 1987); Henri Bergson, *Matter and Memory* (London: George Allen, 1912), 97, 179–81; David Gross, "Bergson, Proust, and the Revaluation of Memory," *International Philosophical Quarterly* 25, no. 4 (Dec. 1985): 374; Samuel Beckett, *Proust* (New York: Grove Press, 1957), 18.

308 ***The required gap***: Proust, *In Search of Lost Time*, 6:261. See also Roger Shattuck, *Proust's Way* (New York: W. W. Norton, 2000), 122.

309 **Nunc fluens facit tempus**: Boethius, *Theological Tractates: The Consolation of Philosophy*, trans. H. F. Stewart, E. K. Rand, and S. J. Tester, Loeb Classical Library 74 (Cambridge, Mass.: Harvard University Press,

1973), 23. The couplet is in fact a paraphrase of Boethius by Thomas Aquinas as found in his *Summa Theologiae*. Its language also appears in an epigraph to Jorge Luis Borges's story "The Aleph," where are found similar concerns with the simultaneous versus the successive. Proust, *In Search of Lost Time*, 1:529, 5:804–5, 6:264.

311 ***Making time***: Proust, *In Search of Lost Time*, 1:606, 4:210–14.

313 ***From the Museum of Forgetting***: Craig E. Adcock, *James Turrell: The Art of Light and Space* (Berkeley: University of California Press, 1990), 19; *James Turrell's Roden Crater*, a film commissioned by the Los Angeles County Museum of Art on the occasion of the exhibition *James Turrell: A Retrospective*, May 2013 through April 2014, online at vimeo .com/67926427.

316 ***The unpaid bill***: Bluma Zeigarnik, "On Finished and Unfinished Tasks," 13–15, online at pdfs.semanticscholar.org/edd8/f1d0f79106c8 0b0b856b46d0d01168c76f50.pdf.

318 ***Zeigarniking Hemingway***: *The Complete Short Stories of Ernest Hemingway* (New York: Charles Scribner's Sons, 1987), 649.

319 ***Sex versus nonsense***: Elizabeth M. Kiebel, "The Effect of Directed Forgetting on Completed and Interrupted Tasks," www.researchgate.net /publication/241552936_The_Effect_of_Directed_Forgetting_on _Completed_and_Interrupted_Tasks.

320 ***Free forgetting***: Edward T. Cone, *Music: A View from Delft*, ed. Robert P. Morgan (Chicago: University of Chicago Press, 1989), 77–93.

323 ***Mr. Forster forgets***: E. M. Forster, *Anonymity: An Enquiry* (London: L. and Virginia Woolf, 1925; repr., Folcroft, Pa.: Folcroft Library Editions, 1976).

325 ***Ambition***: *New York Times*, Oct. 29, 2015.

326 ***Forget marriage***: André Gide, journal entry of May 14, 1921 ("Vous pouvez tout raconteur . . . , mais à condition de ne jamais dire: *Je*."), cited in Michael Lucey, *Never Say I* (Durham, N.C.: Duke University Press, 2006), 1. Oscar Wilde cited in Alan Sheridan, *André Gide* (Cambridge, Mass.: Harvard University Press, 1999), 148.

328 ***Plotless***: *The Essays of Michel de Montaigne*, trans. M. A. Screech (New York: Penguin Press, 1991), 462.

330 ***Meaningless***: T. S. Eliot, *The Use of Poetry and the Use of Criticism* (Cambridge, Mass.: Harvard University Press, 1964), 144–45.

331 ***From the Museum of Forgetting***: Smithson, *Collected Writings*, 194.

332 ***"Instructions for the Cook"***: Dogen, "Instructions for the Tenzo," in *Moon in a Dewdrop*, 53–66.

335 ***The northerner***: Harry N. MacLean, *The Past Is Never Dead: The Trial of James Ford Seale and Mississippi's Struggle for Redemption* (New York: BasicCivitas Books, 2009), 191.

337 ***Closure***: Homer, *Odyssey* 14.484–86; Nicole Loraux, *The Divided City: On Memory and Forgetting in Ancient Athens* (New York: Zone Books, 2006), 156.

338 ***The forgettable life***: Plato, *Republic* 620.

339 ***To the reader***: Frank Kermode, *The Genesis of Secrecy* (Cambridge, Mass.: Harvard University Press, 1979), 14.

340 ***Bird Buddha***: Dogen, *Moon in a Dewdrop*, 167; Shohaku Okumura, *Realizing Genjokoan: The Key to Dogen's Shobogenzo* (Boston: Wisdom, 2010), 2, 90–92; Gudo Wafu Nishijima, "Understanding the *Shobogenzo*," dogensangha.org/downloads/Und-Shobo.PDF.

341 ***The traceless trace***: *Poems of Fernando Pessoa*, trans. Edwin Honig and Susan M. Brown (San Francisco: City Lights Books, 1998), 21–22.

Index

Page numbers in *italics* refer to illustrations.

PERMISSIONS ACKNOWLEDGMENTS

Fernando Pessoa, "XLIII: Rather the flight of the bird passing and leaving no trace," translated by Edwin Honig and Susan M. Brown, from *Poems of Fernando Pessoa*. English translation copyright © 1986 by Edwin Honig and Susan M. Brown. Reprinted with the permission of The Permissions Company, Inc., on behalf of City Lights Books, www.citylights.com.

Transcripts from the CBC film *Mississippi Cold Case* by David Ridgen and from the CBC film *Reconciliation in Mississippi* by David Ridgen are used by permission of the Canadian Broadcasting Corporation and the filmmaker. *Mississippi Cold Case* © 2007, Canadian Broadcasting Corporation. *Reconciliation in Mississippi* © 2011, Canadian Broadcasting Corporation.

Someone Knows Something, Season 3: "Dee and Moore (Episodes 1–7)" © 2018, Canadian Broadcasting Corporation.

Archival photographs of Henry Hezekiah Dee's and Charles Eddie Moore's skeletal remains courtesy of National Archives, College Park/David Ridgen.

ILLUSTRATION CREDITS

85 Francis Picabia, *M'amenez-y* © 2017 Artists Rights Society (ARS), New York / ADAGP, Paris. Used by permission of ARS for the estate of Francis Picabia.

159 *One Accord*, Live Oak Friends Meeting House. Copyright © James Turrell, photograph by Joe Aker. Reproduced by permission of James Turrell.

194 "Worker Frees with a Drill a Bust of Spanish Dictator Francisco Franco, July 8, 2003." Photograph by Miguel Riopa, AFP. Reproduced by permission of Getty Images.

253 *Guernica in Sand* by Lee Mingwei. Two images of the installation reproduced by permission of Lee Mingwei.

265 Louise Bourgeois (1911–2010) © VAGA, N.Y. *Ode à l'oubli* (cover). Fabric illustrated book with thirty-five compositions: thirty-two fabric collages, two with hand additions, and three lithographs (including cover). Page (each approx.): 10¾ × 12¹⁄₁₆"; overall: 11⁷⁄₁₆ × 12¹³⁄₁₆ × 1¹⁵⁄₁₆".

Unpublished. Printer: Solo Impression, New York. Edition: Unique. Gift of the artist. Museum of Modern Art, New York, N.Y., U.S.A. Digital Image © The Museum of Modern Art / Licensed by SCALA / Art Resource, N.Y.

269 Agnes Martin (1912–2004) © ARS, N.Y. *The Tree* (1964); oil and pencil on canvas, 6' × 6'. Larry Aldrich Foundation Fund. The Museum of Modern Art. Digital Image © The Museum of Modern Art / Licensed by SCALA / Art Resource, N.Y.

272 Elaine de Kooning, *Frank O'Hara* (1962); oil on canvas, 93" × 42" (detail), reproduced courtesy of the family of Frank O'Hara.

275 Robert Smithson (1938–1973), *Non-site (Palisades-Edgewater, N.J.)* (1968); enamel on aluminum with stones and ink on paper drawing, dimensions variable. Whitney Museum of American Art, New York; purchased with funds from the Howard and Jean Lipman Foundation, Inc. 69.6a–b. © Estate of Robert Smithson / Licensed by VAGA, N.Y.

279 Aschrott Fountain ("counter-memorial"), reproduced courtesy of Horst Hoheisel.

299 Dan Flavin (1933–1996) © ARS, N.Y. *"Monument" 1 for V. Tatlin* (1964); fluorescent lights and metal fixtures, 8' × 23⅛" × 4½". Gift of UBS. The Museum of Modern Art. Digital Image © The Museum of Modern Art / Licensed by SCALA / Art Resource, N.Y.

313 *Roden Crater* seen from the air. Copyright © James Turrell. Reproduced by permission of James Turrell.